Happy

MW00910320

SEPT. 14, 2014

Love, ELMER & JUDY

FROM MOCCASINS TO COWBOY BOOTS

Happy Birthday,
J Ad.
Sept. 14, 2014.

FROM MOCCASINS TO COWBOY BOOTS

I Followed My Dream

LLOYD ANTYPOWICH

To order additional copies of this book, contact:
Xlibris Corporation
1-888-795-4274
www.Xlibris.com
Orders@Xlibris.com

TABLE OF CONTENTS

Acknowledgments..xi
Foreword xiii
Learning from Grandpa...xv
Introduction xvii

Homesteading in Saskatchewan 1904-1948

CHAPTER 1	My Antypowich Ancestors Claimed to have Come from Poland...1
CHAPTER 2	My Matzner Ancestors Claimed to be German.......................7
CHAPTER 3	Frank Antypowich and Annie Matzner Start a New Life..... 11
CHAPTER 4	I was a Childhood Dennis the Menace 17
CHAPTER 5	Our Cree Indian Neighbors.. 19
CHAPTER 6	Edwards Lake School 26
CHAPTER 7	Hunting and Fishing: Learning from Dad 32
CHAPTER 8	The Sawmill at Junor 34
CHAPTER 9	Lessons My Older Brothers Taught Me................................. 36
CHAPTER 10	Antics of Young Boys on the Farm.. 39
CHAPTER 11	Making Moonshine to Pay the Bills 43
CHAPTER 12	Auntie Barbara and the Rustlers... 47
CHAPTER 13	Charlie and the Bear... 49
CHAPTER 14	Frank Antypowich, the Strong Man...................................... 52
CHAPTER 15	Frank Antypowich, the Entrepreneur.................................... 55
CHAPTER 16	Meeting Neighbors under Unusual Circumstances 60

CHAPTER 17   Pearl School 62

CHAPTER 18   A Whole New World Opens up as "The Hutterites"
Go to See Grandpa Matzner 68

Sawmilling and Logging in Northern Alberta 1948-1953

CHAPTER 19   Alberta Bound 73

CHAPTER 20   Growing up in Logging Camps 81

CHAPTER 21   Going to School at Widewater 87

CHAPTER 22   Moving to Wagner 93

CHAPTER 23   Girls, Girls, Girls! 105

CHAPTER 24   Horse Logging Gives Way to Equipment 109

CHAPTER 25   High School in Kinuso 117

CHAPTER 26   LeeBakken Planer Mill in High Prairie 125

CHAPTER 27   Fun with the Girls from High Prairie! 130

Oilfield Work and Road Construction at Valleyview, Alberta 1954-1958

CHAPTER 28   Homesteading and Working the Cat at Valleyview 139

CHAPTER 29   Working the Oil Patch 144

Farming at Stettler, Alberta 1959-1970

CHAPTER 30   I'm on My Own, Following My Dream 159

CHAPTER 31   New Ventures 170

CHAPTER 32   I Might be a Farmer Now, But I'll Always be a Hunter 177

CHAPTER 33   My Friend, Peter Zahacy, Moves to Stettler 184

CHAPTER 34   We Complete Our Family 187

CHAPTER 35   Buying the Farm 194

CHAPTER 36   Importing My First Limousin Cattle from France 198

CHAPTER 37   Leaving Stettler 204

Coal Mining At Elkford, British Columbia 1969-1973

CHAPTER 38   Now I'm a Coal Miner at Fording Coal 211

CHAPTER 39   I Buy Some Cattle 243

Ranching at Horsefly, British Columbia 1973-2006

CHAPTER 40   Headed for Horsefly, British Columbia:
I'm Going back to the Land 253

CHAPTER 41   Black Creek Ranch..266

CHAPTER 42   I Become My Own Veterinarian..279

CHAPTER 43   Bringing in the Cattle in the Fall..283

CHAPTER 44   Hunting up Black Creek 291

CHAPTER 45   The Irwin Brothers...296

CHAPTER 46   Leaving Black Creek to Go back Home 302

CHAPTER 47   The Rancher Becomes a Trucker..305

CHAPTER 48   I Become the President of the BC Limousin Association... 315

CHAPTER 49   Leo, My Friend and Partner..338

CHAPTER 50   Because I Love Horses So Much, I Made Them My
Retirement Project...345

CHAPTER 51   Rescuing a Fawn...352

CHAPTER 52   My Granddaughter Gives Me Buddy,
My Faithful Companion..356

CHAPTER 53   Traveling with Stu Maitland from Eureka Peak Lodge
and Outfitters 361

CHAPTER 54   Herman Howard and Hank...365

CHAPTER 55   It's Time to Enjoy Life and the Fun Things a Bit 368

CHAPTER 56   It's Time to Think about Retirement 375

Retirement and Wonderful Memories 2006-

CHAPTER 57   Life in Retirement..381

CHAPTER 58   Our Summer Hideout, Beautiful Quesnel Lake!..................386

CHAPTER 59   Looking Back 396

This book is dedicated to

Those I so dearly love: my wife, my children, and my grandchildren. I will try to leave a trail that you may follow from where I came and some of the things I'd done.

ACKNOWLEDGMENTS

Thank you to Sharron Hynes who copyedited this book and cropped and edited the many pictures.

I would like to acknowledge some of the many people who helped me reach my goal of becoming a rancher: my mother and dad who were responsible for nurturing me along the way; my teacher, Hank Lisney, who made a big imprint on my life and whose patience I'm sure I tried many times; Ben and Ole Erickson who helped me get my start as a farmer; Charlie and Hazel Little for raising a lovely daughter who became my partner and the love of my life; to Harvey Tedford, who was the secretary manager of the Canadian Limousin Association and encouraged me and instilled confidence in me to handle the task of being the president of the BC Limousin Association, as well as a director on the board of the Canadian Limousin Association. His support encouraged me on my way to becoming a rancher.

To my wife of fifty-three years for all her help and encouragement; without her this book would not have made it to the publisher.

To my wonderful family, whom I so dearly love, for all your help through the years. I love you all and may this book leave you a trail to your heritage.

FOREWORD

Lloyd's book should be recommended reading for all young people today. If they want to meet an individual and his family and get a history of families who have courage and determination, it is a must. This is what it's like to be a pioneer and inherit the spirit of the pioneers. It is refreshing to find someone looking for the answers to life's questions by looking in the mirror.

It tells the story of people who came to this country with nothing in terms of wealth but had an enormous amount of energy, ingenuity, and determination. They survived and were able to thrive in an environment of hardship, which was the norm.

It is refreshing to hear Lloyd share his story in his own words. It is like being with him on his journey. You don't really know where he is going next because he is truly an innovative and courageous person who will tackle anything life throws his way. He has the ability and courage to apply himself and succeed.

He is truly a man's man, a leader of men. School, the lumber industry, the oil industry, the mining industry, farming, ranching, hunting, the horse industry, the purebred cattle industry, and author all are part of the man developed over a lifetime. Lloyd is a man of honesty, determination, and enthusiasm that allows him to succeed at anything he does.

It is truly an honor to have had the opportunity to work with him and now to read about him and learn of him behind the scenes. I highly recommend that you take the time to sit down and read Lloyd's book.

You will not get the opportunity to meet very many people like him, and if you do you will certainly cherish their friendship and support because they do come along but once in a lifetime.

Sincerely,
Harvey Tedford,

LEARNING FROM GRANDPA

We grew up in his barn, me and my best friend,
Our home away from most every weekend
He taught me a lot, more than he can know,
Like grooming the horses and trimming their toes

And finding the best spot to dig up earthworms
All the important things for a fisherman to learn
Like baiting hooks, and tangled lines and netting the fish
You let us sing Black Socks as long as we wished.

I learned responsibility, chores always came first
Keep your animals free from hunger and thirst
And sit up straight in the saddle all day
Even when the joy of cow chasing has faded away

To leave the show with a warm-hearted grin,
Even if you and your horse didn't win
Because winning isn't always a prize or blue ribbon
If your horse learned just one thing it was worth the time given

You'd come give me pointers when you didn't have time,
Keep your heels down, your head up and jog in a straight line
You'd let us sleep overnight after night,
Knowing Sassy wouldn't foal 'till the timing was right.

You let us come to watch you do what you'd do,
Letting us help out with chores or shovel horse doo
Calving the calves and breeding the mares
I learned more about reproduction than any kid dares

Being strong-willed and hardy and not giving up
Even when that colt landed you on your butt
And cursing in ways I never imagined,
I grew up just like you, now could that happen?

So thank you, Grandpa, for all that you've taught me
Without all that I've learned I don't know who I'd be.

—*Poem written by Jennifer Jackson (my oldest granddaughter)
for my seventy-second birthday in 2009*

INTRODUCTION

From there to here or then till now has been a long time and a long, long ways.

Lloyd Antypowich, the author at about two-and-a-half years old in front of the house where he was born, on the place where his dad homesteaded at Penn, Saskatchewan

I have enjoyed this life so much that if I had a choice I don't believe I would be willing to change any of it. Yes, you might think it was hard, and because of the times and the places where I lived I did experience things that a lot of other young children have never had the same opportunity to experience. And many of you would feel that you wouldn't want to have lived that way! Certainly, even then the children in the cities experienced a totally different lifestyle, with the convenience of electricity, running water, and flushing toilets. I lived close to the elements of nature, where if it was forty below outside, the toilet seat was forty below as well. And the Simpsons Sears and Eaton's Catalogue were something I read while I was contemplating before I had to tear the page. We didn't have toilet paper out there on the homestead!

When one looks back into the past you find many interesting things, and although we might think that we have some tough times now, I'm sure they are nothing compared to what my parents and grandparents endured. In school we learned that many of the immigrants who came to the Americas came for reasons such as freedom of speech, freedom of religion, and a vision of life in a land where they would be free to raise their children and own their own property. Although this vision seemed very inviting, the price they paid for that freedom was more than any of us today would ever want to have to pay.

They had to deal with the anxiety that came with leaving all they'd grown up with to step into an unknown world with only themselves to depend on and to deal with unknown situations at every turn. A land that promised to be so free and enticing could also be harsh and hard and very unforgiving, and only by the sweat of their brow and the strength within them were they able to build for themselves a home, as crude as it may have been, and shelter for their livestock in order to survive the harsh winters of that northern land. Their comfort and conveniences were nothing more than survival, but they were happy to be free, and all their neighbors were very much the same.

There were no such things as unemployment insurance or workers' compensation, hospitalization insurance, or social assistance to kick in. You were responsible for yourself, so you had to do it right if you were going to survive. Although neighbors could be generous and willing to help in every way that they could, they too did not have a lot to give to others. The winters could be harsh with temperatures dropping to -50 °F below zero. They did not have the convenience of fiberglass insulation to keep their houses warm. Their roofs were made out of sod and their walls were plastered with clay. A wood stove was used for cooking and heating. For lighting they used candles that were homemade from tallow and string. After a few years of pioneering they upgraded their lighting to a coal oil lamp.

They truly were survivors off the land. They hunted and fished and grew gardens from which they canned vegetables, and picked wild berries, which they preserved to get them through the long winter. Some dug root cellars in the ground below the frost, where they could keep their vegetables.

But as the days became longer and the sun rose higher into the sky, all the painful memories of their hardships in the winter slipped into the background as spring brought hope that the summer would bring the promise of a good harvest and a better life.

When the pioneers immigrated to Canada, they didn't "shed their skin," so to speak, but brought along with them many old memories and conflicts of the past, which caused problems in the new land. They soon discovered much could be accomplished working together; the past conflicts didn't have the same meaning here in the new land. As a result, in most cases they did very well. There was a blending of religion and nationality, and for those that could bury the hatchet and accept the fact that they were now Canadians living in a new land, things went very well.

Canada Day reminds us we are a proud people, and every first of July I think of the pioneers that braved the elements to make us Canadians. Canadians didn't come ready made. They were shaped by the hand of Mother Nature. Today it is different, and who knows where that will lead us.

HOMESTEADING IN SASKATCHEWAN

1904-1948

CHAPTER 1

My Antypowich Ancestors Claimed to have Come from Poland

I am not a purebred; in a rancher's terms, you would call me a crossbreed. My ancestry goes back to the old country on both sides.

Grandpa and Grandma Antypowich came to Canada in 1904. To the best of my knowledge, they came from Russia, but because of all the fighting that took place in that region, you might have been Polish at one time and Russian or Romanian the next time; it depended on who won which particular war. The stories I have heard indicate that my grandpa was born in an area known as White Russia (an area in Poland). I believe Grandma was born in the Ukraine. I'm not sure where they were living before they came to Canada, but they talked of the Ukraine and a place called Kiev.

Joseph and Juliana (Helen) Antypowich, along with their seven children, arrived in Montréal on the *Halifax*. From there, it would seem that they took the train to Winnipeg, Manitoba, where Grandpa bought a horse, harness, a wagon and a milk cow, and a few other supplies like flour, salt, sugar, lard, tea, and a small rifle and some ammunition so he could shoot grouse and rabbits along the way. They probably bought some cooking utensils and other necessities, like an axe, a hammer, a saw and some nails, as well as wheat and oats so he could grow his own crops. They had to be excited at the prospect of reaching their homestead, their first piece of land in Canada.

My dad's parents, Joseph and Helen (Juliana) Antypowich

They set out into the unknown to cross the prairies. They fought the ongoing battle with mosquitoes, horseflies, black flies, and deer flies, and at times it must have been almost unbearable. They crossed creeks and rivers and bounced the wagon over rocks and rough trails. My dad had been conceived in the old country and it had to have been a miserable journey for a pregnant woman.

They nailed young poplar trees to the sides of the wagon, making a half circle over it, covering them with blankets for protection from the prairie sun and the cool of the night. Grandma and the younger children slept in the wagon box, while grandpa and the older boys slept on the ground under the stars.

They encountered Native Indians who were hunting on the prairies. Grandma described them as lean, muscular men who wore their hair in long braids. Grandpa couldn't understand their language and neither could the Indians understand his, so they used sign language to communicate. When the Indians asked them for food, Grandpa would draw his stomach in to make it look like he was thin and then rubbed it and pointed at his mouth. He tried to tell the Indians he was hungry. Then he pointed at his children, again sucked in his stomach, trying to tell them they were hungry too. Can you imagine how scary it must have been to not be unable to understand them, knowing how vulnerable you were if they decided to be unfriendly?

They gave the Indians some tea and sugar. Grandma said they did not threaten them in any way, but were a scary bunch. I can imagine they'd heard stories of some of the things that had happened to other early pioneers and were very afraid for their lives.

It was frightening for Grandma to hear the coyotes howling at night when they camped out on the open prairies. They saw a lot of animals, mainly deer and antelope, but they were usually too far away to be shot with the small rifle. She said when they stopped to have their supper they would make a small fire from the dry grass and burned the buffalo patties that were old and very dry.

They met very few people with whom they could communicate. They met one man (I would call him a fur trader) whom she described as having a two-wheel wagon pulled by a skinny horse, with many hides and furs he traded to the Indians. She said he must have felt sorry for them because he gave them a blanket for the children.

When they reached their destination near Red Berry Lake, about forty miles west of Rosthern in Saskatchewan, there was more bush than they expected. They settled with Grandpa turning the wagon box upside down for shelter. Grandma and the girls slept under it, Grandpa and the boys slept under the stars. They all worked together to build an eighteen-foot by twenty-four-foot house. The house wasn't completed when Grandma went into labor, and my dad, Frank Antypowich, was born under the wagon box. That is about as close as you can get to Mother Nature.

Grandpa was a slender man about six feet tall. Although I have pictures of him and Grandma, my memories of Grandpa are very vague. Everyone in the family says he was a calm, gentle man who got along with all his children and was well-liked. He apparently was a hard worker and would think nothing of walking for miles to get supplies. When I visited with Donny and Kathy Matzner in 2011, Donny told me that his father, Alois Jr., told them of Grandpa Antypowich packing a big bag of flour home on his back from North Battleford, Saskatchewan to the homestead, which would have been close to one hundred miles. That is unbelievable!

I don't know if he had very much education in the old country, but he did use an abacus to count and calculate mathematically. When he had documents to sign, he signed his name with an X. I don't know if that was because he didn't know how to sign it in English or he simply did not write. I don't believe either he or Grandma spoke very much English, because they usually talked in their native language at home.

When the early pioneers travelled into the outer perimeters of civilization, the land they settled wasn't surveyed, so they were considered squatters. When surveying took place, it created new sets of problems; proposed roads cut through barnyards or fields, and some had to give up some of their undeveloped land to follow the survey lines. If you'd settled on 160 acres it was free until the government required you to file for a homestead, then the cost was $10.

Grandma liked to tell her grandchildren stories of the early times when they came to Canada. I can remember her sitting in her chair in the yard with some of us gathered around her and listening to her talk in her broken English. She sometimes would use Russian or Ukrainian words, and because I didn't know what they meant, it made it harder for me to understand her.

I can remember her saying they lived like a bunch of chickens; when it got light they all got up and went to work, and when it got dark they went to bed because they didn't have anything other than candles for light.

Their house was built out of poplar logs hewn with a broad axe, and the cracks were chinked with a mud and grass mixture. The roof was built using poles laid across the top of the logs with chunks of sod placed on top; a first layer with the grass side down, the next with the grass side up and it had to rain very hard before a few leaks appeared. A window space wasn't cut out until the first flour sack was empty and could be used as a window covering. Although crude, it provided a barrier from inclement summer weather and winter temperatures ranging from -20 ºF to -50 ºF. When they first came to Canada they didn't have cook stoves, so their homes were heated by ovens built out of mud that were used for baking bread (and they made good bread). Modern versions of this type of oven and stoves are still found today in the homes of European emigrants, but now they are made out of better material.

The barn was built next, necessary protection for their precious animals from the weather, as well as a place to store winter feed. It wasn't as nicely built as the house; instead, fresh cow manure was used to chink the cracks, but the rest was done in the same manner.

In between times of building, the family used a hand tool called a scythe to cut hay for winter feed.

I can't tell you just what they ate for meals in that first while when they were waiting for the house to be built, but I do remember Grandma saying they ate a lot of porridge, and the cow was milking, so they had milk for their porridge. Imagine how hard it was to bake bread over an open fire! Whenever someone shot a rabbit or a grouse, they had a special meal, and when they shot a moose or a deer the family feasted "like a bunch of hungry coyotes."

During the winter Grandpa and the boys trapped, then traded the furs for groceries at the trading post. I don't believe there were very many white neighbors living in the area at the time; they were mostly Cree Indians. The reason I say this is because I remember Grandma saying in her broken English that they had to take the cow to the bull at a neighbors so far away that by the time they arrived she was no longer "in love," so they made arrangements to leave her there until she was bred.

The next summer they planted a vegetable garden. Many immigrants brought the seeds with them, and while I don't know for sure if Grandma did, with such a large family it's probable they grew gardens in the old country and would have brought seeds, guarding them carefully as it was one's assurance of having food in the new world.

They made a soup out of the beet greens and the very young beets, to which was added bits of pork and young carrots. This soup is a very well-known Ukrainian dish called borscht. It was fortunate they had a large family as many hands were needed for breaking the soil with spades and picks. The horse would have been used to pull out bigger roots and stumps. Still, they managed to clear enough land to grow a little wheat and oats, and so were much better prepared for the coming winter.

When they acquired a pig and chickens, they felt like they were living like kings. They butchered their own animals, and when they butchered a pig the only thing they threw away was the squeal. After the pig was scalded, cleaned, and scraped to remove the hair, the innards were drawn. The intestines were washed and scraped, cleaned to be used for casings for sausage. The feet were boiled for broth or soup. The head was boiled and then cooled in a pan to be chopped in small pieces to run through a grinder; this was called headcheese. They also saved the blood to make blood sausage, and the fat was rendered into lard for cooking and baking. The small bits of meat left on the fat in the rendering tub floated to the top, becoming very crisp. It would be put between two slices of bread spread with lard as a sandwich. I remember some of the children's lunches being two pieces of home-baked bread spread with lard.

*   *   *

Grandpa and Grandma Antypowich had a large family. In total there were eighteen or nineteen children. Two sets of twins died at birth, and one son drowned. Their living children were Victor, Simon, John, Joe (Bertosie), Mary, Lena, Cornelia, Roman, Annie, Frank, Alec, Joseph, Alan, and Bruce. I don't believe any of them were born in a hospital.

Simon married Warwara Barbara Gromniak. John married Nellie Danyliw. Both Simon and John homesteaded in northern Saskatchewan near Penn. Victor married Lena Melashenko in Saskatchewan and later moved to San Francisco, California. He was one of the chief cable splicer's on the Golden Gate Bridge, and when I met him for the first time in 1954 he showed me a fine cable that he had braided and spliced for his pocket watch. Joe (Bertosie) married Mary Johnson and lived on an acreage in the Penn area; he became a shoemaker. Mary married a man by the name of Dan Nakazny. Lena married a man from Grand Forks, BC named Egnat Pronick. Roman drowned while swimming in Red Berry Lake. Cornella married Johann Peters. Annie married Alex Stishenko. Frank, who is my father, married Annie Matzner and homesteaded in the Spruce Creek area. Alec homesteaded in the Ranger area and married Hilda Tymofichuk. Allan became a sawyer on various sawmills and worked in many different logging camps throughout British Columbia. He and Bruce also did some mining together, mostly in British Columbia. They also rode the rails and lived in boxcars. Work was hard to find, and I do believe that is how they ended up mining in the Kootenays. Bruce was later injured in an accident while cutting cord wood. He never did much physical labor after that and he never married. Allan married Annie Ripka.

Joseph lived with different members of the family most of his life. When he was a baby crawling on the floor while Grandma was whitewashing the house, he found the lime container and stuck a handful of it into his mouth. He almost died from the ingestion of the lime and had to be hospitalized. When he recovered, his mental capacities were diminished; even so, he had a love for trains and worked for the railroad as a laborer for many years, and as a result traveled with the train crews from one end of Saskatchewan to the other without ever having to pay a fare.

CHAPTER 2

My Matzner Ancestors Claimed to be German

Anna Schober Matzner with her three children: Alois Jr. on her lap; my mom, Annie; and her older brother, Joe

Alois Matzner in his Austrian military uniform

Alois Matzner was born in the village of Zottig in the province of Schliesen in Prussia. Now it is located within the Czechoslovakian border and "Zottig" can no longer be found on a map. It is now part of the village (or city) of Sadek.

The Matzners claimed German descent, but they lived at Number 33 Zottig for many generations. There is a story told within the family that many years in the past a Matzner had worked as a gardener for a kaiser in Prussia. The kaiser's only son fell in the river and would have drowned had the gardener not jumped in and rescued him. The kaiser was infinitely grateful and wanted to give the gardener a reward. The gardener was uncomfortable about that because he would have saved anyone's child in the same situation, but the kaiser was not to be deterred, so he gave Mr. Matzner a piece of farmland that became known as Number 33 Zottig. Because they had become landowners, the Matzner family were then considered part of the upper class.

The family property was passed down from generation to generation, and generations later Alois Matzner chose to marry Anna Schober, but because her father was a shoemaker Alois' family didn't approve, as they considered her to be beneath their social status. They opposed the relationship strongly, but Alois knew he loved her and married her without their blessing. In those days the oldest son inherited the family property, and when Alois' father died Alois inherited Number 33 Zottig with the provision that his mother and sisters would still live there and he would look after them. The family never accepted the marriage and did everything they could to make it difficult. In the end Alois relinquished his inheritance to his mother and sisters and moved Anna and the children to Reittendorf, another town about fifty miles away. Alois worked on a farm there, but in time moved back to Neusstadt, which was closer to his family.

He soon realised that he could not live anywhere near his family. Eventually he decided to seek new opportunity and came to the USA. After returning briefly to his family, he traveled to Canada, where he got a job so he could save enough money to bring his family to join him. He sent for them as soon as he could, and Anna Matzner and their three children made the long voyage on the ship called *Cassandra,* arriving in Montreal in October 1913.

They took the train across the prairies to Saskatchewan. When she arrived at Clarkboro she gathered up her children and got off like she was instructed to. No one was there to meet her. It must have been very frightening for her to get off in the middle of nowhere, not knowing anyone, with only the expectation that her husband would come for them. Alois arrived a short time later with a horse and steel-wheeled wagon. He was wearing a pair of coveralls and working man's clothing, and at first she didn't even recognize him.

But they were happy to be together, and he spent some time getting to know his children again. I am sure Anna had many scary stories to share about her journey across the ocean with their three small children. Alois Jr. was the youngest child, just a baby. My mother was about seven years old, and her brother Joe was about a year-and-a-half older than her. They were poor, but they were together.

They spent the first winter in a friend's house. Alois had found a piece of property right close by, but it didn't have a house on it. In the spring, with the help of some of his neighbors, he found a building that would serve as their home and moved it onto his property. This was a far cry from what they were used to living in, in Austria, but it was their own place.

Anna had developed rheumatoid arthritis after her children were born. By the time she arrived in Canada it was much worse, and it wasn't long before she could only walk by using a chair for support as she pushed it around the room. She looked after the children the best she could until she could no longer manage. Eventually she was hospitalized in the city hospital in Saskatoon for the summer months because Alois worked away from home then. This was very expensive, so she was transferred to North Battleford, Saskatchewan, a long way from her family. It must have been devastating for her to be there all alone. I am sure she became very lonely, because it was near impossible for Alois to take their young family to visit her. She wouldn't have known what was going to happen next, or if she would ever be with them again.

It was costing more for her hospitalization than Alois earned, so he basically mortgaged his land to give her the necessary care, and when she passed away it was repossessed to pay the bill. The church wanted money to bury her; something he didn't have, so she was buried outside of the main Catholic graveyard, in the overflow area on the other side of the hedge. The grave marker can still be found there today.

Mom told me that there were times when the family did without many things because there wasn't enough money. They only had one pair of shoes, which was saved for when they went to school; the rest of the time they went barefoot. When there was frost on the ground in the fall, it was cold on their bare feet. When they brought in the milk cow in the morning, they'd stand in the fresh cow pies to warm their cold feet, and after the chores were done, they cleaned and washed themselves and ran to school.

There were times when all they had to eat was homemade noodles and sauerkraut. This situation didn't last too long because grandpa Matzner was a very hardworking and determined man. Soon he was able to provide the necessities for his family, but the children learned the responsibilities of keeping house and doing outside chores at a very early age while their dad worked away from home to provide a better life for his family.

*　　*　　*

Grandpa Matzner, a widower with a young family, discovered a young lady stuck in a creek with a team and wagon on his way to work one day. He stopped to get the wagon out of the mud. She thanked him, then while chatting they discovered they both were single parents. Her husband died of influenza, leaving her with a family farm, while Grandpa had to work away from his young family. It didn't take many visits for them to realize how to solve both their problems. Now the story gets more interesting. You see, the lady my Alois Matzner helped out of the mud hole was Cornella Peters, one of my dad's sisters. So when I was born my aunt was also my grandma. Cornella had five children, Alois had three. They were married in 1919, and in time they had six more children.

Cornella Antypowich Peters and
Alois Matzner on their wedding day

CHAPTER 3

Frank Antypowich and Annie Matzner Start a New Life

One day Frank Antypowich and a friend decided they would go to Vancouver, BC to seek work. On the way, he stopped to see his sister Cornella and meet her new family. Annie Matzner was her step-daughter, and she'd just come in from a day of harrowing a field with six horses. She had dust on her face and baggy patched overalls, and truthfully, she never realized how attractive she was at any time, but at that moment she couldn't imagine any young man being interested in her. However, when they were introduced, Frank decided he wasn't interested in going to British Columbia after all. He had a hard time persuading Annie to even go for a walk with him, but there was a special chemistry between them and eventually she gave in to it. She was seventeen and he was nineteen when they met.

Frank went back home to Penn to work with his brothers and he and Annie kept in touch by mail as there were no telephones. The closest post office was at Witchekan, twenty-one miles from Penn, and every two weeks he would go on horseback to get the mail. One time he tied his horse to the hitching rail and went into the post office, and when he came out the horse had gotten loose and headed home. Dad had to walk twenty-one miles home. And that wouldn't have been so bad, but there was no letter from Annie either. There was nothing he could do but wait another two weeks for the mail to come.

Frank couldn't read and write because he'd never gone to school a day in his life, so he always had to have someone help him with the letters. But he never gave up and on July 20, 1926, they were married at Laventure, Saskatchewan; she was nineteen and he was twenty-one.

My parents, Frank Antypowich and Annie Matzner

Mom and Dad at the ranch

Their first home was a little log house by Edward Lake, near Penn. At first my mother was afraid of the Indians; after all, they'd left a trail of gruesome stories about what had happened to some of the early pioneers that ventured into their areas. The house she lived in did not have many windows, and when Dad was away from home she was afraid to let them in the house. She later learned to trust the Indians as they became better friends.

She was also frightened when the cattle came around the house, with the bulls bellowing and pawing in the dirt. She was afraid that they would push the door in. It was hard for a young girl to stay there by herself without ways to communicate with any of her family.

Frank and Joe Matzner (Annie's older brother) had become good friends. Frank and Annie ended up in a partnership with Joe and they tried to build a ranch near Pelican Lake, Saskatchewan, in an area that was known as Raspberry Hill. There was a lot of good grazing land for the cattle in the summertime, but the hay they'd made was swamp grass with very little nutrition in it. The winter was very hard and the cattle were not accustomed to the North Country. As a result, the first winter was devastating as many cows died during the cold weather because of lack of nutrition. That ended the partnership, but their relationship stayed friendly right to the end of their lives.

I believe this is the picture of the house that Dad built at Raspberry Hill when they lived there

Crossing Chiteck Lake to Raspberry hill where Dad and Uncle Joe ranched; this is a picture of Uncle Joe, Mom, Roman (the baby sitting on her lap) and Doug Blair, a friend of Dad's

The roads in that part of the country weren't much more than trails and there were no bridges. The Indians showed them a shallow crossing on the lake where they could cross with horses and a wagon, but during the high water in the spring runoff they had to tie the box to the wagon to keep it from floating away.

After the ranching venture fell apart, Dad and Joe each went their own way. Joe went to Mildred, Saskatchewan, where he began farming and married a schoolteacher who became my Aunt Ruby. They lived in the Mildred area for many years. They were a hardworking pair and didn't take much time to enjoy themselves. Ruby died from cancer. And Joe, devastated at losing his partner, eventually sold the farm. He later married Dorothy Helm.

Dad took up a homestead in the Spruce Creek area. He was a hunter and gatherer, and although there were many tough times, he always provided for his family. In the summer he would work his homestead with Annie right beside him. In the winter he would trap beaver, muskrat, wolves, coyotes, squirrels, weasels, and mink, creating a source of income or trade.

Frank and Annie had five children: Roman, Ervin, Shirley, me, and Clifford, and I have been very glad to be part of that family.

I believe this is the house Dad built on the homestead at Spruce Creek

Our family before Clifford was born. Dad is holding me.

I was born on a cold and frosty afternoon on November 29, 1937, at home in the old log house on the homestead. A forty-five-gallon barrel converted into a heater supplied the heat for the whole house. Grandma Antypowich was there to assist with the birth. They warmed blankets by the heater for Mom and me, and to this very day I have never liked to be cold. I will be forever indebted to my mom for all the pain and discomfort I must have caused her. There was no anesthetic or painkillers used during my birth. They didn't have the convenience of a proper scale to weigh a baby, so several days later Uncle Alex brought over a beam scale that they used to weigh the bags of grain. So they wrapped me in a blanket and weighed me. I'm told I weighed fourteen pounds. I don't know if I was a fast gainer or the beam scale weighed in the favor of whoever was selling the grain.

One has to appreciate that there were no disposable diapers in those days. Diapers were made out of the flour or sugar sacks. As well, mothers didn't go to the store to buy baby formulas; they nursed their babies. Also, there were no convenient jars of baby food. It was good old meat and potatoes, and they mashed in their own blends of different vegetables. I am told that some women chewed meat, preferably rabbit, and fed it to the young babies.

The ever-present problem of the mosquitoes and flies didn't make it easy either. Oh yes, the early pioneers were hardy people and my roots go back to those times. When I try to visualize just what it must have really been like, I feel very grateful to those who cared for me.

CHAPTER 4

I was a Childhood Dennis the Menace

When I was about two and a half years old I was told to stay in the house while my mom and dad went out to do the morning chores. It was the middle of the winter and very cold, -30ºF or better, outside. I believe that is why I was left in the house where it was warm, but I wanted to go out with Mom and Dad, so after a while I managed to push a stool to the door and tried to open it. I couldn't get it open, so I got a hammer and started banging on the doorknob. It opened, so with no more clothes on than I was wearing in the house, I took the path to the barn. I didn't go very far before I got cold. Along the path there was a load of logs buried under the snow, so I crawled up on the logs and sat there crying, hoping that my mom or dad would come and rescue me, but they couldn't hear me from inside the barn. I am sure that I'd have frozen to death if Uncle Alec hadn't come along. Finding nobody in the house, he was headed to the barn when he found me sitting on the logs, crying. He carried me back to the house, asking why I was sitting outside on the logs with no warm clothes or footwear on.

I told him Mom and Dad had left me in the house, so I was going to the barn but I'd gotten too cold. I wanted him to take me to the barn, but he said first we had to put some warm clothes on. While he was getting me dressed, Mom and Dad brought in the milk. They had found my uncle's team of horses halfway to the barn with no one around, so had hurried to the house to find out what had happened. As the years passed, Alec remained one of my favorite uncles. He always told me how much I was like my dad, and who knows, maybe my second name being Frank had something to do with it. I have to tell you that when he was older and no longer able to communicate or respond to people because of his dementia, I went to visit him at the facility that he was in at Kelowna, BC. The nurse let me take him outside into the sunshine in a wheelchair. She told me that he couldn't communicate with me, so I just sat with him and talked to him just like I would have done years before. When I was telling him how I had called a moose that fall, I thought I recognized something in his expression that told me he understood what I was saying. We just sat there and looked at each other for a while and then he made the sound that you would use to call a moose.

My mother was used to hard work. She worked hard on the homestead throughout her youth, and as soon as she was bigger and strong enough, she'd worked with her step-sister to do the stooking while grandpa cut grain with a binder at harvest time. When I was about three years old, dad was cutting grain with the binder pulled by four horses. My mother was stooking. I was toddling along behind her and when I got too tired she would put me in a box with a net over it to keep the mosquitoes out and I would go to sleep. I guess when I woke up and found nobody there but my faithful old German shepherd, I started to look for my mom. I wandered through the standing grain until I came to the edge of the field that bordered on Spruce Creek. My mother was in a panic when she realized that I was gone. She came running across the field to where my dad was and told him that I had crawled out of the box. Dad looked around the field and could see me and the dog walking through the standing grain near the creek. The old dog was trying to keep me away from the creek and I was trying to go the other way. When dad came to rescue me, I was mad at my dog because he kept me from finding my mom. She must have had a lot of faith in the old German shepherd dog, because a bear or a coyote could have had me for lunch. I guess she never went too far from that box after that.

CHAPTER 5

Our Cree Indian Neighbors

The homestead where I was born bordered right up to an Indian reserve. The Cree Indians taught my dad many tricks for survival with trapping and hunting. He became good friends with them and learned to speak their language very well. They would come to the farmhouse and ask for tea or sugar, and in return would leave a piece of venison or moose meat.

Mom visiting our Indian neighbors

Charlie Pissis, a native friend of Dad's, lived on the reserve and he would come by to visit, and he took a liking to me. He gave me moccasins his wife had made and he'd do a little dance and try to get me to mimic him. I don't think my mother was too impressed. She didn't want her little boy to become an Indian.

Later, when I was able to walk around outside, he would say he was going to make a great hunter out of me. When I was about four he gave me a slingshot he'd made; then he and I would go hunting for small birds. Charlie always encouraged me to become a hunter.

When I was a little older he brought me a bow made from a saskatoon willow, as well as some arrows, and showed me how to shoot it. Boy, now I really was beginning to be a great hunter. He'd take me to the sawmill to hunt for little birds that hung around the slab piles. I still remember Charlie sneaking up on those little birds ever so quietly, teaching me to move slowly so as not to make any noise. I was lucky if I could get an arrow to land within three feet of the birds, so one day Charlie took the bow and shot one for me.

That only made me more determined to learn how to shoot arrows too. He told me I would have to do a lot of practicing, so he set up a box as a target. He said when I hit the dot in the center of the box I'd be able to shoot a bird. I don't know how many arrows I shot before I finally hit the dot. I do remember the first bird I shot. I was so proud of the kill I'd made and took it in to show my mom. She looked it and said, "Oh, poor little bird. Don't you feel sorry for it now?" I said, "No," and asked if I should pluck it the way Daddy plucked the ducks. She said no and told me to give it to the cats. It wasn't long before I was feeding the cats regularly and there wasn't a bird around the yard that was safe if I had my bow and arrow with me. Then one day my dad took me aside and said, "It's okay for you to shoot some birds, but don't shoot the robins."

Charlie would come over and ask me how many birds I'd shot, then he'd say, "Pretty soon you will be able to shoot the big ones." He tried to teach me how to say all names of the animals and birds in Cree. Dad helped me when I needed help with the names. One day he came over with some birch bark and he and Dad made a moose call. I was so fascinated by it and the noises it made that I wanted to go with them to watch them call moose, but of course I was too small. When they returned they had shot a moose, and I remember them laughing and talking about how close they'd called it in before they shot it. Although I wasn't there, I visualized the hunt in my mind. I'm sure I had dreams of calling a moose and having it come to me so I could shoot it, but of course that didn't happen for many years.

*Charlie Pissis at the age of ninety, many years
later in life after he was my friend*

I don't have any pictures of Charlie as a young man. His father's name was Bill Pissis. Although I always knew of him as Charlie Pissis, I was told in later years the family dropped the name Pissis, using only "Bill." All the Pissis descendants are known as "Bill." Charlie was a tall, slender man. He was an exceptionally good hunter and a good friend to the white people who had moved into the area.

In late 2010, I contacted the Pelican Lake Indian Band near Chiteck Lake to find out what had happened to Charlie. No one at the band office remembered Charlie Pissis, probably because they would have known him in the last couple of generations as "Bill." However, someone told me to call Miriam Thomas and she might know. It was sheer good luck to make contact with her. She told me my old friend Charlie had died in 1972. My cousin Ervin Matzner and his wife Evelyn knew Miriam fairly well. Miriam owned a gift shop in Chiteck Lake and she had some booklets of the Indians of that area demonstrating their smoking and tanning technique for the hides they used to make moccasins and clothing. Evelyn bought one and sent it to me, and I found the picture of my friend Charlie in it.

I remember some of the things the Indians did when living near our farm, and one was the women tanning hides. I was pretty young but my memories resurfaced as I watched the same process carried out by the Indians in Northern Alberta, as it seemed basically the same method. I remember seeing hides stretched on frames that they had made from poles.

In the booklet that I received from Miriam Thomas, the process was described step by step and I found it very interesting. The booklet described how the stretching frames were erected and tied at the corners with rope. Then it was set upon a supporting rail at an angle that made it easier for the women to work with the hides. They cut slits around the edges of the hide, then all worked together to position the hide so that they could "sew" the hide by lacing through the slits and around the frame, stretching the hide taut.

One of the hardest parts of the job was removing any remaining flesh or excess membrane left on the hide. They used a leg-bone scraper to work at the hide to do this. After the fleshing was completed, they turned the frame over so the hair was on the top side. Next they would work the hair off the hide by pulling it and pushing a wooden scraper with a metal blade under, along the surface of the hide, taking care not to cut through it.

Then the hide was ready to smoke. The Pelican Lake Indians made a wide tepee of poles and the prepared hide was draped over this framework. A bed of coals was prepared in a fire pot that could have been either a hole in the ground or an old washtub. Punk (decayed) spruce was thrown in so it would begin smoldering under the draped hide. Then the hide was covered with a tarp to keep as much smoke as possible inside. The punk wood gave a cooler smoke and made the hide a lighter colored leather. Apparently the smoking could take anywhere from one to two hours.

When the hide was removed from this first smoking it was very brittle, so next the softening process took place. It is said that a mixture of lard and vegetable oil were warmed over a fire to make a greasy, gooey mixture, and then a feather was used to sprinkle a light application of the grease onto the hide. After that the hide was rubbed with animal brains mixed into water to further soften it. Apparently the rule of thumb is that the brain of every animal is big enough to cover its entire hide (I found this on the Internet). After that the hide was worked by hand for several hours as part of the process of softening it.

The next step took place while the hide was wet. It was pulled back and forth over a long dull blade or a pole until the fibers loosened and it became very soft, resembling something like a flannel blanket. Then the hide had to be shaped and stretched. The wet hide was wrapped around two smoothed poles and two people worked to squeeze all water from it.

After this the hide was draped over a frame for the final sinew removal. At this point the hide took on its final shape and any imperfections were removed, then a final smoking was done, lasting about a half hour.

The finished product was made into moccasins and clothing. The moccasins Charlie brought me as an infant and the ones my parents wore were not fancy and beaded like we see now. They were simple and very durable.

In May of 2011, while visiting family and friends in Chiteck Lake, I phoned Miriam Thomas and made an appointment to visit with her. My cousin, Ervin Matzner, and I went, and when we arrived she told us she had known she was going to have very special company, so she had made bannock and blueberries, which she had picked and canned herself, and tea. She said this was a traditional Indian meal made by a traditional Indian lady.

I hadn't had bannock since I'd last gone hunting in the mountains. I usually made it on those trips, but that day we certainly enjoyed the traditional Indian meal and we had a lovely visit with that charming traditional Indian lady. She is one of native Indians who works and functions in today's world with her people, but preserves and teaches the traditional native Indian ways as much as she can. She still does beadwork and makes moccasins too. I asked her if the natives around there tanned their own hides anymore, and she said no, she got hers from a tannery in Edmonton now.

When I was a child, the Indians camped on a little hill just across the fence from our house and I would listen to them singing and chanting. Sometimes Dad would go there and he learned to sing and chant with the beating of drums as they did. I didn't know what those ceremonies represented to them; to me it sounded like a bunch of coyotes.

Miriam Thomas with bannock that she had made in
her home near Chiteck Lake, Saskatchewan

Moccasins and beadwork that Miriam Thomas still does

Another thing that the natives would do was have a gathering that I always thought was a powwow, but Miriam Thomas told me must have been the sun dance. I'm not exactly sure what all took place, but it lasted for a few days and they'd offer gifts to what I believe was the sun spirit. Most of the articles that they offered were made or carved by their people. However, there was a merchant who sold or traded furs with the native people for brightly colored material, and sometimes this material was offered at these ceremonies. When the ceremonies were over and the people were ready to leave, all the offerings remained at the site, along with the sun dance lodge or tepee, for nature to do what it would with it, because everything was considered too sacred to be kept for personal use. I didn't discuss this with Miriam, but I can remember it being said that after the

Indians had left a merchant would come and collect the material, along with some of the other articles. To my knowledge he never was caught, and it was thought that he probably resold it to them another time.

One summer day my dad took me to a gathering that they were having on the hill. We went into a large tepee. A fire burned in the center and there were tanned hides with the hair still on all around the inside of the tepee. There were many Indians sitting on the hides and we sat down cross-legged beside them and Dad greeted them in their traditional ways. The ceremonies were a series of dancing and singing in all sorts of different costumes. The drumming and chanting was a bit scary to me, but Chief Tom Thomas was very honored to have us at their sun dance. It was an experience that, although a little bit scary, will never be forgotten.

Cree Indians at a sun dance near our home

These are Indian tepees that were set up just across the fence from our farm

CHAPTER 6

Edwards Lake School

The Antypowich family played an active role in building and maintaining Edwards Lake School too. I have included some documents that we came upon in Saskatchewan that record trustee meetings held at Edward Lake School.

Record of general ratepayers meeting dated December 5, 1936, stipulates that all past labor and donations could be applied to the taxes; also recording some of the rates paid for services

*District records from the school, 1936 and 1937,
detailing the work Dad contributed.*

In those days people did whatever they could to keep up with their payments. One thing they did was cut cordwood for the school and what they earned was put against their land taxes. We came across these documents in Saskatchewan.

1938 account of cordwood for the district

Records of trustee meetings; my dad's
signature on the page (Frank Antypowich)

Note of amount of payment received for services provided at the school

The Class at Edwards Lake School

Before I started school, my older siblings moved to Spruce Creek. The school was built of logs with windows four by four feet that would slide open to let in fresh air. It was a one-room school, and the teacher lived in a small "teacherage" built near the school.

The teacher wasn't a lot older than some of her students and she began to invite some of the older ones to her place at lunch hour. My two older brothers were invited too, but when they found out that the teacher and her students were drinking moonshine they didn't go, because they knew they'd be in big trouble if Dad ever found out. That created friction between them and the teacher and the classmates that were involved.

One day when all the kids were picking huckleberries on the way home after school, my second oldest brother had taken the lard pail that he used for a lunch bucket and picked it full of berries. He left it sitting along the side of the road while he helped his younger sister fill hers. One of the older girls came along and emptied his berries into her bucket. He wanted his berries back but she refused to give them to him and asked him what he was going to do about it. So he just started picking berries again, but this time he was behind her. And when she filled her pail, she left it sitting by the side of the road and helped her sister fill hers.

He took a good look at the situation. He knew she was too big and too strong and could probably beat him up, but he thought that he could outrun her if he had a good head start. So he ran up the road as fast as he could, and when he got to where her bucket of berries was, he kicked her bucket like a football punter punting the ball. The berries flew in every direction, and he just kept on running.

The next day the teacher kept him in after school and was going to give him a strapping for doing this. She kept some of the older kids to help her, as she was not very big. They were all standing at the door so he could not run out when she called him to come to the front of the room to get his strapping. He didn't go, so she walked up to him and told him to hold out his hand or she would strap him across the face. I guess he thought he had to protect himself, so he tackled her, pushed her to the window, and threw her out of it. While all the other kids ran out to see what happened to the teacher, he grabbed his lunch bucket, cap, and coat and ran home.

That evening one of the school board members came by our house and told Dad that they were going to expel Ervin from school. He said, "Ye Ervin is all right but he is just too full of hellery." My dad told him that no one was going to expel anyone. He said all the teacher wanted to do was drink moonshine with the older kids, and that if they didn't replace her the whole board could expect to be removed.

That was the last day Ervin went to school. Dad took Ervin and Roman and they went logging. They'd cut trees so that when the muskegs froze they could haul them home with the sleigh and horses. That winter they lived in a tent when they were logging.

The wolves were bad and they'd come around at night, bothering the horses, so Dad built a big fire to keep them away. They used two teams of horses to haul the logs. They would load one team and send them home by themselves. Then, they would load the other sleigh and follow them home. One day, they were surprised to find the first team standing on the road. The wolves were sitting in front of them and the horses refused to go any farther. Dad always had two boards that he put on top of the logs to sit on. He got off the sleigh and took the two boards and banged them together to make a loud noise to scare the wolves away.

Most times, when Dad and the boys got home Mom had the horses fed and supper ready. She used to cook a big roaster pan of cabbage rolls and some fresh baked bread, as well as some gingersnap cookies, for them to take back to the bush with them.

On another trip home they had loaded up old Dick and Tiny and sent them home first because they were a slow-moving team. They'd put too big a load on the sleigh and the horses couldn't turn the corner at bottom of hill, so they went straight into the neighbor's yard. When the dog started raising a ruckus the man went out to see what he was barking at, and there stood the team of horses with a load of logs. He unhooked them and put them in the barn.

It was a clear moonlight night and Dad noticed that they'd missed the corner. When the neighbor came out and helped him hook up the team, he asked my dad if he wasn't afraid to be out late at night when the wolves were so bad. Dad said a gun didn't do much good because the wolves only came out on the road at night. He told him he used two short pieces of board and would bang one against each other and that would make them move off of the road.

CHAPTER 7

Hunting and Fishing: Learning from Dad

When Dad would go hunting or fishing I always wanted to go along. Sometimes he would take me fishing. I can remember him snaring northern pike from the creek that ran through our farm. I can still hear his words of caution as he eased me up to the edge of the bank so I could see the fish slowly swimming by. He would tell me I had to learn to be very quiet if I wanted to be able to catch one. In my excitement I would raise my little hand and say, "There's one, Dad," and of course the fish would be gone. He'd use the same snare wire that he'd set for rabbits. It wasn't very strong, and sometimes when he snared a big fish the wire broke before he got it to the shore and it would get away.

Mom and Dad and I sitting on a log by Spruce Creek
with a northern pike that Dad had snared

There were also times when he'd take me to the creek and we'd sit in the grass and bulrushes to wait for ducks. Sometimes he'd get two or three with one shot. He'd quickly gather them up and come back to sit in the grass with me to wait for more to come by. Sometimes the ones that flew away would just circle around and come back to look for the ones that they'd left behind. There were times when he'd get a shot on the fly, which was always exciting to me. I was about four years old, and I'd have a duck in each hand, proudly walking behind him to the house, where we'd pluck them. All of the fine breast feathers were put into a bag and used for blankets and pillows. When all the fine little hairs and pin feathers were singed, it was time to draw the innards out of the duck. Then Mom would either cut them up in smaller pieces to fry or she would put a stuffing in them and roast them in a pan.

Of course I was too small to go hunting deer with him, but I remember the day a deer came across the field and I watched him shoot it from the window in the house. I also watched him shoot coyotes right from the house. To me this was so exciting that I could not wait until I became older and bigger so I could go with him.

Then Dad sold the farm and we moved. Although it was only eleven or twelve miles away, I did not see much of Charlie and I sure did miss him. On the new farm there was bush that was much closer to the house, so my dad showed me how to set snares to catch rabbits. There were a lot of rabbits, and now I was beginning to be a trapper as well as a hunter.

CHAPTER 8

The Sawmill at Junor

Dad put together a small sawmill to cut lumber to use around the farm. A lot of the men who worked at setting up the mill were neighbors whom Dad would saw logs for. They would trade their wages against the expense of cutting the lumber that they would bring in.

One warm spring day they were digging holes for the big square timbers the mill would sit on and they still had to contend with the frost in the shady places. A preacher came along thinking he would have an opportunity to preach to the men who were working there. He lay on a log and started reading from his Bible. Some of the men did not appreciate it. He was reading a portion of the scripture concerning faith, which made it seem that he was insinuating that they were of little faith. One of the men said that if his faith was so strong he should come over to where they were working and remove the frost for them, but he just lay there and kept reading.

That is, until Ervin, my second oldest brother, threw down his pick and was about to kick his ass off the log. He got up and ran down the road, with Ervin hot on his tail, and Ervin told him he had better have a lot of faith or long legs, because if he caught him he was going to kick his ass all the way to the railway tracks. Needless to say, he never ever came back to preach to them again.

The logging was done in the wintertime because it was easier to pull the logs on a sleigh over the frozen ground than to pull them out through the mud on a wagon. They cut the logs and hauled them to the mill and then sawed them in the summer. This was all done with a sleigh and a

34

team of horses. There were no power saws in those days, so everything was done with a Swede saw and a broad axe.

The sawmill always interested me. It was always fun to play in the sawdust pile and I liked the smell of the fresh-cut lumber. I remember jumping on a slab pile, not knowing that hornets had made a nest there, and it wasn't long before they swarmed around me and did a real number on my bare legs.

One spring day before the sawmill was in production, an old mother cat had her kittens under the log pile, so I crawled under there to retrieve them. There were five and they all had long tails like most cats do. But my uncle had a cat with a short tail, so I decided that I would make short tails on all these kittens. I used a hammer and a piece of iron that was on the bunk of the mill and I whacked the tails off all of the kittens. Of course my dad noticed what I had done and gave me a real shellacking. I think it might have been my first one, but believe me, I never forgot it.

I didn't hold it against him. He still was my idol. Hunting was the big thing in my life and at that time I believed my dad could hunt anything and be successful at it. One day I wanted him to take me down to the creek so we could hunt ducks together. But he told me I could go hunt ducks by myself. All I needed was a salt shaker, and if I got close enough to the duck and put a little salt on his tail, I could catch him. I didn't need any further encouragement, so with my favorite old dog and a salt shaker, I headed for the creek to go duck hunting.

The old dog was my guardian from the time I took my first steps, and of course when I got near the creek he sensed the danger that I might be in and wouldn't let me get any closer. Dad followed me down and was there to assist me if I got into any problems. I guess I was frustrated with my trusty old dog because he wouldn't let me get close to the creek, so when Dad showed up I was all teary-eyed and told him that I was never going to take my dog hunting with me again.

Later my mom clued me into the fact that putting salt on the ducks' tail was just a trick and would never work. Later that summer a neighboring sheep farmer came over to our place. I immediately tried to talk him into taking me to the river to hunt ducks. He gave me a little story about how easy it was to hunt ducks. All I needed was a pepper shaker to put a little pepper on the rock so when the duck smelled it he would sneeze and bump his beak on the rock and then I could catch them. I told him putting salt on the duck's tail didn't work, so I didn't think that putting pepper on a rock would work either. You had to take a gun and shoot them. That was how you hunted ducks.

CHAPTER 9

Lessons My Older Brothers Taught Me

When I was about six years old I'd follow my two older brothers wherever they went around the farm. This wasn't always with their approval.

We had a herd of sheep, and Roman and Ervin were big enough to handle the ram. From time to time they would tease him until he chased and bunted them. But I was too small to deal with him, and I guess they thought this would be their way out of having me tag along, so they decided to have a little fun with me and the ram.

They told me if I could ride him, he'd never chase or bunt me again, and of course I was brave enough to try. Now a sheep isn't all that easy to ride, even though you can hold on to the wool. So they decided to put an old tire around him for me to hang on to, but from time to time I would fall off anyway. Of course, they'd rescue me before the ram could turn around to bunt me. After we had been doing this for a while, the rest of the sheep got up from their afternoon nap and headed over the hill to graze on the creek bottom pasture. The old ram was in a hurry to catch up to them, so when my brothers let him go I went for a merry old ride over the hill. I wasn't doing too bad on the level, but when he started down the hill, he high centered on the tire. We didn't go far before the ram and I ended upside down in the brush along the path. I guess my brothers thought this was a good time to run away and leave me behind. When the ram managed to free himself, he was not too interested in bunting me. He just kept running after the rest of the sheep. When I crawled back up the hill to where I thought my brothers would be, they were gone.

Of course that didn't keep the ram from bunting or chasing me. In fact, I think it made him worse. When I'd go to gather the eggs, he'd watch for me and wouldn't let me leave the barn. I don't know how many dozens of eggs I smashed on his head before he'd go back to the sheep barn. Then I'd make a run for the house, sometimes tripping and falling, smashing all the eggs in the pail. Of course, I would get my ears pulled by Mom because she thought I was being careless and running with a pail of eggs.

After begging and pleading with her that it was the ram's fault and not mine, she came with me to gather the eggs. The old ram came out to meet us and began bunting at her until he broke most of the eggs, then I was in real trouble because I had to tell her that it was the boys who taught the ram to bunt me. They got a real talking too from Dad, and now they were really out to get even with me. They'd let me follow them when they'd go out hunting birds with their slingshots, and when they were a fair way from home they would run away from me. Sometimes when I was trying to find my way back home, they would below like a bull and scare the living daylights out of me.

I was the odd man out. They were seven and nine years older than me, so I was just a pain to them, but little did they know how much I looked up to them. One day when Ervin was ploughing the field on the other side of the creek, my mom asked me to call him for dinner. He unhooked the horses from the plough and told me if I wanted to be like him I would ride one of the horses, so I did. All was going really well until we got to the creek. Ervin stopped to let the horses drink, but the horse I was riding decided to paw in the water and then lay down. Of course I fell off, and while the creek wasn't dangerously deep, I sure got wet!

One other time I went with him to bring the milk cows in from the pasture but some of the cows had crossed the creek. This was in the spring of the year and the creek was running full bore. Ervin told me that he'd throw me across the creek so I could chase the cows home from the other side. Although reluctant, I let him try and I almost made it to the other side but fell backward into the roaring creek. I surely would have drowned had he not jumped in to rescue me.

Another time when we were bringing in the cows, we were having difficulty finding them as there was so much bush in the pasture, so he decided I would crawl up a poplar tree to see if I could find the cows. I crawled up ten or fifteen feet, only to find a hornets' nest in a woodpecker hole. When they came after me I lost my hold and tumbled down. I thought he would catch me, but he missed and I landed on my back. It knocked the wind out of me and I couldn't talk for a few minutes. Although I wasn't badly hurt, I had a very bad headache. The hornet bites were secondary as we still had to find the cows. He made me promise that I wouldn't tell anyone that I'd fallen out of the tree, and for all I know my mother thought that my headache was caused by the hornet bites.

I don't know why I always wanted to go with him because he was forever playing mean tricks on me. He always liked to race horses. One nice balmy day in the winter when I was about seven years old, he decided we should have a horse race. There was a foot of snow on the ground, so I guess he thought I wouldn't get hurt if I fell off. We were riding bareback and that didn't leave much to hang on to. I can still remember I was in the lead and then his horse passed mine and we were flat out as far as old farm horses were concerned. I was having a hard time hanging on, so I tried to grab my horse around the neck. It wasn't long before I was hanging around the horse's neck, but she wouldn't slow down and finally I had to let go. I was afraid she was going to trample me as I fell right in front of her. Somehow she managed to not step on me and all that got hurt was my pride. And of course I lost the race.

Two things that stand out in my memory of those early years was a love for hunting and horses. I used to love watching the teams pull heavy loads of logs on the sleigh. I'd cut two willow sticks and use them for my stick horses. Each one had a special name and in my mind reminded me of the various horses that I watched work. It is no wonder I love horses because in those days the only transportation was by a horse and wagon, toboggan, or sleigh. My dad ploughed the fields, seeded, and harvested, all done with horses.

One would think that after the bumps and spills I had on horses I would have a dislike for them, but to this very day they are my favorite animal; and the hotter and faster, the better I like them. I have had many spills, but many thrills as well. It has just been in the last couple of years that I quit breaking my own young foals. At seventy-one, I thought it is just too hard to try to keep the old apple box in one piece. I still enjoy a good ride on a well-trained horse, but now I let my granddaughter, Jen, do all the frisky stuff.

CHAPTER 10

Antics of Young Boys on the Farm

For a young boy growing up, the farm was a great place to live. There were always chores to do: bringing in the wood, gathering the eggs, sweeping the snow off the step, or feeding and watering the chickens. After the chores were done, I could go out and play. There were no TVs or videogames, so I would go outside and entertain myself by making igloos and snow tunnels.

On schooldays, my time was laid out for me and I pretty much did what I was told, although my sister might not agree and sometimes my teacher probably wouldn't have either. In those early days we didn't have buses to take us to and from school in Saskatchewan. Just getting to and from school was a challenge. In the wintertime, it was cold and snowy. In the summer, bears and bulls wanted to use the road we traveled on as well. That meant we would have to detour around, sometimes as much as three miles, to get home safely

On the weekends and during the holidays, my cousins would come over and we would create our own activities, which I'm sure our parents didn't always appreciate or agree to. My three cousins and I were close in age, and when we got together we terrorized the farm.

One day when they came to visit we decided to pick on the ram. We ran past the door of the sheep shed, and when the ram came out to chase us, one of us waited with a shovel to whack him on the head. This wasn't too successful as the shovel would bounce off his head and hit us in the shins, so we decided to get something smaller and easier to handle. We found an iron rod from an old buck rake. Now we were ready for the old ram. When he came out, we took turns at whacking him on the head. Our aim wasn't always that good, so we repeated it many times. I guess eventually he realized he was losing the battle and he quit chasing us, so we went on to something else.

These are my three partners in crime, my cousins Walter, Ervin, and Harry Matzner, and their mother on the left of the wagon, and a young schoolteacher, Vera Lavachek, who was boarding with the Matzners at the time

The next day Dad noticed there was something wrong with the ram. His head and nose were swelled and one eye was very cloudy. Dad couldn't figure out what the ram had been fighting with, unless it was the bull, since my older brothers encouraged him to fight the Hereford bull. They'd feed the bull some grain and the ram would come to get his share. The bull wasn't about to share his grain; he would bunt him away. Then the ram discovered he had just as hard a head as the bull, so they had battles over a pile of grain. The ram even knocked the bull right off his feet because he hit him so hard, and then sometimes the bull would rough up the ram. This was a David and Goliath affair.

When my dad found out, he explained to the boys that this was very dangerous and somebody was going to get hurt, because the ram was getting uncontrollable. I don't know what he thought happened to the ram for sure, but I wasn't about to tell him that I had anything to do with it. The ram took a long time recuperating and I don't think he ever saw properly out of that one eye again.

It was not long after that Dad traded the ram to another sheep farmer who wanted new blood in his herd. Now, Louie was an old shepherd, and he'd feed his sheep a handful of grain and they'd follow him wherever he wanted them to go. However, when he tried to do it with that ram, he wanted the whole pail, so he bunted Louie around until he managed to crawl up on the hayrack to get away from him. Louie knew Roman and Ervin very well, and when he came over to see Dad he told him that his boys had wrecked the ram, now Dad would have to come and get him because Louie couldn't handle him. Louie walked with a cane for quite a while after the ram bunted him in the leg.

Another time when my cousins were visiting, we decided to play in the straw stack. This was a huge pile of straw that was blown into a heap by the threshing machine. In the fall, the crop was cut into bundles by the binder. The bundles were stooked by hand into small groups to dry. They were picked up and stacked onto a hayrack, then hauled to the thrashing machine, where they were forked onto a conveyor that fed them into the working mechanism of the threshing machine. The machine would break up the bundles and shake the grain out and separate it from the straw. Then the straw was blown into a huge pile, which would be later used for feed and bedding for the animals on the farm.

These were large piles, and if they were near the barnyard, the animals were turned into them to self-feed. When pigs were turned into the straw pile, they'd dig their way into the middle. Usually, only the sows and the boar were turned into the straw pile, but sometimes Mother Nature would play a little trick on the farmer, who'd find a litter of piglets too. They usually did quite well, and one day when the pigs came out to feed at the trough there would be a bunch of little pigs following the old sow.

The horses and cows would eat around the edges of the straw pile. When the wind blew from the north, they'd feed on the south side; and when the wind blew from the south, they'd feed on the north side. They'd waste quite a bit of the straw by tramping and laying on it, but it saved the farmers so much labor most of them used this method to feed their livestock.

One day my cousins and I decided to dig into a straw pile, and after we managed to make a few holes we tried to make one larger so we could all sit in it. We were jumping up and down, trying to pack the straw, but unbeknown to us the pigs had their room right below us, and the jumping wasn't really packing the straw, but was pushing it into the area that the pigs had rooted out. All of a sudden the floor fell out of our little room and we ended up in the middle of their bedroom; as you can imagine, quite a lot of straw came down with us on top of the pigs that were sleeping nice and comfortable. When we landed, let me tell you, all hell broke loose. There were grunting, squealing pigs going in every direction, with four kids desperately trying to get to the outside, right along with about ten pigs that had no respect for anyone they ran over. We managed to make it out, a little scraped and bruised, but still all in one piece. Have you ever been run over by a big pig? You should try getting run over by ten of them. It's a real treat. And let me tell you, there are two reasons why we never did try it again: one was that we didn't like the beating we took from the pigs as they ran over us, and the other was the thought of the beating we might get from our dads when they found out what we'd done.

So we looked for something else to do. We liked playing squirrel on the backs of the cows. The milk cows were all housed in the barn and their heads were locked in individual stanchions. We would jump from one cow to the other; this worked the cows up a bit, so when Mom and Dad would go to milk one, the cow would haul off and kick them. It didn't take Dad long to figure out what was causing the cows to act up so badly. The next time my cousins came to visit, Dad and my uncle sneaked out to the barn to see what we were doing. We were caught in the act, and I'll let you guess what happened! All I'll say it was quite dramatic for a few minutes, but it was effective, because I don't believe we ever did that again.

I wouldn't want you to believe that we'd turned into little angels. After that, we just went on to something different. Now, I can understand why my mom said, "When you raise a bunch of boys, you just give them a licking every time you see them, because they're either just going to get into trouble or are coming out of it."

CHAPTER 11

Making Moonshine to Pay the Bills

In the early days when people started settling in the northern areas of Saskatchewan, many of them found it very difficult to come up with ready cash that was required to pay their taxes, or the leases on their property, so they relied on the skills that they had learned in the past, probably from the old country.

Many people knew how to make their own liquor; better names to describe it might be homebrew, white lightning, or just good old moonshine.

Many of the homesteaders, including some of my relatives (although to my knowledge my dad didn't resort to it), found themselves in need of money, so they made clear moonshine and delivered it to a bootlegger who would give them cash. Although this was considered illegal and they could be fined or go to jail if caught, many still took the chance.

I will tell you a few stories that actually happened, and some of them are quite comical. One of the homesteaders loaded up just enough grain in his sleigh to cover a number of gallon jugs of moonshine that he was delivering to the bootlegger. The RCMP happened to have come to town, and when the homesteader pulled up to the post office, he was approached by an RCMP officer who asked him what he was hauling in his sleigh.

The homesteader told him he was delivering a load of grain to the elevator, but the RCMP asked to have a look at his grain. When he rolled back the blankets, the officer commented that he didn't know you had to keep grain warm when delivering it to the elevator. He began digging around in the grain and found the gallon jugs of moonshine. He confiscated the team and sleigh along with all the jugs, then tied the team to the hitching rail in front of the courthouse. He took a jug into the courthouse for evidence against the homesteader. I am not sure if the officer intended to seize the horses, sleigh, and grain, but he left the rest of the jugs in the sleigh, taking only one for evidence.

The homesteader was summoned to court. When he arrived, there were a few other cases ahead of him, so he had to wait his turn. He wore a fur cap, a buffalo coat that fell to his knees, and felt boots he'd tucked his pants into. While he was walking around inside the courthouse, he noticed the evidence sitting unattended. He picked up the jug of moonshine, put it under his big buffalo coat, and went outside. When he was stopped and asked where he was going, he said he had to relieve himself. He was told to make sure that he came right back and he promised he would. While outside, he put the jug back under the grain, untied the horses, and sent them down the road toward home. He went back into the courthouse to wait his turn and finally he was called before the judge, who read the charges against him and asked the RCMP officer for evidence to prove the accusation. When the officer went to retrieve it, the jug was missing. The judge said there wasn't a case without the evidence.

The officer asked for a moment to get another jug for evidence and his request was granted. The officer went outside to discover that the horses and sleigh, as well as the jugs of moonshine, were nowhere to be found. He came back into the courthouse and asked the homesteader where his horses and sleigh had gone. He shrugged his shoulders and lifted up his hands and said he had no idea, they'd been tied to the hitching rail. When the police officer told the judge the predicament, the judge threw the case out of court. I guess it would be safe to say that is like having your grain and moonshine too.

One day while us kids were playing at the neighbors', we came across a pile of sweet smelling barley on a shed floor. The neighbor kids said their dad was feeding it to the pigs and the turkeys. The younger girl said we couldn't give them very much or they would get drunk and fall over. That sounded like it would be fun to see, so we filled a pail with barley mash and poured it in the trough for the turkeys. They gobbled it up, so we gave them some more, and it wasn't long until those turkeys were doing the "funky chicken." Now that was fun to see, so we fed the pigs as well. After a couple of pails full, some of them began squealing and bumping into the pen. Some fell down; others just lay down, squealing.

Hearing the noise, the neighbor came out of the house to find thoroughly drunk turkeys and pigs surrounded by a yelling, hollering, excited bunch of kids. He scolded us, saying that feeding too much mash wasn't good for the animals. We were relieved that we didn't get a spanking.

Moonshine wasn't something new; it had been around from the beginning of the first settlements in North America. Rum was the preferred liquor, so the fur traders spiked it with molasses, brown sugar, and even iodine to give it that darker look. They traded it with the native Indians, who had a low tolerance for alcohol and would foolishly trade their furs for a few jugs of alcohol. The situation caused fighting among them, and in some cases children starved while their parents were in a drunken stupor.

One of the native Indians where we lived was called Homebrew Pete simply because he had a "nose" for it. He'd go hunting and not return home for two or three days because he had "sniffed out" a hidden still, and when the homesteader came to check on it, he'd find old Pete lying there, passed out. They never really did anything to him, because they didn't want him to tell anyone that they were making moonshine, but it meant they'd have to change the location of their still or he'd have been there all the time. When I talked to Miriam Thomas from Chiteck Lake (whom I mentioned earlier), I asked her about some of the older natives who had lived in the area where I grew up. I wondered if she knew Pete's last name, and she said she wasn't sure; it had been lost through the years as he became known as Homebrew Pete.

When the railway was built from Prince Albert through Leoville, then on to Meadow Lake in the early 1930s, life became a little easier for the people in the area. In those days people went into the forest and used a Swede saw to cut wood in four-foot lengths and hauled it to the siding along the railroad. The train would stop to load the wood on a flat car that was pulled behind the engine. The wood was used for fuel to heat water to produce steam to run the steam engines. They were paid sixty-five cents for a pile four feet high by four feet wide by eight feet long, which was the measure of a cord of wood. If a man worked a long, hard day he could cut two cords, and depending how far away it was from the railroad, he might get it unloaded at the siding the same day.

New development was costing the government a lot of money, so they put pressure on the settlers to pay income tax. One day the income tax man came to my Uncle John's place and said, "John, how much money did you make last year?"

In his broken English, John said, "I not make it money."

The tax man said, "But you must have made some money."

John said, "No, I tell it you true. I'm not make it money."

The tax man said, "But, John, you have eight more cows, three more horses, and ten more sheep. You must have made some money."

Again, John shrugged his shoulders and lifted up his hands and said, "I tell it you true. I not make it money."

The taxmen tried to explain how the income tax worked and that John would only have to pay on the profit that he showed. He said, "John, show me where your can is with all your money and I will help you out and show you where you've made a profit. And if it is big enough, then you will owe a little bit on the profit."

John thought for a while and then he said, "You want see my profit? Come, I show it you."

Now the taxmen thought John was going to show him the can with all his money in it, but instead he took him out to the barn, opened up the backdoor where he had been piling all the manure from the long winter, and said to the taxmen, "See, it all is my profit," pointing to the manure pile.

CHAPTER 12

Auntie Barbara and the Rustlers

On the fringes of the frontier in those early pioneer days, the people were tough and used to hard physical work. They protected their possessions with pride and fierceness. Simon Antypowich had gone to town with a team of horses to get supplies, a trip that would usually take him four days to return from. Barbara stayed home to look after the ranch while he was gone, and she decided to take her saddle horse and go to the meadow to check on the cows. As her horse leisurely jogged along on the trail, she was reminded of what a beautiful country it was. They'd built a small ranch for themselves and were enjoying life even though they did without a lot of the conveniences other people in cities farther to the south had. While she rode, she made note of how dry the trail was, thinking that a good rain would be welcome before haying time. As she neared the edge of the meadow, she saw two deer that were so occupied with something going on in the meadow that they hadn't noticed her approach them.

The first thought that entered her mind was a wolf was trying to kill one of the calves, and she hadn't strapped on the scabbard that contained Simon's .303. As her horse reached the edge of the meadow, she wasn't quite prepared for what she saw. There wasn't one wolf trying to steal her cattle, but three of them, and they were riding horses. They had separated ten or twelve head from the herd and were trying to drive them out of the meadow.

If Simon had been there with her they would have taken care of that situation very quickly. But she was alone, and although she knew it wasn't going to be an easy task as she was outnumbered three to one, she still couldn't let them take their cattle, so she was going to have to do it on her own. She was enraged and I doubt if she even gave a thought to the fact that she was one woman against three men.

She took down her lariat, built herself a good loop, tucked it under her arm, and rode her horse directly but slowly toward them. They were so busy trying to keep those twelve cows from going back to the main herd they didn't notice her approach until she was within speaking distance of them. She spoke loudly, saying, "It looks like you boys could use a little help."

They were so surprised that they immediately left the cows to make a run for it. She spurred her horse in hot pursuit of the rustlers, and when she was close enough to the last rider, she dropped a loop around him and jerked him off his horse. Now if the jerk hadn't been severe enough to cause damage to the rustler, I'm sure hitting the ground did. Can you imagine being roped around the midsection with your hands by your side and being jerked off a horse at full gallop? She wasn't too sure what she was going to do next but she took out her pegging string and tied his hands and feet. When he was able to talk, she asked him why they were trying to steal the cows. He said it was the other two riders' idea; the plan was to sell them to a rancher in the south country. She wanted to know who the other two fellows were. When he said he'd tell her if she untied him, she told him he was in no position to make a deal like that. When he finally told her who they were, she said, "I'll give you a message; you can take it to them to show them what will happen if we ever catch you trying to steal cattle again."

She turned and walked to the edge of the meadow, where she cut several sturdy willow switches that she used to lash him mercilessly. When she thought he'd endured enough, she untied him and let him up, telling him that he was lucky that Simon hadn't caught him or he'd be hanging from a limb of a big pine tree.

I don't believe that Simon and Barbara were ever bothered with rustlers again. It was sometime later that Simon was at the trading post talking to the man behind the counter, who said, "So, Simon, I hear somebody tried to rustle some of your cows."

As Simon smiled through his big handlebar mustache, he said, "If you know someone who needs a remedy for cattle rustling, tell them to come and see Barbara. She has a good one."

CHAPTER 13

Charlie and the Bear

One day I was with Mom when she was stooking bundles in the field, and one of the Indians from the reserve came and asked her for some iodine. Although his English wasn't very good, she managed to ask him what he needed iodine for, and he said, "The bear scratch 'em Charlie." Mom asked him how bad, and he motioned arms, legs, and stomach. Thinking this may be more serious than a scratch, she told him that he should go talk to Frank.

He did, and after some conversation, Dad stopped cutting grain and came out of the field with the horses. When he arrived at the tent, Charlie was lying on some blankets, moaning. The Indians were sitting around his bed, chanting. Dad asked if he could have a look at Charlie's injuries and when he rolled back the blanket, he could hardly believe what he saw. The bear had ripped his stomach open and you could see his intestines. Dad came home and got some bandages and warm water. He went back and tried to clean Charlie up and put some clean bandages over his wounds. Then he took him by horse and wagon to the little town of Penn, where there was a railway station and a store. He asked them if they could use a speeder to take Charlie to the next town where there was an old truck that would take him to a hospital. I'm not certain, but I believe the distance would have been somewhere in the neighborhood of twenty to thirty miles.

Charlie was in the hospital for about two months. When he came home, the first thing he did was come to visit Dad. I remember him taking off his moccasins to show us where the bear had bitten right through his feet in several places. He also showed us the scars on his hands where the bear had bitten through when he grabbed it by the bottom jaw and wrestled with it to keep it from chewing at his face. I remember him telling Dad about his encounter with the bear, but when he spoke in Cree I couldn't understand him. Later, Dad told me it must have been a gruesome battle. I will try to describe what I remember of the encounter.

Charlie had gone moose hunting with a team and wagon. When he arrived where he thought he'd find moose, he unhooked the horses, tied one to a tree, and rode the other one. He didn't go far before he found some fresh moose signs, so he tied his horse to a tree and began to track the animal. He found the moose and was about to shoot when he heard a twig crack behind him. He turned to see a bear coming. He didn't want to shoot the bear; he wanted the moose, so he tried to discourage the bear from coming any closer.

I don't know if the bear was confused between the moose tracks and Charlie, or if he was simply intent on killing whatever was in front of him. The bear kept coming and Charlie realized he was about to be attack, so he shot it. He was shooting a .30-30 with open sights.

The bear fell down, then got up and kept on coming. Charlie shot twice more, but it still kept coming. He waited until it was right beside him, planning to shoot it in the head, but when he pulled the trigger the only sound he heard was a loud *click*. In Charlie's mind his gun was fully loaded, but he'd lent it to a friend, who used a few rounds and didn't replace them. Charlie was out of shells!

The bear grabbed him by the leg and threw him to the ground and tried to crawl on top of him. Charlie kicked him, and the bear bit through his feet, then crawled on top of him anyway. The bear tried to bite his head, so Charlie grabbed the bear by the lower jaw, trying to hold him off, and the bear bit down on his hand. When it let go of his hand, it grabbed his stomach, tearing a hole in his side. The bear tried to chew his head again, so Charlie grabbed its bottom jaw with his other hand. The struggle seemed endless, but finally Charlie managed to roll it off him. He said he could hardly see because of all the blood flowing from the bear's chest and splashing on his face. The bear crawled a few feet from Charlie and collapsed.

When Charlie got up, he said there was blood everywhere. His expressions were, "*Wa, wa,* lots of blood just like when you shoot 'em moose." He said his stomach was starting to fall out, so he put it back in, picked up his gun, and walked back to his horse. He walked back to the other horse and wagon, hooked up his horses, and drove back four or five miles to where some of the other boys that were hunting with him had made a camp. By this time Charlie was barely able to stand, so they wrapped him in a blanket, laid him in the wagon box, and drove eleven miles back to the reserve.

Two weeks after Charlie came home from the hospital, he and his two boys went out moose hunting again; this time, they just shot moose.

Incidents like these were just another day in the lives of the natives in those early years, and after they recuperated from these traumas, as gruesome as some of them may have been, they carried on with their lives as usual. Charlie was one of the providers, not only for his family, but also the reserve, making it his responsibility to help the old, those who were crippled, or sick by gathering food for them. Charlie was a keen hunter who knew and understood the habits and the language of wild animals, and he passed that knowledge on to his sons.

Later, my dad had an opportunity to talk to the doctor who had sewn Charlie up. He said it was unbelievable, leaves, dirt, and twigs were mixed in with his intestines. The doctor said he was sure Charlie would to die, but he had more hunting to do.

CHAPTER 14

Frank Antypowich, the Strong Man

*When Frank Antypowich was young, he exercised and did a
lot of weightlifting to build a strong physical body*

My dad was a very strong man. He'd done a lot of weightlifting to build
a very physical body, and some of the things he could do shocked me.
He would take a six-inch spike, put the head of it in the palm of his hand,

make a fist, and punch at a two-inch plank and it would go clean through. I lived for the day I could do that, and when I was in my later teens I was able to. This feat expresses your punching power. It requires a strong wrist and a straight punch from not more than a foot away from the plank, keeping your punch straight is very important. I should add that we used a glove to help protect the palm of the hand.

One day when a farrier was putting some horseshoes on the skid horses, Dad told him that the shoes weren't strong enough. He told Dad that if he could bend them he'd put the shoes on for nothing. Dad took the horseshoe, put it over his thigh, and literally stretched it apart. The guy looked at him and asked, "How did you do that?" Dad took the other shoe and did the same with it. The farrier said, "Stop! Stop! Don't wreck my horseshoes. I've never seen anyone that could do that before. I have to do it with a hammer on the anvil and you just pull it apart by hand." I have tried many times since I became a man and I have never been able to do that. I guess I never was as strong a man as my dad.

Frank Antypowich, stretching a horseshoe apart over his thigh

I can remember him telling us boys that when he practiced for wrestling he did a lot of weightlifting. He made a pouch out of rope and a piece of soft leather. He'd put the leather between his teeth and have a 175-pound man lie in the pouch, and then he'd lift him off the floor and carry him across the room. This was the way he strengthened his neck muscles. He did some exhibition wrestling at small towns and fairs. It was common for men to match their strength against other men at these fairs and exhibitions, and although I don't know if there was ever much money to be earned, people would bet on them. What percentage of the take they got, I'm not sure.

Dad played many tricks on merchants who didn't know him. He'd ask to buy a bag of flour; after having a look at it, he'd tell the storekeeper the bag was no good because it wasn't very strong. He'd say, "I bet I can poke my hand right through that bag." The storekeeper often would say, "I bet you can't, and if you can I'll give it to you." Needless to say, he could punch his fist right into a bag of flour. He did it many times to get a free bag of flour. He'd also tell a storekeeper that a fifty-pound block of salt was not fifty pounds. He'd put two blocks together and lift them over his head with one hand and say see they're not fifty pounds. To the amazement of the storekeeper, he would say, "I bet I can even lift three blocks over my head." Of course, the bet would be challenged and Dad had three free blocks of salt.

One day he went to visit his brother-in-law Joe, who was thrashing grain. Joe didn't see him arrive. Dad put his back against the rear wheel of the tractor, squatted down six or eight inches, grabbed the spokes on the wheel, then he straightened his legs and lifted the tractor enough to throw the drive belt off the pulley. The thrashing machine plugged and stopped.

He stepped behind the granary so Joe couldn't see him. After Joe got the thrashing machine unplugged, the belt on, and running again, Dad snuck out from behind the granary and did it again. My uncle Joe was inclined to be a little short-fused, so after it happened a second time he said, "Damn you, Frank, you must be around here somewhere," and went looking for him. They had a great laugh and Dad helped him unplug the thrashing machine and get things going again. When he was older, Dad had a lot of back trouble. Do you wonder why?

CHAPTER 15

Frank Antypowich, the Entrepreneur

My dad never failed to amaze me. Although he never had a day of schooling (my mom taught him how to read), he ventured into many different enterprises and was quite successful. When I was six years old, Dad sold the homestead and moved eleven miles south to Junor, where he bought another farm with a nice house and a large barn with a cement floor. The farmland was good, but rocky.

The house at Junor as it was when we lived in it

Gloria and I visited the old farm at Junor in August of 2007. The barn was much the same as it was when we lived there, except a lean-to had been added to the side of it. The property had been bought by an Indian reserve and First Nation's family lived there.

The house is much the same as it was when we lived there, except for a few modern renovations, which included window changes, etc. There was a satellite dish and a trampoline in the yard; things that didn't even exist when I was a child.

In the summer, Dad worked to help pay the taxes, building road with a four-horse team and a Fresno. He also bought a W30 McCormick

Dering steelwheeled tractor and a breaking plough, and he'd do custom breaking. He also had a threshing machine and he used to do contract threshing as well. The old threshing machine is still there, overgrown, in a patch of poplar trees on the farm of my cousin Ervin Matzner.

The old threshing machine Dad used to do custom work with in the 1940s

The steamer that powered the mill

The W30 McCormick Dearing tractor that powered the planer;
Roman feeding the planer, Ervin shoveling shavings

Air-dried lumber piles at the mill at Junor

Dad bought a steam engine that powered the sawmill, and he cut logs for his own use, as well as to sell as lumber. He also did custom sawing for the neighbors.

A load of lumber leaving the Junor mill site, headed to Mildred, Saskatchewan

The roads were so bad in the summer that trucks couldn't make it through the mud holes, so they'd come after it froze up in the fall to buy lumber. I can remember when the trucks wouldn't start on the cold mornings, Dad and my two older brothers would pull them around the yard with a team of horses to get them started.

CHAPTER 16

Meeting Neighbors under Unusual Circumstances

I remember one nice summer day when the wheat fields were blowing in the wind and there was promise for a good harvest. The rain that fell during the night ensured the heads would fill properly and a bumper crop could be expected unless something unforeseen happened, like hail or frost.

Dad was out in the yard working on the binder so everything would be ready for the harvest. I looked toward the barn and I saw a woman running through the wheat fields. She was wet and muddy from the rain and she was yelling in a language I didn't understand, Russian or Ukrainian. She came running for our house as a man appeared out of the wheat field carrying about twenty feet of rope and threatening to beat her.

She didn't stop to knock on the door, just opened it and ran into the house, muddy shoes and all. She ran right up the stairs and locked herself in one of the bedrooms. The man had the same intention, but Dad stepped in front of him and asked where he thought he was going. He tried to push my dad aside, but Dad grabbed him by the shoulders and pushed him up against the porch wall, telling him to calm down.

He said he was after his wife; he was going to beat her with the rope for something they'd been fighting over. Dad told him to stay outside and he'd go into the house and get his wife. He obeyed, but Dad had a real problem convincing her to open the door. Dad told her that her husband wasn't going to kill her; he'd convinced him that they needed to work out their differences at home, not at the neighbors'.

When she came down the stairs, she hit the porch steps running, and had Dad not stepped in front of him, he might have had her in his grip. Dad intervened for a few minutes, telling him to calm down and go home and talk about their problems like civilized people.

When Dad let him go, she had a head start on him and he went running after her, yelling all kinds of profanity in their native language. I'd never seen anything like that before. When we went into the house, Mom was cleaning up the mess that the woman had created when she ran through the house. It was the topic of conversation at our supper table that night as Dad tried to explain what had happened.

A week later, Ervin was in town. It was train day and the mail came then, so he was in the store waiting for it to be sorted. He noticed the woman standing by the end of the counter beside the block of cheese. She looked like she had been roughed up, so he told her he hoped things turned out better for her and her husband.

She grabbed the big cheese knife and started yelling in her native tongue and took after him. He jumped over the counter, ran past the storekeeper, and out the door. When he got home, he asked Dad if he was sure the guy shouldn't have beaten his wife up, because he thought she was crazy.

She probably did not understand English well enough to know what Ervin said to her; she obviously had taken offence to it. Those people scared the hell out of me, and when I found out that her daughter was attending the same school that I was, I wasn't sure I wanted to go to school.

CHAPTER 17

Pearl School

Pearl School in 1945

I began school at Pearl School, and attended there until grade four when our family moved to Alberta. Pearl School was a one-room school and the teacher taught grade one to grade eight. Shirley and I had to travel four miles to school in the summer; in the winter we could take a shortcut across a farmer's field, so it was only three miles. In the summer we either drove a horse and buggy, or we walked. For the most part it was a lot of fun, except for scary incidents when we encountered a bear eating saskatoons along the trail or a neighbor's bull pawing in an ant pile. It always seemed that we encountered these things when we were walking, and we'd have to make a detour and run the long way around.

In the winter we used a toboggan that Dad had made, in which we could take enough horse feed and a couple of rocks warmed in the oven to keep our feet warm. We had a lot of fun with that toboggan, except when the temperature dropped to -50°F. It was a sight to see all the different rigs coming down the road to school in the morning. Some kids would use a team of horses with a caboose on a sleigh. In the caboose, they'd have a small wood stove with a little four-inch stovepipe out the top and when it was very cold little puffs of smoke would keep time with the jogging of the horses as they came down the road. There were no indoor toilets or running water, just a large forty-five-gallon barrel converted into a heater to warm the school. On very cold days, the teacher would let us sit around the heater and we'd drink hot chocolate that we made at school. We heated the water in a small pail on the heater and added cocoa. In the evening, before leaving the school the teacher would make sure the water bucket was empty so it didn't freeze. The farmers would get together and cut a big pile of wood to burn in the heater during the winter, and that is how they paid their part of their school taxes.

In the summer, we'd sit on the pile and entice gophers to come up from under it for a small piece of bread tied to a piece of twine. Then we would catch them.

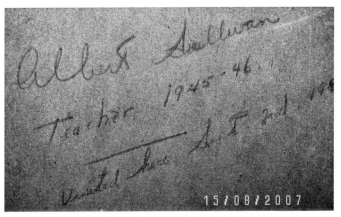

When I visited Pearl School in 2007, I took this picture of Albert Sullivan's autograph that he had left on the old wall of the school when he visited it many years after he taught there

When I was in Chiteck Lake in 2011, I visited Albert Sullivan, who had been my teacher at Pearl School. He is eighty-four years old and amazingly active and sound of mind. He remembers that previous to 1945, the school term was from July to November, and March to June. He believes lack of discipline in the school, the home, and the lack of church guidance have all changed teaching. The new rules of discipline came into effect in 1982 and he retired in June of that year. He thinks most teachers retire after thirty years because of the lack of order and discipline. He taught for thirty-six years before retiring, and has been retired for thirty years now.

I asked Albert to write a few lines explaining what it was like to be a teacher in those early days. The following is what he wrote.

My First Teaching Position,1945, as told by Albert Sullivan in 2011

I had taken all of my high school grades by correspondence at our homestead home at Penn, Saskatchewan. I had completed grades V1, V11, and V111 at the Penn School. It was a log school, with all grades from one to eight taught by one teacher.

I was accepted as a graduate of the Leoville High school in June of 1945. I left the farm, with two cream cheques totalling $11.00.My bother Tom loaned me $200.00 to cover my Normal School.I graduated from Normal School with an A average and a 12T Teaching Certificate after six weeks. I applied for and got my first school at Pearl School at Junor, Saskatchewan.

I stayed at Joe Murkowski's home for two months. They moved to Blaine Lake, so I had to find another boarding place. Bill Doijk invited me to stay with them and share a room with their 18 year old son, Mike. I learned a lot of Polish there and Mrs Dorijk learned a lot of English as we dried the supper dishes. She also took her grades one and two that year.

Pearl School had been operating since 1935.There were thirty more or less in attendance. Edward Lake School had no teacher, so two families came to Pearl School. There were nine grades and my six grade ones did not speak English, so I had to use an interpreter for the first two weeks.

I was most fortunate in having a wonderful experienced teacher at the Penn School, who gladly became my mentor for the whole school year. Mrs. Gagnon had 15 years' experience and willingly guided me.

The first thing she pointed out to me was that there were only eight months in the school year to complete your year's work. You can't count

December because it is all taken up for the Christmas concert and exams. And June likewise was a review month, track and field, nature trips, and final exams.

She prepared the October exams and I prepared the Christmas exams. I prepared the February exams and she prepared the Easter exams. The Department of Education sent out exams for all grades from two to nine.

Almost all schools required the teacher to put on the Christmas concert. We prepared plays, drills, recitations, and songs. Everyone took part. The teacher was often judged by the success of the concert. The teacher had to arrange fundraising for the concert so that every child in the school and all the youngsters at home would receive a small bag of candy, a Japanese orange, and an apple. Money was raised usually by a box or pie social and dance.

After the concert, three of the girls from my class played guitar and led the packed one-room school with Ukrainian Christmas carols for an hour. Then the dancing started and continued until 5:00 a.m. There was lunch served after the concert.

Pearl School was constructed of hand hewn logs. The size of the one room was 22 x 30 feet. It was heated with a barrel stove. It was a woodstove. The stove was near the door and the chimney in the opposite corner. I was obliged to do the janitor work, light the stove in the morning, clean the pipes every month and clean the outdoor toilets, and supply drinking water.

I was paid three dollars a month for doing the janitor work and I paid that out to the Halko family for bringing a five-gallon cream can full of fresh water every day.

I was not allowed to start school until near the end of September because the children were needed to help with the harvesting. In January I was not allowed to start classes until all the Ukrainian Christmas celebrations were over. I had to work an extra year before I retired to make up for those two months.

My total wages for my first year was a little over five hundred dollars, and I had to pay out thirty-five dollars a month for board and room.

Two important principles had to be carried out fairly and sternly. They were organization of your classes so that all students received the help and guidance they needed. And the second requirement was discipline, without which nothing could be accomplished. Again, discipline had to be fair and sensible as a wise parent would treat his family.

I'm 84 years old now, with a head covered with shingles. I thank God that I have good sight, good hearing, and am mentally alert. I walk without a cane and can look after myself. I'm a good cook and enjoy photography. I love music but I cannot play an instrument.

When I look back to 1945, as an 18 year old farm boy I was eager indeed to make a success of my teaching. One of my grade six boys became a renowned architect in Toronto.

We had no TV, very few had radio, ballpoint pens came to our school in January. We used gelatine pads in cookie sheets to make copies for exams, etc. Scrub was our main softball game. And I taught them the Russian-German game of "Mutka."

I did not like corporal punishment, so I used it very sparingly and only under very trying conditions. In thirty-six years of teaching I can count on one hand serious problems with student behavior.

At the end of June 1946 I bid farewell to my students and parents. I was hired to teach at Chetek Lake and I remained there for eight years. I bought property by the lake and today I enjoy my home that has a fantastic view of the lake. I'm also an avid gardener and florist.

I do take friends and former students to see Pearl School. The old barrel heater is outside of the old log school. There is a lovely two-room school built in the yard five years after I left. It also has been closed for twenty-five years or more.

The thought that comes to my mind from Grade X1 poetry is

> "The old order changeth
> Yielding place to the new
> And God fulfills Himself
> In many ways."

It's sixty-six years ago that I started teaching at Pearl School, Junor, Saskatchewan.

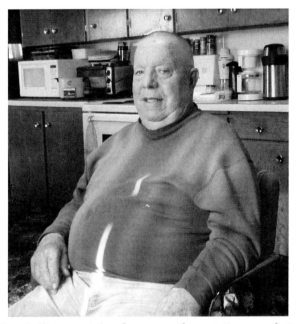

*Albert Sullivan at eighty-four years of age, sitting on a chair in
the kitchen of his home at Chetek Lake, taken May 2011*

CHAPTER 18

A Whole New World Opens up as "The Hutterites" Go to See Grandpa Matzner

Grandpa Matzner had moved from Saskatchewan to the lower mainland of British Columbia and worked hard to build a big dairy farm. He didn't see his daughter Annie very often due to distance and travel difficulties. One summer, he surprised us by coming for a visit, arriving by train in Junor.

I'd never met him before, but he was so good to me and I really liked him. We went hunting together and of course this was all I needed.

His youngest son, Uncle Alois, lived ten or eleven miles from our farm. One day he decided that he and I'd walk to Alois's place. We prepared a big lunch, made two slingshots, picked a lot of fine stones, and started out on our long journey. Mom and Dad would come to pick us up with a team and wagon in four or five days. It was a time I never forgot; having a grandpa that would walk with me and hunt all the way on such a long journey was very, very special for me.

After meeting Grandpa, I looked forward to every letter he wrote, and made sure my mom read it to me. One sad day, she began to cry as she read his letter; it brought the sad news that he had been diagnosed with lung cancer and there was no cure for it at that time.

Earlier that summer, my dad had bought a brand-new two-ton Dodge truck. He built a box on it from the lumber he cut with his mill, and fit a tent over the box so we could have shelter for the night or if it rained. The whole family, with the exception of Ervin, left in it for Vancouver to see Grandpa. We stopped at North Battleford to pick up my dad's sister (Annie) and her two younger daughters, Margaret and Katie, who all came with us. Traveling like that, we must have looked like a bunch of Hutterites going to pick fruit in British Columbia.

Frank Antypowich and my uncle, Joe Matzner, with their two new trucks. Dad is standing in front of his new 1947 two-ton Fargo on the left. This is the truck that we went to Vancouver with when we went to see my Grandpa Matzner.

This trip was a tremendous learning experience for me. I remember seeing the gas pumps for the first time. The gas was pumped by hand with a long handle into a big glass container that was elevated so it would gravity feed into the vehicles. On this glass container was a bunch of marks and numbers to show how much gas you had purchased.

You can imagine what this all looked like to a young lad of my age. I remember stopping to have lunch just west of Calgary and I saw the mountains for the first time. They impressed me so much I couldn't wait to get closer and see them towering above my head. But for my mom it was totally different. She did not like the mountains and was terrified by the steep, winding roads. Actually, I don't believe she was very comfortable riding in the truck at any time in those days, as I'm sure the change from a team of horses and wagon to a truck traveling at fifty miles an hour was hard for her to adjust to.

I remember stopping along the road in the mountains just so we could see the scenery, but my mom was so afraid she was almost in tears. This was the first time she had seen the mountains as well.

The roads in 1947 were nowhere near what they are today. When we were going through the Kicking Horse area, there were places where the road was little more than single-lane traffic. In one spot we met a large truck and trailer hauling gas, and the road was so narrow we weren't sure if the two trucks could pass each other. For the other driver to back down would have been very difficult because he was pulling the trailer. Dad and he talked about the situation and decided if Dad drove as close as he could to the rock wall that towered above the road the trucker would stand on the running board and try to steer the truck past us and up the inclining grade. He said that if the truck slid off the road, he would jump off and let it go. He made it past without mishap, but I remember Mom sitting in the truck, crying because she was afraid rocks might fall off the mountain above us. All ended well, except we got a small tear in the tent that covered the box of our truck.

For me it was one of the greatest experiences in my life; seeing the mountains for the first time and seeing the ocean as well. At that time, I'd no idea how big the world was in which we lived. Eating fresh fruit from the trees in my grandpa's orchard was just awesome to me. I remember going for a walk through the orchard with him and coming across a snake. I wanted to kill it, but he said not to because it ate the insects in the orchard. We talked about the time he and I walked to my uncle's place in Saskatchewan. Little did I realize he knew it would probably be the last time he and I would do things like that together.

I remember how dry and desolate everything seemed when we were returning to northern Saskatchewan. At home, the summer was hot and dry; the crops were short and did not yield very well that fall. It was such a change for me to have seen so many different conditions and not really realize what caused them.

I looked with even greater anticipation for Grandpa's letters to arrive. Now I knew where he lived, but couldn't understand why he was going to die. Then one day the sad letter came. I had lost the only grandpa I had. I can remember my dad trying to comfort my mother in her grief.

SAWMILLING AND LOGGING IN NORTHERN ALBERTA

1948-1953

CHAPTER 19

Alberta Bound

Uncle Alec moved to Alberta in the late 1940s. When he was selling his farm, I stayed with them for a day to play with my cousins. My older cousin brought Grandma to Uncle Alec's place with a team of horses, as Grandma was an old lady at that time and she wanted to be at his farm sale. I recall she was not feeling very well that evening and some of her sons were quite concerned about her. It was sometime near midnight when we children were awakened as two of her sons were trying to walk her outside to get some fresh air. We could hear her saying something like *"dia-boisha, dia-boisha,"* which I believe meant "God save me" in Ukrainian.

A short while later, my Auntie Hilda came and told us that the angels had come for Grandma. She was buried beside her husband on one of her son's property. Their caskets were made out of the lumber that might very well have been cut by my dad's sawmill.

When Gloria and I were there four years ago, my cousin Ervin Matzner showed us their gravesite. He owns the property now, and when he cleared the land to make more hayfields, he left about an acre undisturbed and built a little fence out of iron pipe and welded the Antypowich name on it. Apparently, three other unknown infants are buried there as well. Ervin said he wanted to make sure the cattle could not walk over their gravesite. It had become overgrown so much with trees that I would never have recognized the spot.

A picture at the funeral of Grandma (Baba) Antypowich's
coffin, taken at Uncle Joe Antypowich's place

At that time the government of Saskatchewan was making it difficult for small sawmill operators to get timber, so that fall Dad and Roman and Ervin took the new truck and headed for Slave Lake, Alberta. They rigged up a pole trailer on the truck and found work hauling lumber from the small mills along Slave Lake to the larger centralized mills that bought most of their production.

It's amazing they could haul such big loads with such a small truck and trailer. I don't know if the trailer even had brakes. They didn't have metal bull boards to protect the load from crushing the cab and operator if they came to a sudden stop. The bunk on the truck was just a square timber with a pin through the bunk into the deck of the truck to hold it in position.

Today the Department of Transport would permanently park a rig like that. I don't know where Dad got the idea to rig his small farm truck up like that, yet they hauled lumber all winter without any serious mishaps. I guess at the time you made do with what you had and got the job done. Today we haul logs with much bigger trucks and trailers in a similar fashion but they are built of iron, equipped with airbrakes, and are a much safer on the road.

*These are my brothers, Roman and Ervin, hauling lumber
with a truck from Slave Lake Alberta to Kinuso*

*Roman and Ervin were driving a new 1947 two-ton Fargo
truck that they attached a pole trailer to. They hauled
6,000 to 7,000 board feet of lumber per load.*

Mom, Shirley, Clifford, and I stayed in Saskatchewan to feed the animals and look after the farm. The burden lay on the shoulders of Mom and Shirley. Mom was responsible for our safety getting to and from school in -50º F, keeping the animals fed, milking cows, keeping the chicken house warm so they would lay eggs, which was an important part of our diet. For me it was fun and games. I'd snare rabbits for the dogs, not understanding the help I was providing. It was a very cold, harsh winter and farmers were short of feed for their livestock. When we were short of feed, we dug into an old straw pile with a pitch fork, shook the straw over a tarp to save all the fine chaff, the weed seeds, and the light grain, then dragged it to the barn to add to the good feed to make it go a little further. The snow was so deep I remember going to school with a horse and toboggan right over the top of fences without any problem.

The sleigh Uncle Alois used to come and see us that winter;
Uncle Alois is in the far left side of the sleigh

Mom's youngest brother, Alois, arrived one Sunday with a team of horses and a sleigh. He didn't think he'd come back as the roads were drifted in and the snow was too deep for the horses to pull the sleigh through. Mom's diary mentioned there wasn't a thaw from January till March.

Sometime in March, arrangements were made to sell the farm and move the family to Alberta. Dad came back home by train to finalize the deal, selling the farm for $3,000 and a 1947 four-door Monarch car. Snow blocked roads, making them impassable for motorized vehicles, so our household and personal possessions, as well as two horses, a sleigh, and the car, were loaded into a boxcar at the Junor siding. All I remember is the long train ride.

Moving from Saskatchewan to Alberta was a big change for me. I learned so many things in that transition; besides the long ride, I was amazed at the country I could see from the train window. It was fascinating to see Lesser Slave Lake for the first time. Lesser Slave Lake is eighty-five miles long and sixteen miles wide at the widest point at Widewater. And living near the highway, which was the only road between Edmonton and Alaska at that time, was a new thing for me. The Alaska

Highway from Dawson Creek, British Columbia to Alaska had just been completed. The highway along Slave Lake was the main thoroughfare for movement of low-beds carrying road-building equipment both ways. Army vehicles and other military equipment were constantly moving too; it was common to see army convoys of one hundred vehicles or more travelling the road. There were all kinds of big trucks and vehicles I had not seen in Saskatchewan.

A picture of my sister Shirley and two of her friends in front of the train car that we took to Alberta when we moved

In the undeveloped part of Saskatchewan where we lived, transportation had still primarily been horse and buggy or sleighs in the wintertime. In fact, my dad was one of the few who owned a vehicle where we lived. Roads were pretty primitive, basically wagon trails, yet not far away in North Battleford it was very different. There were better roads and people had vehicles and lifestyles were more developed.

The move to Alberta took place in the month of March and I didn't go back to school to finish my grade, which left more time for me to snare rabbits as there was a lot of bush right close to the yard.

The house we moved into at Slave Lake was the old log schoolhouse at Canyon Creek. It was not anything like the house we'd left in Saskatchewan. I have wondered how Mom really felt about the change in circumstances, but her life hadn't been easy over the winter, so it may have been a relief to be with Dad and the older boys again and looking ahead with hope of something better. She never complained though; she just did what was necessary.

While Dad and my brothers were unloading the boxcar and moving our possessions into our new home, I was exploring the yard when three young native boys came to see what was happening. One of them was my age; the other two were a little older. They asked me quite a few questions, but the last one was, "Are you tough?" I said I was. Then the older, bigger one punched me right in the stomach, almost knocking the wind out of me. It wasn't a very good way to start out. I soon discovered white children were outnumbered here five to one. I remember going home crying after getting a beating from little native boys. Ervin taught me how to fight and protect myself and I was able to hold my own on a one-on-one basis and not get caught where three or four could gang up on me.

That summer, Mom, Shirley, Clifford, and I moved to a house along the highway that Dad rented from the Menzers. He had bought Rimmer's logging camp, which was two miles off the highway. Dad built the typical logging camp facility, which was a shack made of rough lumber with tar paper and no running water or electricity. The road still had to be fixed because it was only a winter road, which meant in the summer it was impossible for trucks to get in or out to haul the lumber so it could be shipped. That was done by laying slabs on the ground, covering them with sawdust, another layer of slabs, more sawdust, until we had the road firm enough to haul over. It took a lot of time and labor to do this without heavy equipment, but we worked like a bunch of beavers to get it done.

Tom Rimmer, the previous owner, thought he'd get the logs cut for nothing since the high cost of rebuilding the road would be prohibitive. That spring he told many locals in the area that he'd put us on a sloop in the fall and pull us down to the railway station so we could go back to Saskatchewan. We prevailed with Dad's persistence and the hard work of everyone in the family.

The sawmill was bigger than anything Dad had owned previously. It had a large power unit to drive the mill and the edger. The trim saw was powered by another small stationary engine. The mill yard was approximately ten acres in size, with logs decked and ready to be sawed. I believe the deal Dad had was that if he sawed all the logs decked in the yard he would own the mill.

Loading sawdust to build the road into Rimmer's camp

Here we are loading slabs to corduroy the road into Rimmer's Camp

After this, Dad got small sales through the forestry, logged the timber with horses, then milled the logs, and sold the lumber. This was the beginning of good and prosperous times for the family, although prosperity didn't come quickly and instead grew every year. A planer was added to the mill, and after the lumber was air dried it was planed, then loaded into a boxcar and shipped by rail to destinations across Canada and the Eastern United States. Some of the lumber was sold to Nelson Homes in Edmonton Alberta.

*Roman and Ervin with loads of logs that they hauled
in with horses at Rimmer's Camp*

Ervin riding on a load of logs at Rimmer's Camp

CHAPTER 20

Growing up in Logging Camps

This new country held opportunity for things for me to do. It was bush country and there were lots of squirrels, weasels, and mink to be caught, and of course I thought that should be my job. But Dad had different plans for me and there never was much time to play because he always had something for me to do around the mill. It was my job to shovel the sawdust that would build up at the bottom of the conveyor below the head saw, and I had to pull the slabs away from the mill with horse and a logging chain. Even when I went to school I had to do that as soon as I got home.

Although this was a family operation, there were hired men at our table, and my mother was informed by a local health nurse to be aware of possible problems such as syphilis and gonorrhea, warning that care must be taken to clean all utensils and dishes in boiling water with lots of soap. She threatened that there would be a big needle waiting for us if she didn't, because the nurse's job was to clean up such messes. I remember her as a very hard, rough-looking lady who was very well suited for the job.

With such a large undertaking at the sawmill and the responsibility of so many workers, there was little time for Dad to spend hunting and fishing with me. I remember the day a bear stole the bacon and wieners that were buried in the sawdust pile where Mom kept them on ice to keep them fresh during the summer. Dad and I crawled up on the mill roof and lay there till the bear came back, looking for something else to steal.

It was almost dark when he showed up. I'd seen bears before but hadn't been there when one was shot. Dad made certain he wouldn't come back to steal anything else.

There were a lot of mink ranchers along Slave Lake and they all had fishing boats and nets that they used to catch fish to feed their mink. They used a small mesh net to catch a fish about the size of a herring that they called a tulabi. They ground the fish with horsemeat and a special concentrate to make feed for their mink. They all had freezers where they could freeze fish to use at a later date.

When I started school in the fall, I made friends with Howard Engelbertson. Whenever I could get away on weekends, I'd go with him on his dad's fishing boat. Howie's dad, Cliff, made work fun, and I liked going with them. They used nets to catch fish to feed their mink, and while Mr. Englebertson was pulling in his nets, Howie and I would cut a small fish in half and tie it to a fishing line and throw it into the water. A seagull would swoop down, pick it up, and swallow it. We'd have it on the end of the line and we'd pull it to the boat. We'd let it fly until it came to the end of the line and crashed into the water, then we'd drag it in again. Most of the time, they were able to regurgitate the fish bait and free themselves.

Suckers (fish) were a ration that the mink ranchers didn't use very often since they had to be boiled first because of the iodine in them. Most of the time, any suckers were hit on the head and thrown back to be picked up by seagulls and pelicans. Cliff showed us how to tie a sucker fish to a fish line and throw it out to catch pelicans too. You had to give a pelican a little more time than a seagull, because you had to make sure they swallowed the fish and didn't just keep it in their pouch. It was quite a job to pull that big bird back to the boat. The pelicans were the most fun because they could swallow a whole sucker and it seemed harder for them to regurgitate it. So it was more fun to see a pelican thirty feet in the air, tethered on a fish line. Sometimes he would come crashing back down to the water if he couldn't regurgitate it fast enough.

One memory that stands out in my mind when we moved to Alberta was the smell of the mink ranches along the lake. I learned to accept it. In a short time I realized that quite a few of the domesticated mink would chew their way out of their pens and became fair game to trap. Dad got me some leg hold traps and showed me how to set them. When I caught a mink, I would sell it back to a mink rancher. They gave me an average of $10 apiece. I didn't get many and didn't really know how much they were worth. That wasn't a bad price for the standards, but the pastels were worth a bit more.

I soon realized that those little buggers could really bite. My dad warned me to always wear a big mitt, but they could still bite right through it.

I spent much of my free time with Howie Englebertson and Cliff, who bought most of the mink I caught. He showed me how to make a box trap to catch the animals alive. These boxes or live traps were made with one-by six-inch boards to measure six inches square and about twenty inches long. They had a sliding door that was held open by putting a nail on the end of a string that ran through a small staple fastening it to the top of the box, then down to the end of the ramp where bait was placed. When a mink was drawn in by the bait, his weight tripped the ramp, pulling the nail out from under the door, and he would be caught without injury. I'd take the mink to Cliff. We'd let it loose in one of his empty pens, and after looking it over carefully, he'd pay me accordingly.

This worked well until I had to make a longer run with the mink; then it wasn't long before everyone knew I was trapping them. When the game warden stopped me, I repeated what Cliff told me to say: I was trapping mink that had escaped the pens. The game warden only asked how I knew the mink was Englebertson's.

One day he came to the sawmill (he was the forest ranger as well) and Dad asked him if it was possible for me to get a small trap line for mink, squirrels, weasels, etc. He said he would look into it and see what he could do. Nothing seemed to happen for a while and I was sure he had forgotten about it. When I was about fourteen, he came to my dad and said he'd give me a small area along the lake to the height of land to the south where I could legally trap. I'm not exactly sure that my dad didn't have to sign for me, but I had a trap line. Now I was busy building another ten or twelve live-trap boxes and setting them all along the lakeshore in every culvert under the railway tracks, as it seemed to be a place that mink and weasel would travel.

I caught mink and weasel in foothold traps during the winter and I learned to snare fool hens in the spring as they ate the willow buds. If I was careful and quiet, I could sneak up to them; then using a pole and a piece of snare wire, I'd slip the snare over their heads and jerk it, taking the head off. Sometimes I'd get three or four before they flew.

Although I never got to be just a young boy who could play and do all the things I liked, this was a great place for a young boy who loved hunting, fishing, and trapping to grow up.

During the winter I'd go with Dad to help him fell spruce trees, and at the same time he showed me how to snare squirrels by leaning a long dry pole against a spruce tree. When the squirrels ran up the dry pole, they would run into one of my snares. Sometimes I'd have two and three squirrels hanging from the pole. He taught me how to skin and stretch the hide properly to sell later.

I would catch weasels in foothold traps, and in the winter I would catch mink the same way.

As I grew older, I learned many things with him. I'd help him fell trees with a Swede saw and I learned how to make an undercut and place a wedge so that the tree couldn't tip back and pinch the saw. I also learned to "buck" the tree into short logs. I learned what the "bite and the bend" meant quickly, because it wasn't fun to chop the saw out of a log after it pinched. Also, the branches of the trees had to be trimmed off with an axe.

I was also taught to never fell a tree into another tree and to always look for dead trees that were standing near the tree you wanted to fell. I also learned to always step away from the tree that you needed to fell and to step behind a tree when it was possible. Although I knew how to do all these things, I wasn't big enough. Still, I'd help Dad and he would school me, telling me what would happen if I did things wrong.

In some ways I enjoyed the hard work because it made me strong and more capable of looking after myself when I was confronted with some of the young native boys. After supper, some of the men boxed with each other for entertainment and to hone their skills in self-defence, so I'd practice with them. There always seemed to be someone who had boxing experience and he'd help others learn the skill. Although my father had boxed and wrestled when he was younger, he didn't like to see his boys enter into such a rough sport, although he was in favor of us learning how to protect ourselves. When he saw me doing something wrong, he'd correct me, then show me how to do it properly.

I always looked forward to going berry picking. We'd pick raspberries, gooseberries, and high bush cranberries so Mom could make jelly for hotcakes at breakfast. We'd go by boat across Slave Lake to the north side to pick saskatoon and blueberries. We picked pails and pails and washtubs full and brought them home.

My mom and Shirley would can them in two-quart sealers and store them in the icehouse with canned moose and deer meat. All the canning took place on a wood cook stove that Mom also used to bake bread, cookies, cakes, and pies for the family, as well as the millworkers.

I can remember helping to make sauerkraut in a forty-five-gallon wooden barrel. It was a big job cutting mounds of cabbage, then pounding it down into the barrel with a big club that looked like something that caveman used. She'd sprinkle on the salt and then put in a layer of whole cabbage heads and then a layer of cut cabbage over the top of them. After repeating this process at least three times, the barrel was packed full. Several boards were placed on top, inside of the barrel, and weighted down with heavy stones. Then the barrel was covered with cheesecloth. It took quite awhile for the cabbage to become *sauer*, and the cabbage heads inside of the barrel would become soft. After using some sauerkraut, Mom would take out the cabbage heads, peel off the leaves, then wrap rice and raisins with other spices to make cabbage rolls, filling a large roaster and then baking them in the oven.

The sawmill workers who boarded at our camp always commented on how good the food was; homemade preserves, homemade bread, homemade pies, cake, and cookies were very much appreciated. I just don't know how Mom and my sister Shirley were able to do all that work on a wood cook stove.

It was always fun time for me to go picking berries. When my mom, sister, and I were picking cranberries, she would call to me occasionally so when I answered her she would know where I was. Sometimes I'd play a trick on her and not answer. Once when she called I didn't answer. She had heard something making a noise very close to her and thought it was me. She said, "Answer me, Lloyd, I know you're there," but I didn't answer. We were surprised by a black bear that had been picking berries in the same patch. After that scare, I always answered when I was called and Dad insisted we take the dog with us.

One hot, dry summer several forest fires broke out in the area. A dry lightning storm started a fire not too far from our camp. It was a very scary situation as the fire came closer to camp; Dad told my mother and sister to pack everything they could and be ready to leave at a moment's notice. The smoke was so thick it was hard to breathe, and it also bothered our eyes. The only good thing about it was that it took care of the mosquitoes.

In those days, we didn't have water bombers and helicopters to help extinguish the fires. It was done mostly by hand with mill and/or logging crews. They had backpacks with pumps attached to them, which would squirt water about twenty or thirty feet. They had larger pumps placed beside a swamp, creek, or wherever they found a water supply and dragged hoses to deliver water to check the fire. Bulldozers made trails, pulled sloops with water tanks on them to get closer to the fire. They would "backfire" in the path of the fire to burn up the fuel so that when the fire came it had nothing to burn; however, in most cases it was the rain that eventually put the fire out.

The fire had burned some good timber that my dad was able to log with the permission of the Forest Service. Afterward it made excellent pasture for the horses and wildlife. After a fire, a plant called fireweed and another called pea vine grew in abundance, making good pasture, especially the pea vine. And the next year new growth was succulent to the wildlife. The area became a good place to hunt deer and moose. It also gave the animals some relief from the constant pestering of the flies and mosquitoes, which could be bad in the bush country.

I can remember a big tall Sewed saying, "Oh, the mosquitoes aren't too bad here; they are yust the lettle ones. When I worked in Alaska they had big ones. Yaw," he said, "one time I tied the horses to a tree and when I came back later two mosquitoes were playing horseshoes for the harness. One said to the other, 'We better hurry up and get this over before the big ones come.'"

CHAPTER 21

Going to School at Widewater

I took most of my public schooling at Widewater. It was a one-room school from grades one to eight. The health nurse came to the school and told the teacher that the schools were going to be supplied with paper cups and that it was no longer acceptable for the students to all drink out of the same dipper. The dipper was to be used only to fill the paper cups. In the public schools, there was a water bucket on a stand as there was no running water in the school. The public school at Widewater was pretty clean and I was lucky to be able to complete my public schooling in that school. Some of the other surrounding areas were not that lucky.

Because the bus had a long way to go from Slave Lake to Kinuso, I'd have to meet it at the road by 7:30 a.m. and would get off at 5:00 pm. Then I still had to walk home to camp, so in the wintertime I would walk in the dark both ways. One cold stormy day in the winter, I was waiting for the school bus and it was about half an hour late. I was getting cold standing out in the open along the road, so I decided to crawl into a big culvert, thinking I'd hear when the bus came. I didn't hear it come but I heard when it started to leave, and when I came out of the culvert it was leaving me behind. I was afraid to hitchhike, so I walked all the way back to camp.

When I was in about grade six or seven, the teacher was a man from Saskatchewan by the name of Mr. Douglas. He was a big man, someone you would have thought could be a football player rather than a schoolteacher, and he had a special way of dealing with the children.

Many of them were very undisciplined; some that were in grade five or six could be as old as fifteen or sixteen because they hadn't gone to school when they were younger as their parents lived too far away from school. Most of them were Indian or Métis children, and it took a man like Mr. Douglas to be able to take those kids in the hand to teach them but also be able to enforce discipline.

When some of the older boys got into trouble and did damage to the school, he'd get even with them when he came out and play with us, which he made a point of doing every day. He'd get those bigger boys on the ground and rub their ears so hard I am sure they felt it for days.

Most of us liked Mr. Douglas. When he went back to Saskatchewan to get married, the substitute teacher (who had taught in the school before but was then semiretired) could not handle the students. He was a staunch Englishman, a regimental man, and we saluted the king and queen twice a day. He treated us like soldiers and would appoint different ones to do different tasks, making some generals, lieutenants, or corporals. We didn't learn much, as most kids wouldn't listen to him and didn't complete their assignments.

When attending Widewater School, several of us caught the same bus the high school kids rode to Kinuso, which meant we'd be at school early. One morning as we entered the schoolroom, one of the boys kicked off his boot and it flew up, hitting the ceiling and leaving an imprint of the sole. The in thing was to wear bomber jackets and flight boots which were never laced up. This incident created quite a laugh from the rest of us, so he proceeded to keep doing it until it looked like someone had walked on the ceiling. Then he hit the light bulb and broke it. Now he knew he was in trouble. Mr. Douglas ignored the footprints, but wanted to know who broke the light bulb. Eventually Gordon's ears got a real good rubbing, enough that he didn't try to do it again.

I loved sports like baseball and boxing, and although I was good at them, I could only participate at school because Dad would always find some work for me at home—anything to make it impossible for me to go when I needed to if I'd been on a team. In his opinion, sports were an even bigger waste of time than schooling.

My class at Widewater School in grade eight. Howe Englebertson is at the far left in the front row next to me. He was a good friend of mine. At the right end of the row is Morley Mouger. Because he was small and quick, he was hard to tackle when we played football.

A few years later they built another school for grades one to three, just in time for Clifford to begin his education. I always enjoyed sports, but track and field was what I excelled at. We were at a disadvantage in the small public schools because we didn't have the same facilities that the larger schools enjoyed. Our pole vault beds were made of a mixture of sawdust and sand, and the poles were made of dry spruce. One day when I was trying to clear the bar at the fifteen-foot mark, my pole broke and nearly killed me. It scraped along my ribs, tearing my T-shirt off, and when I fell to the ground I fell on the pole on my right thigh and was severely bruised. It hampered most of my other track and field events for the year. The next year I was back, more determined than ever, except for pole vaulting. I was competitive in most of the other events and came home with many first-place ribbons. I guess this was something that I inherited from my mother as she was quite an athlete in her younger days. I loved to play ball as well, but never was able to join a team.

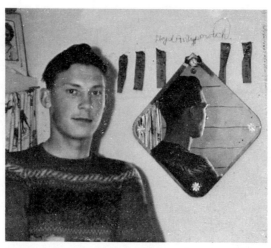

Me, aged fifteen years, standing in front of my first-place ribbons for track and field competitions from Kinuso to Slave Lake. The sixth ribbon is missing from my collection from the time when my pole vaulting pole broke, eliminating me from that event.

In the mill business, we moved many times to where we'd be close to better timber as we could not haul the logs very far with horses. Our next move was closer to Slave Lake Town, about two miles off the highway, near a family called Bayers. My dad bought some private land with a nice stand of timber on it.

He logged the timber, and then sold the land. It was a long ways to walk from camp to the highway to meet the school bus and bears were a problem. In the winter, timberwolves were a concern, as they were like ghosts, you rarely saw them but could hear them and sometimes they would not be very far away. I walked home after school in the dark from the fifteenth of November to the middle of February because it was dark by four o'clock in the afternoon. I didn't get off the bus until 5:00 p.m. and if there was no moon it was dark. I remember the school bus driver telling me I needed a flashlight, but I knew the road so well I'd jog it in about twenty five to thirty minutes. And if the wolves put a little pressure on me, I could do it faster.

One afternoon when I got off the bus there was a fresh skiff of snow on the road. I started out on a fast jog, but after about a mile I became a little winded, so I settled into a walk. I hadn't gone a hundred yards when a wolf howled really close to me. I stopped in my tracks. Then four or five more came, howling even closer, and they were on both sides of the road. The adrenalin kicked in, telling me to run as fast as I could. I don't know how fast I was running, but I had the after burners wide open until I saw the camp lights and had a feeling that I might win the race. The next morning my brother drove me to the bus, and sure enough the wolves had followed me almost right to camp.

When I started high school I rode the same bus to Kinuso. I caught it at seven o'clock in the morning to be in Kinuso in time for school. In the winter that mean I'd walk in the dark to and from the bus. When you live that far north in Alberta, it would be dark by four o'clock in the afternoon.

My biology teacher, Mr.Brendonfeld, was from Romania and was a different sort of guy. I think the many wars that he had lived through in that country must have affected him, or at least his thinking. He used terms like *regimes*, and everything had a political flair to it. One day I drew a big bug and a few other plants and shrubs on my new biology book and I called it "Bugology." When he noticed it, he had a conniption fit and stormed around me as if I was a Communist. He showed it to the principal, and the next day he made me copy everything into a new book. When the principal finally talked to me about it, he told me he thought my art was very creative but I shouldn't be writing on my book. However, he didn't reprimand me.

When I was in high school, my physical education teacher, Mr. Dumont, also taught science, which I enjoyed, although I never seemed to get a very good mark for the efforts I made. Anyway, when we were playing football, he'd usually be our referee, coach, and linesman all combined. In order to have two football teams in that school so we could play against each other, the main team was made up of the better athletes from grade ten, myself included, with grades eleven and twelve; while the secondary team were from grade nine, ten, with some from grade eleven. Even though some of the grade ten students were older, it was only because they didn't attend school on a regular basis.

Mr. Dumont cheated when he stepped off yards or when he refereed penalties or rough plays. All of the grade eleven and twelve boys on the main team took the game seriously, as we hoped to compete against other schools and show them that we could beat them, which we did. When he cheated and favored the younger team, it would frustrate us. When he played, it would always be on the secondary team. Since my position on our team was running back or right tackle, I'd look for a chance to hit him. I'd ask the quarterback of the other team if he could get Mr. Dumont to play with them and then make sure they gave him the ball because I wanted to tackle him. He was a good player, but then he was a lot more mature. Some of us were pretty tough, and were prepared to match our strength against his. One day my chance came, and because I could outrun him, I let him get a full head of speed, thinking he was going to outrun me to make a touchdown. When I tackled him by the ankles, he hit the ground so hard his head nearly popped off. That ended his playing football with us boys. He told the principal that we were getting too rough. Also, if we were going to continue to play that kind of football, the school would have to provide better protective gear or someone was going to get seriously hurt. That actually turned out good for us because we did get better football gear to protect us against the hard hits and the hard ground.

Mr. Dumont also taught boxing. I might not have been the best boxer, but I was probably the second best. I could probably punch harder than anyone else, but not as fast. One day, I hit a guy who was much larger than me with a body shot and he went down, a technical knockout. Mr. Dumont reprimanded me for not holding back on my punches. He put the gloves on and was going to give me a lesson in the art of boxing. Teddy Bajer, a very good boxer, was acting as referee. Of course, the boys were hoping that I could beat him, but I did not know how good he really was as I hadn't boxed with him before. He was fast and tried to explain to me that I should concentrate more on my jab and my hooks. My defence was doing fairly well, keeping him from getting through to me, so I decided that it was my turn to show him what I could do. I could see Teddy was encouraging me to take him. Teddy slipped a corner stool into the ring, so I immediately took advantage of it. I put a lot of pressure on Mr Dumont, backing him up toward the stool, and then I drove him in the midsection with everything that I had and knocked him backward over the stool. There was an awful roar and yelling from the rest of the kids, enough to catch the principal's attention, and he came in to see what was going on. I think only two of us saw him, Teddy and I, as he came in from the back of the room and we were the only ones facing him. Mr. Dumont was so busy trying to get the gloves off himself I don't think he saw him either. Regardless, the uproar temporarily ended our boxing lessons. Later, when we were reprimanded by the principal for spending too much time and attention on the girls, the trade-off was for him to give us back the boxing gloves, and he did.

CHAPTER 22

Moving to Wagner

From Bayer's, we moved the mill to Wagner, where Dad was able to get larger timber sales. The logging and milling were doing well. He had bought two larger logging trucks. One was a lumber truck, the other was a truck that had come from the oil field. It had a winch and a set of gin poles and he could skid full-length trees out of the bush to the mill with it. He also bought an HD7 Allis Chalmers crawler tractor that he could build his own logging roads and campsite with. He also built a new camp with a much larger kitchen, family living quarters, and a large grocery store. The problem for me was that it was my job to haul all the wood in, and since the camp was so much bigger, it took a lot more wood. I still remember the day Mom caught me roasting a wiener through the air hole in the heater in the storeroom. I am sure that is why I have one ear longer than the other.

The sawmill at Wagner camp

Air-dried lumber piles at Wagner Camp; the planks that are sticking out on the side of the stacks were purposely left that way so they could be used as steps for the workers to walk up to finish the pile

Some of the crew dismantling a pile of air-dried lumber and stacking it to be taken to the plainer by the gin-pole truck

Me driving the gin-pole truck and Roman standing on a pile of lumber that we were moving to the planer; we would put a cable around the pile of lumber and lift it off the ground

As I grew bigger and stronger I had to take on more responsibility at the camp. I fed horses, milked cows, and fed the chickens and turkeys. The chickens were mainly used for meat, so when they were big enough Mom would slaughter them and can them in sealers. Shirley helped Mom, and I think that's why she is such a good cook today. She also looked after the store and did the books for my dad.

Mom feeding her chickens and turkeys in the barnyard at Wagner Camp. The chickens supplied eggs for cooking and meat as well. The turkeys were for camp meat also (Christmas dinner).

Two loads of hay that we made at Nine Mile Bay at Wagner along the Slave Lake to feed horses and cows for the logging camp. In the picture, Ervin and Clifford are on top and I am standing on Roman's shoulders. Wagner Camp House is in the background.

*Clifford and I feeding a Hereford heifer calf a little bit of grain.
This was a calf that I made a pet of from the herd of nine or
ten cows that we raised for beef for the mill crew.*

*The stuffed owl that Gordon Beavess (a lumber buyer) gave me, sitting
on the corner of a rough-cut plank from the mill that was twenty-two
inches wide. Spread out on the plank is my day's catch of twenty-five
jack fish. I fed the fish that I caught to my mink. At times I would set
the owl in the yard to lure in crows and magpies. I would hide behind a
lumber pile or a pile of rocks and shoot at them with a slingshot when
they came in to dive bomb the owl. I got lots of crows that way.*

When I was about thirteen years old, a neighbor boy and I decided we'd get rich fast by trapping muskrats in the fall of the year. The bays of the lake would freeze over and rats would come from the shore, swimming under the ice. They made push-ups where they could sit and eat the roots of various plants that grew in the shallow waters of the bay. We'd set a few traps in the push-ups and then lace our skates on and try to chase the rats to the push-ups where our traps were. The ice wasn't very thick and you could see the rats swimming under it. In all the excitement of trying to chase a rat where we wanted it to go, we sometimes forgot to pay attention to thin areas of ice and fell through. Although it wasn't very deep, only two or three feet at the most, we'd get soaking wet. Then we'd run home and change so we could do it all over again.

My friend got the bright idea to shoot through the ice with a .22 so that we'd get more rats. The rats could only go so far under the ice before they had to come up for air and they'd come up in one of the push-ups or an air pocket under the ice. So when the rats went to one of the air pockets, the neighbor boy would try to shoot them in the head. This was working quite well, but to get the rats we had to chop a hole in the ice, and before long we had too many holes. Now this was a lot of fun, but when you were hot on the tail of a rat you weren't paying attention to where you were going. This one particular time, I was watching Herman chasing a rat, trying to shoot it on the go, when he skated over some holes that we'd already cut and fell through. The water was deeper in that spot, which made it harder to get him out. When his parents found out what he'd been doing, they put a stop to him rat hunting with me. The weather turned cold and snowy, and we couldn't see the rats through the ice anymore, so I just trapped the push-ups.

On weekends I'd take my dogs and sleigh and go trapping squirrels and weasels. I wasn't allowed to pack a .22 to hunt squirrels until I was older, so I used a slingshot with some small round stones handpicked from the railroad tracks as my "gun." I killed many with a slingshot, but some squirrels were just knocked out, so when I'd go to pick them up they'd bite me. I still have scars on my fingers to prove it. In the spring, I'd trap muskrats along the lake. I even caught the odd coyote and lynx.

A lynx that I shot with a shotgun because it was eating Mom's chickens

My pet owl sitting on my shoulder; I took it from the nest and raised it

A picture of my fox called Foxy Loxy

I caught a fox in one of my mink traps, so I bundled him in a gunnysack and brought him home. I put a collar on him and tethered him with a chain. Mom learned to hate him because he would challenge her and she was afraid of him. He never became tame to anyone but me. He would eat anything, and in the end he died after eating a groundhog that I'd caught on the railroad track. Later, I wondered if it had been poisoned or something, because normally feeding it to him shouldn't have been a problem.

An American tourist admiring my pet crow, Black Jack, sitting
on Dad's shoulder; Clifford and Roman watching

I had a pet crow that I'd taken from the nest and raised. If you asked him a question it sounded like he'd say "No." He was very friendly to all the men in camp since he had no fear of humans. He'd come through the door and hop down the hallway, making noises to let everyone know he was there begging for food. Someone would throw him food and he would grab it and fly away. Mom would always get after them because she didn't want them to encourage him to come into the kitchen to eat.

We had bought Racer's mother for a skid horse, later discovering that she was bred. When the colt was born, Racer was finer boned, too slight to be a skid horse. Tracing back, we found that her sire was a thoroughbred. Dad agreed to let me claim her and train her. She learned to do many tricks: count by pawing, communicate yes and no by nodding her head or shaking it sideways, and under a silent command from me she would act viciously, running toward me, baring her teeth, and laying her ears back. When she was a few feet from me, she would slide to a stop at my hand command. I scared many a person with this trick, and they'd dive under the fence or run for dear life, fearful that she would attack them. I taught her these things from a horse-breaking and training course I got from Professor Jess Barry from Pleasant Hill, Ohio. At the time it cost me $25.

I am riding Racer, a horse I raised from a newborn

In the fall when the Eaton's catalogue came out, I set my heart on a guitar. I asked my dad if he would buy it for me. When I told him it cost over $85, he told me to snare squirrels and trap mink and weasel to make money to buy my own guitar. So that's just what I did. My oldest daughter, Cindy, has it now. Take good care of it, Cindy, because I'm sure it's an antique by now.

Me playing my first guitar, Roman playing the violin, Shirley is the one with the accordion. This picture was taken at Wagner Camp.

Me playing my guitar while sitting on my horse

When I set out to make enough money to buy my guitar, I didn't have funds to buy .22 shells, so I used my slingshot. Before the snow came, I picked nice round stones of about the same size and put them in a bag so I could use them later when I went out to snare my squirrels. It was important to use stones of the same size and weight in order to shoot straight. It is no different from the bullets for a rifle. A hundred-grain bullet travels at a different trajectory than a 150-grain bullet.

Many times there'd be a squirrel sitting on the lower branches scolding at my little dog who came along with me. I'd shoot it off the branch to put it in my bag, but the odd time I hadn't quite killed one and when I went to pick it up it bit my finger.

I'd set five or six snares on a pole and lean it up against a spruce tree where the squirrels had made a big cache of cones. When they'd run up the leaning pole to sit on a limb to eat the seeds inside a cone, they'd get caught in one of the snares and hang themselves

I'd hook my two dogs to the sleigh and go farther into the bush to get more squirrels. One weekend I picked up several squirrels, but a few of them must not have been dead when I put them in my bag. When I dumped them on the floor behind the heater in the storehouse where we kept a small amount of produce for the millworkers, one of them was very much alive and began running through the shelves, looking for a way out.

Shirley looked after the storehouse and she wasn't impressed with this rodent running through the shelves over chocolate bars, chips, cookies, and gloves and socks. She told Dad that I had to get it out of the storehouse, insisting I had to go somewhere else to do my skinning and stretching. That was a good place for me to work in, so I had to do a lot of sweet talking, promising that I'd never let a live animal get loose in there again.

I had a limited amount of leg-hold traps for weasels. One of the loggers showed me how to use an inch-and-a-half drill bit to make a hole about three inches deep into a tree. Then I'd place my bait in the hole and put a horseshoe nail in on an angle. The weasel would stick his head in the small hole to get the bait, and when he tried to come back out the nail would get him behind the head. When I caught the weasel, I pulled the horseshoe nail out and put the weasel in my bag. Then I put the horseshoe nail back in the hole and it was ready to catch the next weasel. I caught a lot of weasels that winter using this method.

I'd built all my trap boxes by mid-September and I set them out, mostly along the lakeshore. One day, I had a martin in my trap. That was a big surprise; it was the first one I'd ever caught in my life. Two days later I had another one, but I didn't catch any more that winter, as there were not many in that part of the country.

When I caught a mink, I'd take it home and put it in the pen I built myself. I'd feed them fish that I'd chopped up with a big cleaver and mixed with some mink concentrate and some eggs that I snitched from the henhouse. The fur developed a good shine; Cliff Englebertson said it was because of the eggs.

There were quite a few different breeds of domestic mink and they varied quite a lot in price. The standard, which was the black, was probably the cheapest. The pastels were the next most expensive. The breath of spring or the silver blues and 97 percent whites were the most expensive at that time.

One day when I was going down to the lake to catch fish for my mink, a young buck deer stepped out on the path in front of me. I used my slingshot to shoot him in the head with a ball bearing that I'd taken from a wrecked bearing on the planer mill. He went down like a sack of potatoes, then immediately jumped up and ran down the path right into the lake. The ball bearing must have screwed up his thought process, because it was unusual that he would do that when he could have run back into the bush. He stood there looking at me. I didn't want to waste any more of my precious ball bearings, so I tried nailing him with a few small stones I picked up off the lakeshore. When I finally bounced one off of his back, he moved out into the lake even a little farther.

I ran back to a cabin where an Indian who worked at the mill was living. I asked him if he had a gun because there was a deer standing in the lake. He came down to the lake with me. The deer had come back closer to shore, but was still standing in water about belly deep. When he shot, it retreated back into the lake until it was swimming. He tried to shoot it in the head a couple more times, but couldn't seem to hit it. After it swam quite a ways out into the lake, I guess it decided that the lake was too wide, so it turned and came back toward the shore. When it touched bottom, it just kept on walking, and he kept shooting until he finally knocked it down. I helped him dress it out, but it had been shot in the belly a couple of times, so I told him I didn't want any of it. I would have liked to claim the horns for the first deer I had knocked down with the slingshot, but that didn't happen.

One of the older Indians that worked on the sawmill asked me to go hunting moose with him. He cut a piece of birch bark off a tree and rolled it up into a funnel shape and made a call that sounded like a cow moose in estrous. When a bull answered, my adrenaline began to flow. Suddenly, I wondered how good this Indian could shoot, because that bull moose was acting like he was ready to take on the whole world. He just demolished an old rotten birch tree, then got down one knee and ripped up some moss and grass. He stood there for a while and then with every step he took he would let out a deep grunt. The old Indian lifted his rifle ever so slowly and shot him right in the hump. He went down, tried to get up with his front feet, but his back legs didn't seem to be working. All he could do was thrash around. He'd been shot in the spine and the back half of his body was paralyzed.

The Indian jumped up, ran right close to him, and shot him in the head and killed him. Then he waved his hand for me to come. He was excited, saying, "Wa wa! He's a big one." He was shooting a .32 Remington, which was hardly big enough to shoot coyotes with, let alone a big bull moose. The stock was all taped up, but I guess it shot quite straight and that's all that really mattered. He definitely knew where to shoot that moose, because once he had knocked it down he knew that it couldn't get up and then he shot it in the head. When we got back to camp, I looked up Dad and told him what the old Indian had done.

He asked who I'd gone with. When I told him I'd gone with Constance, he said I was brave to go with him; he looked to be nearly blind. I told him he could see real well when it came time to shoot a moose. It was an experience that I will never forget.

I must admit, though, every time after that when I went hunting with an Indian, the first thing I did was check his rifle to see if it was big enough to shoot a moose. And you know, to my surprise, they never had a rifle bigger than the 30:30. The Indians were expert hunters. They never shot anything farther than 100 yards away, and most often it was much closer and they knew just where to place a shot. They were excellent trackers and read signs in a way that was just amazing.

CHAPTER 23

Girls, Girls, Girls!

By now I was becoming a teenager and my hormones were starting to kick in and I was looking at all the pretty young girls, thinking how much fun it would be to play with them instead of my boyfriends. Dating was pretty much out of the question. I was too isolated and still wasn't old enough to get a driver's license, even though I'd been driving for quite a while. I still had to wait for the big birthday. When that day arrived, I drove Dad's car to the police station to get my driver's license. The police asked me if I knew how to drive. I said I did. Later he asked me how I'd gotten there and I told him I'd driven. He looked at me and smiled, then said, "You didn't have a driver's license." I told him, "Well, I do now." He just laughed, wished me well, gave me a few pointers, and told me to be careful with speed as he didn't want to have to give me a ticket. He was a real nice fellow and I appreciated his advice.

At that time a few of my friends were getting their driver's license as well, and they'd get their fathers pickup to go tearing around the country. From time to time they got into little skirmishes with the police. I think the reason this happened was because they'd get together and one would challenge the other or dare him to do things that usually netted him trouble.

One time three friends picked me up and without my dad's knowledge we ended up at a dance. Of course somebody got hold of some beer and I didn't want to be chicken and not try it. It didn't take many bottles of beer to spin my world; I was not used to drinking. When we got to the dance, I asked a girl that I had a crush on for a dance, but I wasn't in very good shape to dance. She looked at me and said, "What have you been doing? You're drunk!" She knew I didn't drink, so I said to her, "Don't blame me, blame those guys," as I pointed to my buddies. Then I told her that I loved her and I wanted to dance with her. She was a good enough sport to try to hold me up as we wobbled around the floor. At the end of that tune, I decided it was safer for me to sit down because my legs didn't want to go where I wanted them to. It wasn't long before more of my school buddies gathered around and were laughing at the state I was in. Evelyn said, "You guys got him drunk. He can't even dance."

Gordon said, "Sure he can. Just give him another beer!"

I started telling the guys I'd come with that I had to get home because I had to load lumber early in the morning. They said they'd have me ready for work, so they stuck my head out the window and drove real fast, trying to sober me up, but it really didn't work. My oldest brother, Roman, got me up at five o'clock the next morning to load the load of birch lumber we were shipping to Edmonton. I was as sick as a dog and promised myself that I'd never do that again, and I never did. Alcohol wasn't really a problem for me and neither was smoking. I had my sights set on track and field and neither smoking nor drinking did anything for me.

As I grew older, the workload also increased. First I started piling lumber; from there I graduated into various jobs on the mill, and before long I could do everything except saw, as I was never given the chance to try. I enjoyed the job of being a canter on the mill, and would look forward to all the school holidays with anticipation just so I could cant (roll logs in for the saw). It was clean and you were at the beginning of the production line instead of at the end.

I remember a winter when my dad did some commercial ice fishing on Slave Lake. I had to help him, but ice fishing was not as much fun as fishing with a hook. First we'd cut a hole through the ice, which was anywhere from three to five feet thick and we didn't have ice augers like fishermen do now! Then we'd put a jigger in the hole, and by pulling on a small cord, could make it crawl along under the ice. After we had jigged it for 100 yards, we would cut another hole through the ice to retrieve the rope. The trick was to be able to cut that hole above the jigger. Then we'd pull the fish net with the rope from one hole to the other. The bottom of the net was weighted down with led weights and on the top were wooden floats. We would tie a rope with a weight to submerge the net deep enough to keep the floats from freezing to the ice. Then we'd work the jigger from one hole to the other until we had a thousand yards of the net in the lake. A day later (or not more than two), we would go back and rechop the hole and pull the net out. If the net was in the right place we could catch a lot of fish. In -50° F weather, with the wind blowing across such a big lake, it wasn't a very comfortable job. Then to make things worse, sometimes we would catch a twenty- or thirty-pound northern pike or a large ling cod that could twist twenty or thirty yards of the net into a rope. Trying to untangle such a mess in the cold, with the wind blowing, was really miserable. Netting in the summer from a boat with Cliff Englebertson was much more fun.

Although my dad did quite well at commercial fishing that winter, we never did it again. And to be honest with you I was really glad, but that was another learning experience for me. I would rather ride bronco skid horses, even though they beat me up badly, than to stand out on that cold, cold lake with the wind blowing thirty miles an hour and the temperature anywhere from -20 °F to -50 °F. But even after that, I still love to go fishing.

Lesser Slave Lake could be harsh and very cruel to the inexperienced persons who thought they were going to have a pleasant ice-fishing experience. I can remember lying in bed at night when it was −50 °F and all the nail heads on the bunk house wall had a quarter of an inch of frost on them; and the unforgettable noise, a booming sound rather like thunder made by cracking ice. The next day when you went to pull nets you had to be very cautious and look for the fresh cracks that created during the night. Sometimes the cracks would only be six inches wide; other times they could be eighteen inches wide. They could go down the full depth of the ice, anywhere from two to five feet. A person could fall into them, and although I didn't know of anyone who lost their life, I knew of several who ended up with their leg wet up to their knee, a very uncomfortable feeling. The cracks were hard to detect because snow would form a crust over them, leaving the ice too thin to hold a man's weight.

Although my dad never used a Bombardier, I knew of people that had them. If they were unfortunate to drive parallel with one of these cracks, the front ski would go through the thin ice, and in some cases, it would break off.

It was always exciting when the ice broke up on the lake. Most times it seemed to drift to the north shore, but when it drifted to the south shore, it would come right up on shore. It would move in very slowly and just keep pushing everything that was in its way; first the small willows and trees, then the railway's snow fence, telegraph poles, and eventually the railway track itself, sometimes pushing up several hundred yards of track. It began approximately 100 yards from the lakeshore and the sounds it made are hard to describe. It would screech and grind, and at times a piece would push up into the air, eventually falling to break into many, many pieces, sounding like breaking glass.

Shirley helping Dad with commercial ice fishing on Slave Lake

Ice that came off of Slave Lake, pushing its way up onto shore and across the railroad track below our camp at Wagner. When this picture was taken the ice was still moving, and several hours later it piled the whole rail bed (ties, rails, and everything) against the bank, breaking the telegraph poles as well. The train was shut down for several days until the railroad crew could come and clear the ice off and replace the bed and ties so that the rails could be laid down again. This line had an average of seven trains a day, so it was a major disruption.

CHAPTER 24

Horse Logging Gives Way to Equipment

Ervin bought some horses from a lady in Athabasca. She had a team of grays that he wanted to buy; however, she didn't want to sell the big gray gelding, as he had run away with her husband and killed him. He was a nice big horse and Ervin insisted that he could handle him if she'd sell him. She finally agreed to sell him for $80.

Ervin called him Big Silver. This big gray weighed 1,800 or 1,900 pounds and was a bit nervous. After putting together the biggest collar and the heaviest harness we had for skidding, Ervin took him out into the bush and hooked him to a big butt log and let him go. He didn't go very far before he ran into a stump and broke the single tree in half. So Ervin put one on that was made of iron. After hooking the horse to another log, Ervin let the gray go again. This time he went even faster and hit a birch tree, breaking the hame straps, the belly band, and the birchen straps. He wouldn't stop for the guy on the landing, but instead ran all the way back to the camp with just a halter and collar on.

After repairing the harness again, it was plain to Ervin that he had to slow this horse down somehow. I was home on Christmas break, so he decided I should ride this horse while he skid logs. Riding a horse with a harness on wasn't my interpretation of bronco riding but Ervin was sure I could handle him. The next morning he put a bridle on the horse as well as a halter, then tied the halter shank real short to the top of the hames. The next thing was to see if I could ride him, and just getting on him was a job. When Ervin finally got him dallied to another skid horse that he

109

rode, I climbed on Big Silver. He did a lot of jumping around but after a while he seemed to accept the fact that I wasn't going to hurt him. Then we went off into the bush on the haul road. Big Silver tried to run away several times but because he was dallied so close to Ervin's horse he gave up and pranced all the way out to the landing.

We went into the bush and hooked him to a large butt log again. I took a good hold on the reins, and when I asked him to go, he went full throttle for the landing. I pulled back on the reins as hard as I could but wasn't able to control him. We were going much too fast when he hit another stump, which almost set him back on his haunches. I slid up his back with my thighs squeezed as tight as I could; had it not been for the hames, I might have ended up by his ears. Before I could get myself collected and in place again, we were off down the skid trail, hell-bent for leather. I managed to get him stopped at the landing just barely long enough for the guy to unhook my skid chain. I had quite a time getting him turned around to go back down the skid trail to get the next log. Ervin managed to get the skid chain hooked, and we were off again, this time going past the rollway before I could get him stopped. I turned him around and headed him down the skid trail again. When I got back to Ervin, I asked him to hook Big Silver to another big butt log because I was having trouble controlling him. He did, and we were off to the landing again.

This horse was so strong he could still run to the landing with a big log while I was pulling on the reins as hard as I could. We kept hooking the biggest logs we could find to him to see if we could tire him out. Eventually he began to slow down, but when we hooked a smaller log to him he wanted to go fast again. He'd run into a stump or tree and I'd go sliding right up to the hames again. The inside of my thighs were getting so sore I didn't know if I was going to be able to finish the day, so we kept on hooking the big logs to him. Before we were finished that day I was able to get him back to a walk with a big log hooked on behind him. I rode him for several days before he would skid by himself.

Although he was so big and strong, he wasn't a very safe horse to skid with, as he'd only give you one chance to hook the skid chain and he was gone; you'd better be out of the way or he would simply run you over with the log. Most other skid horses were slow and steady; if they hit a stump, they would pull to the side and slide the log off the stump themselves, then carry on to the landing. When they were turned around to go back down the skid trail, they'd walk slow, sometimes stopping to nibble on whatever they could find. But when you turned Big Silver around, he wouldn't go back down the skid trail, so he had to be ridden or led back.

It was hard work logging with horses. Although I loved horses and loved to work with them as well, I must admit it was much easier with the gin-pole truck, which could skid seven full length trees at once from the bush to the mill yard. Then we got the Allis Chalmers cat and it could do so many tough jobs. One was hauling the short logs on sloops behind the cat, except we had a problem when going down a steep hill as the loaded sloops would run up against the cat, pushing it down the hill. It could push sawdust and slabs away from the mill. As well, it was so much more efficient to build roads and landings with it than by hand.

A sloop load of logs pulled to the mill by an Allis Chalmers HD 5 Crawler

Seven full-length trees pulled by a gin-pole truck (that sure beat horse logging!)

*Ervin, Chester Maryfield, and Roman rolling logs up two
small skid poles onto a five-ton truck (hand loading)*

*A sixteen-foot high pile of hand-decked logs made by rolling
the logs up to the top on a couple of roller logs*

Two cats pushing slabs and edgings into a pile (beats doing it with a horse!)

The transition from horse logging to mechanical logging with trucks and cats came quite quickly for my dad. The use of power saws also sped up the falling and bucking of timber. Soon we were logging two and three times as much timber in a season as we did with horses, Swede saws, and broad axes. Now the time had come for bigger horse power in the power unit running the mill, and bigger and faster head rigs so that a third more lumber could be cut in the same eight hours. Although the horses were never far away, they were mostly turned out to pasture, used only as a backup, and it wasn't long before they were permanently retired. These changes increased production, which in turn meant more income, and Dad's big problem was income tax time. After his accountant fine-tuned his books, he still had eleven thousand dollars to pay the government. That was a lot of money in those days!

The planing crew at Wagner, from left to right: Ervin, Joseph, Alfred Giroux, Lazard Giroux, Roman, Chester Maryfield, and the sawyer that we kept working on the planer until the milling started again

A Monarch planer that Dad soon realized was not large enough to handle the volume of lumber that we were milling

*Me driving the gin-pole truck, moving lumber to the planer;
Roman and Clifford standing beside the truck*

*Ervin and the three-ton Fargo with a load of lumber that was too long
and over balanced the truck, lifting the front wheels off the ground*

The millwork and logging continued throughout the winter, so there was an overrun of logs that were decked for spring breakup. With the cat, it was possible to clear a bigger area for the logs and for lumber to be air dried until June, when the planing would begin. The lumber was planed and then loaded into a boxcar at the sliding in Wagner. This process lasted until late fall, then the logging and milling began again.

Our five-ton truck, hauling short logs to the mill at Wagner

*Logs that were skidded with horses, decked, and waiting to be hauled
to the mill; Ervin and Joseph doing a little comedy at coffee break*

Dad was doing very well with his logging and milling operation; in fact, maybe a little too good, as some of the big lumber companies were complaining to the forest service that he was cutting too much timber. The competition was strong from the bigger companies when he tried to bid on the timber sale. He logged at Wagner for a few more years, and then Roman and Ervin expressed an interest in working with equipment cutting seismic line for oil companies, as they had been offered several good jobs. Dad still wanted to stay with the lumber business, so he decided he would try his hand at a much larger planing mill at High Prairie, Alberta.

CHAPTER 25

High School in Kinuso

I finished my public schooling at Widewater, and then did a year and a half of high school at Kinuso, which was a much larger school with each grades having their own room and I had several teachers for different subjects. The principal was Hank Lysine and I got along with him really well.

My physical education included boxing and football as well as track and field. In 1954, I participated in the northern Alberta track and field, and although I won some ribbons, that competition was much tougher than at the local level. I felt I was much more capable of doing better if I had had some better coaching, as I pretty much did all my training. I also may have been able to do better if I hadn't spent so much time playing with the girls.

One time on a nice warm spring day about five of us boys, along with Hank Lysine's two daughters and three other girls, were lying in the sun behind the backstop. I don't know if Hank had seen us go there or somebody snitched, but it didn't take him too long to haul us all into his office. We were totally innocent of any hanky-panky. All we were doing was using the girls for a pillow to lay our heads on and were chatting and enjoying the sunshine. In his office he gave us all the "what for" and promised to send a note home to our parents.

That's the part that scared me the most, so at the next recess I went into his office to have a chat with him. I told him that I didn't think my dad would take too kindly to me bringing that kind of note home. I pointed out that we were all innocent of any wrongdoing, that we were really just enjoying a nice warm spring day. He had a very down-to-earth talk with me and explained the problems and where they could lead. He told me that although he trusted me he didn't know if he could say that for all the others. I told him I'd give him my word that although we enjoyed the company of the girls, it wouldn't go beyond that. He told me he wouldn't send a note home to my dad, but that he'd keep a close eye on me.

One day I put a frog down one of my classmate's neck. She and her friend were walking back from the little café near the school. I walked up behind them and put my arms around their shoulders and walked with them. One of the girls was well developed and her blouse gaped open just a wee bit, so I lined up and let the frog drop into her blouse. It may not have been so bad except he just kept on kicking and scratching, trying to find a place to hide. She became so afraid, she fell down and I thought she was going to pass out. I'd never seen anyone get so scared in all my life, so there was only one thing that I could do. I had to get the frog out of there, so in I went and it wasn't as easy to find that little devil as I thought it would be. I would have him by the leg and he would pull away, then I'd have to start all over again. This was a blind situation; everything was done by feel, and she wasn't cooperating with me at all. Believe me, I did a lot of exploring before I got that little fellow out of there. While all this was happening a grade four student called her teacher, and when the teacher saw what I was doing she called the principal. Thank god I was done exploring and had the little fellow out and back on green grass by the time Hank came along. We were still sitting on the grass when all the questions started coming fast and furious. You'd think a serious crime had been committed. I told Hank that I was responsible for what had happened. He said, "Okay, all of you into my office."

I was glad because quite a crowd had gathered. We told our story to Hank and he asked what I was doing with my hand in her blouse. I just looked at him and said, "Hank, did you ever put a frog in a girl's blouse?"

He just looked at me with a slight grin and said, "I'm not sure what the frog has to do with your hand being in her blouse." But when she and the other girl told their side of the story, I think he had it figured out. When I saw a smile on his face, I thought I might get to go to school a little longer. He told me, "Lloyd, you could do yourself a favor by running a few laps around the track, but I think you need to spend a couple of days in your room on detention first."

So into my room I went, but it was sure hard to stay in there when it was so nice outside. I persuaded some of my buddies to catch three frogs and bring them to the ping-pong table at the back of our main classroom and we could have some frog races. I drew three chalk lines on the table and we'd start the frogs at one end and race them to the other end. This turned into a lot of fun; the bet was on with our nickels piled up at the end of the table.

I guess Hank thought he'd better check on me, and came sneaking around the corner to witness the frog race. He stomped his foot and clapped his hands and said, "You boys get the hell out of here. And, Lloyd, you don't only run two laps around the track; you had better run five and be in by the time the bell rings for class." Well, that was impossible because the noon hour was soon over and the track was a quarter of a mile, so while everyone was in class I was doing my laps around the track all by myself.

At that time, two young girls from Edmonton had come to teach school at Kinuso for the last two months of the school term. They were fresh out of normal school and getting their feet wet as a teacher.

One of them was a redhead and she was only eighteen years old and I was seventeen. It would be fair to say that we were attracted to each other. I remember one day when she and her friend were walking back from the little café. I walked out to meet them and was going to walk with them back to the schoolyard. She said, "You stay away from me. I don't trust you. You probably have a frog or snake in your hand or in your pocket, and if you come any closer I'll scream and holler until somebody comes to rescue me."

I assured her I didn't have anything in my hand or in my pockets. She said, "You are so crazy, I can never tell what you are going to do next. After what you did to Margaret the other day, I don't know if I can trust you."

I tried to sweet talk my way into her trust, but I'm not sure I succeeded before we reached the school. Since it wasn't all that bad, it only gave me a chance to try again.

And I did try again, but I guess she was right. There must have been a little more devil in me than I realized, because what I did to her next was not going to gain her confidence. You see, I had this little book that was kind of a tricky thing. On its cover it said, "All you ever wanted to know about sex." And although it looked like a real book, it was a fake, and when you opened it, there was a battery in it that would give you a nasty little shock.

So one day I got enough courage to walk down the hall, and when I passed her room and saw she was there, I walked in and handed her the book face down. I told her that being a teacher and all she might want to read the book. I turned and walked out of the room without seeing the expression on her face, because I didn't want to be in the room when she opened the book and got the shock. I knew she would probably scream and that would draw the attention of the other teachers. I was just a few steps out the door when I heard the scream and then I heard her say, "You devil."

Now, I wasn't supposed to be at that end of the school, so I just kept on walking. But her classmate from across the hall heard her scream and hurried into her room to see what was wrong. She said, "It was him again." So she asked her what I'd done, and she said, "That book on the floor. If you are brave enough to pick it up, you really should read it." Her friend looked at it, and it looked quite harmless to her, I guess. So she picked it up, turned it over, and when she read what was on the cover, she said, "He is a bit of a devil, isn't he?" Then she opened the book, and of course she suffered the same shock. I guess that's what you'd call a double whammy. Now I had two of them to suck up to, because neither one of them would trust me. Besides, they threatened that they'd to give it the principal.

I said, "Don't do that. Just give it back to me as I haven't even read it yet." She said, "There's nothing in that damned thing but a battery and some wires."

I asked her if it tickled and laughed at her. She asked where I found something like that, but I just laughed and said, "It sure is a lot of fun, isn't it?" But I promised that I'd never pull a prank on her again and I didn't; however, it took quite awhile for her to trust me.

I was very involved in track and field sports and was scheduled to go to the Northern Alberta track and field day at the Waterhole sports ground at Fairview, Alberta. I really did appreciate having Hank as a principal because I had a lot of respect for him. He was the one who arranged for me to go, as I don't think my dad would have let me go if Hank hadn't had a talk with him.

Hank had great hopes that I would come back to Kinuso with some first-place ribbons. He had chosen the young red-headed normal schoolteacher to be one of his assistants; little did he know the big favor he had done us.

I was entered in five events, and even with strong, tough competition,

I managed to bring home five ribbons. Although I didn't get a first-place, her encouragement helped me bring in second and third ribbons. I don't think Hank would have been any prouder of me if I had been his own son, and although my expectations had been higher than my ribbons, it was still a great achievement.

Besides that, it gave me a chance to spend time with her, and even though she still thought I was a bit of the devil, she kind of liked me. I said I felt the same way and asked her if she would like to come to the rodeo on the last day of school. She said she would love to. She had a few things to do in the morning, but after that she would be free. I said I'd meet her at the school and we could walk across the road to the rodeo at the fairgrounds. I did that, and who do you think we'd meet as we were leaving the schoolyard but Hank Lysine. He asked me where I was going and I told him I was going to show this city girl a good old-fashioned western rodeo.

I'd done a lot of planning and manipulating to get this far because I knew Dad wouldn't let me go to the rodeo. I asked Ervin and Shirley to pick me up after school and meet me at the rodeo. I told Ervin that I was going to take the pretty redhead to the rodeo, but we had to take her to the station so she could catch the train back to Edmonton that night.

Ervin and Shirley didn't make it to the rodeo in time to see most of the in-field events, and maybe it was a good thing because one of my classmates and I decided we'd go in the wild-cow riding competition. Gordon got bucked off, but I rode my cow the required eight seconds. He suggested we ride one cow double. I told him as long as he planned to ride backward I was game, if they'd let us do that. He said, "No fair, we will flip a coin," and I lost. So I rode backward, and let me tell you, that was one hell of a ride. We banged heads and thumped each other in the chest as that old cow did her best to throw us off. I guess we were a little heavier load than she expected and we rode her to a standstill. I can still hear the rodeo announcer telling the rest of the contestants and spectators this was what you got when two young guys fresh out of high school thought they could take the whole world on.

One of the pickup men knew me because he'd worked for my dad at the logging camp. George came to me and said, "I have something for you. Why don't you ride some of the fresh horses that haven't been tried out yet? Some of the cowboys don't want to draw them because they aren't proven buckers."

Gordon said, "You can't do that. You'll get bucked off."

I said, "No, I won't."

George said, "Good! When they call your name you can ride number seven." I had no idea what I was getting into. I had ridden horses that bucked before, but never at a rodeo. I didn't have my own bucking rigging. I didn't even have a cowboy hat, but Gordon had a beat-up straw hat that he was wearing and he pulled it down over my ears and said, "Now you're a cowboy."

I don't think I would have had enough guts to pull it off if that little redhead hadn't been sitting in the bleachers. George said, "Make sure when you come out of the chute you don't get your legs caught on anything. Keep them high and lean back so you don't let yourself get sucked over his head."

When I nodded toward the gate to indicate that I was ready, they opened it, and George was right there beside me on the pickup horse. He kept telling me to lean back more, and believe me, I thought I was going through the biggest explosion that I had ever experienced. It felt like the world was flying apart and I was about to be launched up into the clouds. Somehow I hung on for dear life, flailing away with both legs, hoping they'd both come down on the right side of the horse's neck. Before I knew it, George had me under the arm, rescuing me from that hurricane. He asked if I was all right as he let me down.

I said, "Oh yeah." I wouldn't have said otherwise even if that horse had jerked my arm right out of joint. I went back and crawled up on the bleachers beside my date, and the first thing she said to me was, "Now I know you really are crazy. How many times did you do that before?"

When I told her not many, she said, "I want you to stay here beside me and quit going in there before you kill yourself." Here I thought I'd impressed her, but instead she was scared stiff that something terrible was going to happen to me. We sat there and watched the rest of the rodeo. When Ervin and Shirley arrived, we walked through the midway and played a few games, which I lost every time.

Then they announced that there was going to be a boxing card that evening featuring some heavyweights, middleweights, and lightweights. My brother was set on watching the boxing events, as he liked boxing as much as I did, and we missed the train and had to catch it at Slave Lake in order for her to get on it to go to Edmonton.

When we got to the logging camp to drop Shirley off, Dad was on the board step in front of the house. He told me to get into the house. I told him that one of the teachers had to catch the train at Slave Lake, but he was not buying any of it and insisted that I get into the house right then. He said Ervin could take her to the train.

Boy, did he know how to deflate my bubble. I'd been flying high, feeling like I was ten feet tall and now all of a sudden everything came crashing down around me. It was one of the biggest humiliations I think I'd ever experienced. Although I didn't agree with him, I told her that I had to respect him as my parent and I was sorry our date ended this way. I gave her a peck on the cheek, wished her well, and said maybe someday our paths would cross again. She slipped me a piece of paper that had her name and phone number on it and asked me to please call her, and I turned and walked away from the car in the dark of night. I didn't really know what awaited me when I reached the porch. Dad said, "What do you think you're doing?"

I said, "Nothing more than you'd have done under the same circumstances when you were my age." I don't think he was expecting that kind of reply. I didn't want to have any more conversation with him concerning the day's events, so I walked into the house and went to bed.

I didn't go to sleep for a long time. I believe that was a turning point in my life. I decided then that I didn't want to be under someone else's control for everything I did, and although he held all the cards now, it would only be a matter of time before I took control of my life. I never did call her number for one reason or another. First of all, we didn't have a phone in the logging camp and I knew that unless she came back into that area, it wasn't likely that I'd get to see her again.

One day a lumber buyer stopped in with a note for me. He said, "I don't know if I should give this to you or to your dad." I asked him who it was from and he said as near as he could tell it must have been one of my old flames.

I said in that case he'd better give it to me. Apparently she was teaching school in Edmonton and the lumber buyer's two daughters, one in grade five and one in grade three, told their teacher that they were going to Slave Lake with their father and they were going to stop at a logging camp and spend the night with the Antypowiches. She asked them if they knew me and they said they'd met me when they were on a trip with their dad the year before. They said I was the guy with all the animals, a crow, an owl, and a pet fox.

The note read, "Lloyd, please call. I can be reached at this number. I had the most wonderful day of my life, even though I nearly missed my train. I highly respect you for the way you handled the situation with your dad that night. I don't know if I could have done that. Signed with hugs and kisses, Angelina."

I never called the number and I'm not really sure why. I don't know if it was lack of confidence or what, but somehow our paths never crossed again.

CHAPTER 26

LeeBakken Planer Mill in High Prairie

Dad purchased the LeeBakken Planer Mill at High Prairie and had a contract to buy and plane lumber for LePage Lumber Company. Some parts of the planing mill were run by big electric motors, and when the millwright sharpened the planer knives, he used an electric jointer that would do the job right on the planer without having to take the knives out, a procedure that saved a lot of time. The trim saw was run by an electric motor as well.

We had a large lumberyard where lumber was dry piled as it came off the trucks from the various mills in the country. Each load was hand scaled. The mills would get paid for their lumber, and the trucks for their hauling. The load slips would go into the office and the bookkeeper would do the necessary calculations.

Living at High Prairie was quite a change for Mom, who no longer had a crew of men to cook for. She had the benefit of running water, an electric stove, a fridge, and furnace. There was no more wood and water to pack!

The first winter, we needed to build an inventory of wood to plane, and Alfred Martinson and I dry piled all the lumber purchased by the planing mill. We used horses and sleigh to haul the various dimensions from where the trucks unloaded lumber in the yard to the area where we dry piled it. Dad did the scaling.

*Me driving the team; Alfred Martinson standing on lumber that we were taking
to the dry piles in the lumberyard that we rented from Horoshko in High Prairie*

*Martin Martinson and I loading lumber onto a sleigh from
a load that had come in from one of the mills that we bought
lumber from to plane in the High Prairie mill*

Alfred Martinson was an excellent man to work with. He lived in a
house on the mill site. Piling lumber requires a lot of physical strength,
and with synchronized teamwork we could do that without saying a
word to each other. We did this all winter. I'm sure when he first hired
on and learned that I was going to be his partner, he must have had

some reservations about working with a "kid" just out of school, but after the first week I was still there and going strong. When he realised I was sneaking out after work and spending time with the girls uptown, he said I had hormones that he didn't have anymore and that must have been what kept me going. I spent a fair bit of time visiting with Martin and his wife and their eighteen-month-old son, who was a lot of fun. He was very energetic and talkative and he loved pickles. After he'd eat one, I'd ask him where the pickle went, and he'd point at his stomach and say, "Here it is."

In June of the next year, the planer started running. A lot of the lumber that we planed was shipped to the North Eastern United States. The mill was much larger than anything we had ever operated before. The trim saw, green chain, re-saw, three planers, and the big power unit were all under cover. There was a small toolshed where the planer man, who was like a millwright, could hammer the re-saw blades and sharpen them. Not every mill could hammer its own saws at that time; they'd send them away to be sharpened and hammered, but we had the tools to do our own. The trim saw and green chain were run by electric motors. The planers had a huge blower that sucked up the dust and shavings and blew them directly into the beehive burner. We loaded lumber directly into the boxcars on a twelve-car spur. When one car was full, we'd pull it ahead with the Dodge power wagon and the aid of several wheel jacks. If we were planing dimension lumber, two by six and greater, we could plane three carloads a day, but it took considerably longer if we had to re-saw it into one-inch or window sashing.

Once the mill started planing, I hauled lumber from the lumberyard to the trim saw, where it was trimmed, then run up a green chain to the re-saw or to the planer. Since I was very familiar with the operation, I could haul with two trucks. I'd take a loaded truck to the mill and dump it by the trim saw. While I was gone, the crew loaded the second one, and when I came back I'd take the loaded truck, leaving the empty one for them to fill again. I did a steady turn around all day long.

Eventually Dad had trouble finding someone fast enough to keep the green chain going steady, so he took me off the hauling truck and put me on the green chain. I understood how it worked and could keep it going flat out. Eventually I worked in every aspect of the mill, except to millwright the planner. Joe Nome was a master at that and it was his job.

The planer only worked from June to October because it took that long to plane the lumber that was air dried in the yard.

During those years the compensation board had begun encouraging all the smaller mills to have someone that had a first aid ticket onsite. I took two courses and passed them both with very good marks. I really enjoyed first aid and was good at it. The guy from the compensation board phoned to ask me if I would be interested in a job doing first aid and booking in the supplies that were flown by plane to Coppermine in the Northwest Territories. He told me that the pay would be very good and that they would fly me out once a month for a week, then fly me back in.

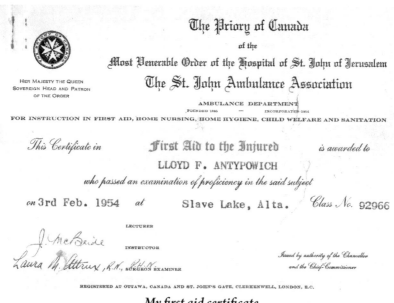

My first aid certificate

When I asked Dad if I could go he said he needed me to work on the planing mill. I realised that he wasn't prepared to release his control over my life, yet I had nothing of my own and I would have to leave home if I wanted to take that job. So that squashed my first job opportunity. It would have been a good experience, even if I was young.

Dad told me they would pay me $24 per day if I scaled the lumber as it came in during the winter. The trucks hauled day and night, so I stayed in a bunkhouse and the truckers woke me up when they came in to unload. I'd scale the lumber and then go back to bed. Sometimes I'd hardly get to sleep before the next load came in. During the day I scaled loads as they came in and then helped the bookkeeper tally the lumber. I was young and gung-ho with dreams of being able to save for the future, but like most of the other promises, I didn't receive cash for my labours. I was told it went back into the company, which I would own a share of. It was then that I realised the carrot was being hung in front of the donkey and I was the donkey. I chased the carrot, with all its promises, for five more years and never caught it.

CHAPTER 27

Fun with the Girls from High Prairie!

The planning mill was located on the west side of the West Prairie River, just a stone's throw from downtown High Prairie. I remember a day when I went uptown with Shirley to do some shopping. There was an attractive young girl at the till and she was very friendly. One day my mom asked me to run uptown and get a few things from the store. When I went to pay at the till, the same girl was there. When she handed me the receipt, she had written on the back, "I am U-nice. Who are you?" I told her I'd be happy to meet her after work and tell her who I was.

She said she got off work at five o'clock. I got off at six and would still have some cleanup to do around the mill, so I wouldn't be free until seven. She said we could make it work; she would be at Thelma's Café.

I was there at seven o'clock. Her name was Eunice Reagan; she was a lot of fun and she also had a lot of girlfriends. On weekends, we'd go down to the river and have a wiener roast. I'd play my guitar and the girls would sing all the western songs they knew.

Shirley was Dad's bookkeeper until she married Ben Erickson and moved to Donalda, Alberta. Then Dad had to hire a new one. He hired our neighbors' daughter, Marie Horoshkow, and she did a very good job but she had matrimony on her mind, and as a result she married Carman and moved away.

Marie and Carman were a very nice young couple. I was a best man at their wedding. She was Ukrainian and the wedding lasted the better part of three days. I played guitar for them every evening after work. As was usual with Ukrainian weddings, there was lots to eat and lots to drink. Marie's mom knew how much I liked cabbage rolls and even while I was playing she would be handing me a cabbage roll, saying, "Eat, boy, it's good for you." Marie's dad always tried to hand me a glass of moonshine or some drink concoction, but I didn't drink very much. It was hard for him to understand how I could play and sing without having something to drink all the time. When I asked him for a glass of water, he brought me a glass of pickle juice. He said it was good for my vocal cords and if I drank it I'd be able to sing like a bird all night.

Me playing at Marie and Carman's wedding

Dad hired a cute girl and I wasted no time trying to court her. It was fun, but she had her sights set on a higher paying job and quit. Dad said he'd had enough of the young girls and that he wanted someone more stable. He hired a lady to do the books and her husband worked on the mill. That worked for Dad, but it meant I had to go uptown and look for young girls for fun; there were a lot of young girls in High Prairie.

Our mill was right on the outskirts of town, so I didn't have far to go. After work it was my job to make sure the trim saw blocks and sawdust were hauled to the burner. Also, the area around the burner had to be wet down to make sure that nothing would catch fire. If we'd planed three boxcars that day, the burner would really be burning. And although it had a big screen on the top, sparks would get through, so there was always a danger of a fire starting.

I suspect my dad thought if he gave me that much work to do I'd be too tuckered to go uptown. One evening the girls called and asked Mom if I was coming uptown, so she called me and I told them I didn't think I could make it because I had a lot of work to do. They said they'd come and help me if I'd take them back uptown after. I said I would, and in a short time Mom saw six or seven girls walking across the railroad bridge. When they turned and came into the mill yard she really was curious. I was loading the trimming blocks into the back of a Ford truck to put them in the burner. They asked what they could do to help, so I told them that some could help me with the trimming blocks and the others could hose down the yard around the burner.

My dad was at the back of the planing mill, and when he stepped out he saw the girls hosing down the yard. He asked them what they thought they were doing. They told him they were wetting down everything around the burner and turned the water hose on him. He had a tussle to get the water hose away from them, but he soaked them with it. They told him if he did that to them again they were never going to come back and help me clean up around the mill.

I'm not certain, but I suspect that may have been his strategy all along. When I got to the burner with the load of trimming blocks, they looked like drowned rats, wringing out their blouses and combing their hair. They told me a man had come by and they'd turned the water hose on him, so he took it away and gave them a good soaking. They couldn't have minded it too much, because they came back several times a week and helped me clean up around the mill.

The first summer the planer ran, a young fellow named Peter Zahacy asked Dad for a job. He was slight, but told Dad he had a big heart and was strong. He talked to Dad in Ukrainian and Dad hired him. He turned out to be a hard worker. Peter was an orphan raised by his relatives in the High Prairie area. He was unable to finish high school because he had to go to work to help support himself and his sister. There wasn't a lazy bone in his body and he had a jovial way about him that made it easy to like him. Peter and I became fast friends. Also, he was a local boy who knew a lot of the young people in town; with his help, we were never short of female company and we'd spend weekends together with as many girls as we could find.

When we were moving the mill from Slave Lake to High Prairie, Peter and I were left at the camp to look after things. For something to do, we took my crossbow and went looking for deer. Not finding one after walking around in the bush for a while, we came back to the mill site, where we had a water pond for fire protection. There were four ducks swimming in the pond, so Pete said that since we hadn't shot a deer, I should shoot a duck and he would cook it for supper. I leaned over a stump and took aim at a big male pintail. I don't know if it was my aim or the arrow that was crooked, but I hit the duck right behind the leg and it went through the rear end, running clean through its tail. We could tell the duck had been hit because when it tried to fly, it couldn't steer where it wanted to go and it headed right for a big birch tree. Peter said, "Look out, Mac! You are going to hit that tree," and sure enough it smacked right into it. It was a pretty sad looking mess when we got to the base of the tree. Peter took one look at the duck and said he didn't think we would want to eat that one anyway, it was too busted up. So we had hamburgers instead. Peter was a good cook and he cooked for the small crew that was left to clean up the mill.

As we began to mature, we took different paths in life. Peter found work at various different places and did well at whatever he chose to do. The next time we connected he was in Edson, Alberta, working at an electrical shop where they repaired small electrical equipment and rewound smaller electrical motors. He was married and had a small son when we stayed with them on our honeymoon.

We have stayed in touch ever since. Although Peter may have had a struggle in life at first, he has done exceptionally well for himself. Eventually he settled near the city of Edmonton and pursued a career in electrical motor rewinding, starting his own electrical motor rewinding company and doing very well. I chose a rural lifestyle, ranching, farming, mining, and logging, and my entertainment was hunting and fishing.

When we lived in High Prairie, I loved hunting. There were many farmers in the area who were plagued by Canada geese and ducks doing a lot of damage in their fields. I bought a new Ithaca 12 gauge pump shotgun from Mike Kosub, who owned a hardware store in High Prairie. Mike told me I should look some of the farmers up, so one weekend I took the old Dodge power wagon, loaded up a half a dozen girls, and we went looking for geese. I found several places where geese were coming in to feed, but when I asked the farmer if I could hunt in his fields, he gave me a funny look and didn't give me an answer.

I went back and told Mike I'd found geese but the farmer didn't seem too interested in having me hunt them. He said he would give him a call and ask him what was wrong. The farmer told Mike that I had all of those girls with me and he didn't know if he could trust me.

Mike said, "Lloyd, Lloyd, if you are going to hunt geese you will have to leave the girls at home and pay more attention to hunting." I told him I wanted to hunt the geese, but I wanted to take a few girls with me too. He said he'd assured the farmer that I wouldn't damage his fields, and I'd only bring a couple girls with me the next time I came.

We had a couple of pretty good hunts, but I needed Dad's decoys, and I needed to dig some pits. I asked Dad for the decoys and he wanted to know where I was going to go and said he'd go along with me. I told them I had some company that wanted to come with me, but he said he didn't think they could come if he was going to go hunting with me, so that ended my fun hunting with the girls. However, Dad and I had a lot of fun hunting geese and shot a lot of geese from the pits we dug in the farmer's field.

One foggy morning we crawled into our pits, and when we heard the geese coming in there was still quite a lot of fog over the field. I don't know what kind of radar system they have, but they hit the exact spot they were at the night before. And when they saw our decoys, they just glided in for a landing. When the banging was all done there were twelve geese on the ground.

Mike Kozub was a fun guy to go geese hunting with too. One weekend we planned to do some scouting in a new area that a farmer had told me about. He told me he'd go with me but he didn't want me to take the girls along; he thought his wife would like that better!

It had rained, so we parked the old power wagon and walked down through a ravine that ran across the field, because we didn't want to cut up the farmer's road. When we were almost up the other side, we heard geese honking. I hurried to the top, and sure enough, I saw nine geese flying in low. So I told Mike I'd move to the left of him and if we were lucky the geese would come in right between us. And sure enough, they did. For just nine geese, they sure were making a lot of a racket. When we stopped shooting, there was just dead silence and Mike said "Lloyd, that is a dirty crying shame. We never even left any for seed." He asked me how I managed to shoot so many times. I said, "I just let them have it."

He asked me if I had a plug in my gun. I said no, I'd taken it out because I thought if I was going to help the farmers get rid of the geese I could do a better job without it. He told me I was a lot of fun to go hunting geese with, but he thought I was a bad influence as well.

In the spring I had to take the Dodge Power Wagon and scale some lumber at Salt Prairie. I loaded up the old wagon with some shells, and of course, all the girls that would come. That was one fun day! The ditches were still full of water and there were a lot of ducks. I lay the windshield down and shot ducks on the go. The girls thought they could shoot some too, so I let them try. They made a lot of noise and surprisingly managed to get a few ducks before we finally ran out of shells.

Mike Kosub and I were good friends and he treated me like a son in many ways. I always dreamed of having my own ranch and I heard about a ranch that was for sale at Cherry Point along the Peace River. I went out and took a look at it; at that time of the year it looked good to me. The ranch consisted of 1200 acres, much of it bottom land. There was a small lake on it and about 400 acres under cultivation. The poor guy had the rug pulled right out from under his feet when he discovered that he had a health problem similar to muscular dystrophy and he would never be able to operate his ranch again. He said he'd take $2,800 for it because he was in need of money.

I went to Mike and talked it over with him. He said he'd lend me $2,000 but I had to put up the extra $800. The plan was that I'd keep working at my dad's mill until I made enough money to pay back the $2,000, then he would set me up with enough equipment to farm the 400 acres and I would be able to pay him back on a crop-share basis. I didn't have $800, so I asked Peter Zahacy if he could help me out. Peter was happy to; in fact, he was eager to become my partner in the enterprise.

When Dad learned that Mike had offered to do this for me, he was upset and told Mike to quit meddling with his son's life; he would look after me and my place was at the mill with him. When Mike told me this, he said he didn't want to make enemies with my father, so although he thought it was a good deal, the timing was probably not quite right. He said if part of the plan hadn't been that I would keep working for Dad, he would have lent me the money, but under the circumstances he thought it was better that he withdraw from the deal. My dream was shot down.

The planing mill was a good business and financially Dad was doing well. Ervin wanted to continue working in the oil field cutting seismic lines around Slave Lake and Valleyview, as he and Roman had been doing since Dad had moved to High Prairie a year and a half previously. Roman had married Arleen Lauder while we were still at Wagner Camp.

Roman and Arleen were ready to start a family and didn't like the constant moving and living in camps while cutting seismic line for the oil companies. Roman decided he would come back to High Prairie and help run the mill. Arleen would do the books and the whole operation would be back in the family again. Dad was happy with this idea. Roman's first child, Gervin, was born in High Prairie. He was Mom and Dad's first grandchild, a boy to carry on the Antypowich name.

OILFIELD WORK AND ROAD CONSTRUCTION AT VALLEYVIEW, ALBERTA

1954-1958

CHAPTER 28

Homesteading and Working the Cat at Valleyview

Shortly thereafter, a huge area of land opened up for homesteading in the Valleyview area. That triggered Dad's interest and each family member applied for a half section of land under the Homestead Act. Dad sold the planing mill and we moved to Valleyview and started a new venture in farming and ranching. I was happy, as that lifestyle was a big part of my dream.

The land around Valleyview was flat and had very few stones. The trees were mainly small second-growth poplar that had grown up after a fire had burned through the area many years earlier. We had two cats, one D7 and an Allis Chalmers HD15. We'd clear land by angling the blade and going a full half mile before turning around to come back. When the windrows were big enough, we'd put the two cats together and push the windrow as far as we could. Then we'd bring the rest of the windrow back to the pile we'd just made. We made many of these piles in the field, and when it dried the next spring we'd burn them. Then we started to break the soil with a Rome disc pulled with a smaller cat. Next, the fields were worked with John Deere tractors pulling disks and harrows. After the disking was done, there were still roots to pick. We hired Indians from the Sturgeon Lake Reserve to pick and burn the roots. Clearing a half section of land took a lot of time and hard work.

After the move from High Prairie to Valleyview, Roman went back into the oil field to work heavy equipment. I was hoping to work on the farm with Dad because there was a lot of development to be done on all the land we'd acquired, but I had to go to work on the cats. It was a lot cheaper to pay farm workers than cat skinners.

For financial reasons, Dad's lawyer advised him to form a limited company when we moved to Valleyview, so Frank Antypowich and sons formed North Wood Contractors. When the company was finalized, Dad, Roman, Ervin, Clifford, and I were equal partners. Because Clifford was so much younger, his shares were entrusted to Dad. The wages for those of us who were working was supposed to be eight hundred dollars a month, but because the company was in its early growing stages, Ervin and my wages were cut back to 190 dollars a month. I paid thirty dollars a month for room and board and made my share of the payments on the car that I bought jointly with Ervin. That didn't leave much to spend on having fun with the girls or anything else. Dad and Roman were paid eight hundred dollars a month, so somehow this scale had different strokes for different folks. When I questioned how long this was going to go on, I was told it would only be until the company got on its feet, then we would be paid what we were owed in back wages and go on to the regular wage. That never did happen for me. While I dearly loved my dad and did so right up until the day of his passing, I did not always agree with some of business transactions he made within the family.

In the spring I worked for the Highways Department, digging gravel from the river and stockpiling it along the highway so it could be crushed later and used to pave the highway from Whitecourt to Grand Prairie. I spent one spring working at the Little Smoky and soon realized that I didn't want to be a cat skinner for the rest of my life. I guess I just worked too many hours without getting a break; one time I worked over thirty hours without getting any sleep. I was pushing gravel to a loader, creating a pile ten or twelve feet high for him to load from. I fell asleep going up the pile with the blade full of the gravel and went right over the end. It scared the hell out of the loader operator; luckily he wasn't digging into the pile at the time. He said I was crazy to work that many hours without sleep. Someone was supposed to come and do the nightshift, but they never did show up, so I just kept working. I slept for four hours on the cat and then went in for breakfast at the camp.

The foreman asked me when the other operator was supposed to come. I told him he should have been there already, and I didn't know why he hadn't shown up. He asked me if I could work another shift and he would go to the farm to find out why they hadn't sent an operator to relieve me. At supper time he told me that Dad promised they would find an operator. Although it meant the loader would have to shut down along with twenty-five or thirty trucks, he didn't want to see me run another shift. I said I would push gravel for the loader and when I got ahead I would sleep for a while until he cleaned up the pile. That way we could keep the loader going as well as all the trucks. When an operator finally came, I had to work the nightshift anyway because he refused to work at night.

The next spring I got to work on the farm at bit, but soon I was sent back on the cat to work at the gravel pile we'd made the previous winter. I pushed gravel from the pile into a huge drum that rotated; it was part of the process of making asphalt. We paved many miles that summer. I'm sure the only reason I could stand to do that monotonous job was because there was a nice young girl named Muriel Heglund in the camp kitchen. She did the serving and helped her aunt. Of course, with so many truckers onsite a girl in a camp was like ants on a honey pail, but she seemed to fend them off quite well.

One evening I came in for supper late because I'd had to clean up around the mixer. They had my supper ready for me and asked me if I could eat quickly because they wanted to go to town. I asked how they were going because they didn't have a vehicle of their own. Her aunt said they hoped the foreman would take them. I ate real quick and told them I was going back to the farm and I would be glad to give them a ride to town. They took me up on the offer. I stopped at the farm and got the things I needed for the cat and then took them into Valleyview.

They did their shopping and we went to a café for some pie and coffee before we went back to camp. I felt the trip had "broken the ice," so one night I stayed in the kitchen until all the other men had left and chatted with Muriel and her aunt. I asked them if it wasn't boring to be in camp like that all the time. They said it was, but it wasn't easy to get into town. I didn't tell them that nearly every trucker, at least all the young guys, would give their right arm to take Muriel to town. Instead I asked them if they'd like to go to a show one evening after their work was done. They told me they would but they didn't want to inconvenience me in any way and I said it would be my pleasure. It wasn't long before Muriel and I did a lot of things together. Her aunt was great. She'd say, "You take Muriel to the show and I'll stay and clean up the dishes." That summer seemed to go by quickly. The camp moved several times until we finished paving for the year, then it moved northwest of Grand Prairie and my cat didn't have a job with them. Although I made a few trips to see Muriel, it seemed that work was getting in the way. I continued to work on the cat for sixteen hours a day and didn't enjoy one of them.

That winter I worked at another gravel camp at Crooked Creek, Alberta, operating a Michigan loader. There were about 200 trucks hauling gravel and I'm not sure how many loaders and cats.

There were a lot of young fellows my age driving gravel trucks. One was Roy Rankin (he should have been called Roy Rang-a-tang). He was from Eckville, Alberta, and he asked if I was going to go to the dance at the community hall on Friday night. I told him I didn't think so; I didn't have anyone to take anyway. He said he'd pick up a few girls and bring them out. I could have my pick. Well, sure enough, on the next trip his truck was full of girls. He told me I'd have to take one in the loader so the foreman wouldn't give him a bad time if he saw him.

There isn't very much room in the loader, but one of the girls jumped out of the truck and started climbing up the ladder. Her name was Irene Logan. I had a dusty old blanket that I rolled up to make something for her to sit on while I kept loading the gravel trucks. Because my loader wasn't as big as some of the other ones, I just loaded single-axle trucks. The only way I could get a break was if I worked real fast and loaded all my trucks before the next one got back. Then I would have a few minutes to relax.

I was having one of these relaxing moments, trying to get to know something about Irene, when a tandem gravel track pulled under my loader. I found the biggest frozen chunk of gravel that I could and dropped it in his box. He came out of the cab cursing at me, and I told him that if he didn't like the treatment I had given him, he could get back in line and load where he was supposed to.

The trucker was so mad, he stopped the foreman and told him what I had done and that I had a girl in the loader with me. I saw the foreman coming, so I told Irene that she had to hide under the blanket. The foreman asked me why I'd dropped a frozen chunk in the trucker's box, so I told him he was under the wrong loader. He said he didn't realize that he wasn't one of the trucks I was supposed to be loading, and he'd make sure that truck wouldn't pull under my loader again. He took a good look around inside and left without saying any more. I was glad Irene was so small, because she did a good job of hiding. When Roy came back for his next trip, I told her she had to go but I would see her at the dance Friday night.

Friday night Irene came with her mom and introduced me to her. I was getting kind of nervous because they seemed too serious to me. What I didn't know was that she wasn't quite sixteen yet, and her mom wanted to see who she was at the dance with. We had a lot of fun that night, but I can still remember when Irene's mom came and said it was time to go home. Not knowing how old she was, I thought it was only appropriate that I would get to take her home, but I could see that her mom meant what she said and Irene was going to have to go home with her. So I said, "All right, go home with your mom." She didn't want to go, but knew if she was ever to get to come back to the dance again she'd better do what her mom told her.

And after the orchestra quit playing, any of us that could play musical instruments picked up where they left off and played until it was time to bring the cows home. About ten of us went to the home of the girl that Roy had taken to the dance and her mother made us a breakfast of hot cakes, homemade sausages, and eggs. During the breakfast preparation, she and Roy began throwing a dishcloth at each other. From there it went to throwing eggs at each other. Oh boy, what mess that was!

Irene and her mother were at the next dance and she came across the floor and sat down beside me, apologizing as she told me she'd just had her sixteenth birthday and had talked her mom into letting me take her home, but that she had to be in by twelve o'clock. I was a little shocked; I thought she was older than that. I respected her mom for her concern and promised her I would have her home by twelve o'clock, and I did. There was a dance nearly every Friday night for the rest of the winter and we were there for most of them. I think her mom felt quite safe letting her go to the dances with me because I didn't drink.

When that job ended, I went back into the oil patch and our relationship ended. A number of years later after I was married and living at Stettler, I went to the bank and this young girl came to assist me. She asked me if I remembered her, and I had no idea who she was. She asked me if I had ever worked at Crooked Creek and I said yes I had, but it had been a few years ago. I still did not make the connection. She looked at me and asked, "Do you remember the girl you told to go home with her mom?" I think my face must have gotten red as I realized who I was talking to. We had a little chat and she was beginning to ask me quite a few questions until I told her that I was married and had a farm seven miles from town.

CHAPTER 29

Working the Oil Patch

When I finished the job at Crooked Creek, I went back to the farm at Valleyview and helped my dad and the hired man build fence. I worked around the farm until an engineer from Triad Oil needed to hire a cat to clear some seismic lines and make a few new short ones. John Miller was an older fellow, but good to work for. The morning I started to work for him, he wanted me to wait until he came with his pickup. I waited for quite a while, and when he still hadn't shown up, I decided to start clearing the line. Shortly after he caught up to me and told me he was going to leave his pickup and I would just use the cat to take him to check the seismic lines.

That made my job much easier, but if something broke down on the cat it meant we wouldn't have a good trail to get a service truck in to make repairs. We went several miles before we came to a place where the beavers had made a small dam across the line to back up water. It didn't look too bad, so I decided that I would push some snow and small trees over it and walk the cat over it. I was about halfway across when the front of the cat seemed to fall right out from underneath us. I couldn't use the winch to pull myself back because there were no large trees to hook the line to. We had to walk back to his pickup and he took me to the farm to get another cat to pull us out.

John said not to worry about needing to bring another cat in as Triad Oil would pay for it. I made sure I constructed a better crossing and then we continued on. After several days of just running around with the cat, checking out the seismic lines, he decided that we'd build two short lines so they could do more seismic testing. Then I went back and ploughed the snow off the seismic line so he could follow me with his pickup.

One Sunday I was working on one of the short lines and John, his wife, and a friend from Valleyview came out. I was surprised to see that he had gotten all the way in with his big Chrysler car, but in his Texas drawl he said, "Hell, man, you been doing such a good job I could even drive my Cadillac here."

It was a mild, sunny day and it was melting quite a bit. I was not far from the end of the seismic line, so he decided to wait until I had finished it. I'd moved several hundred yards from where the car was parked and thought everything was safe. I was pushing a medium-sized poplar tree over when it broke off at the stump and came backward. That normally wouldn't have been a problem, but when I looked back they'd decided to catch up to me to take some pictures, and there was the car and the three of them throwing snowballs at each other. John's wife had her back to me and was totally unaware of what was happening. I tried to put the cat under the tree as it fell back, and while I managed to break the fall with the canopy of the cat, the top of the tree hit her right on the head. The thing that saved her was that the cat took all the weight of the tree, and it was just the whip of the top that actually hit her. She went down like a sack of potatoes and I thought I killed her.

I jumped off the cat and ran to her. When I got there, she was moaning. The three of us moved her onto the backseat of the car and John rushed her to the hospital. Before he left he said, "Don't you worry about a thing. Everything will be all right." It was hard for me to keep working, so I quit early and went back to the farm.

I told Dad and Roman what had happened and they phoned the hospital immediately. The hospital said she had been examined and sent to Grand Prairie to be further checked out. When she left Valleyview, she was conscious and they were quite sure that she would be all right. I called the motel where John was staying and left a message for him to call me as soon as he got back. That evening John and his wife came to our place. I was glad to see her up and walking on her own. The first thing I told her was how sorry I was for what happened. She said, "Oh, sonny, don't you worry one bit about me. Us Texans are real tough! Why, land, you can't hurt us by hitting us with a stick on the head." They had put nine stitches in her scalp, but other than that she seemed okay. John apologized for coming so close to the cat and said not to worry about a thing; if anyone was to blame, it was them.

Myself and Jack Hutchinson at a battery site that I had just completed building for Triad Oil

Curly Gavel and me (leaning on my service truck) discussing a few things that needed to be done on the oil location to make the job complete (1956)

That summer we contracted a lot of work with Triad Oil. They were drilling Triassic wells at approximately 4,800 feet and we made sixteen oil locations for them with two cats and a scraper. Many of them were near the farm and several were right on the farm. By the time we'd have a location made, they'd have completed the hole they were drilling. This went on seven days a week for the entire summer. Ervin and I worked sixteen hours a day and then did our own servicing. That didn't leave much time for sleeping. When you finally got into bed, it would seem to be shaking as if you were still operating the cat. What we needed was another shift, but the work was so close to home and they were drilling so fast, we just kept working longer hours to stay ahead of them. To complicate things even more, the rain made the soil like gumbo, which slowed down road building because we had to put on more gravel so the big trucks could make it in and out of the oil location. Sometimes the cats would be required to assist the rigs by pulling the trucks.

One day I was checking on some Indians that were doing logging on a road right of way. Dan MacLean was in charge. As I was walking up to them, there was a rough grouse sitting on a log. Dan said, "Do you see that chicken?" I said I did. He told me if I was a good warrior I would take a stick and kill it, then I could marry his daughter. I picked up a stick and threw it at the grouse. My aim was a bit high, but the grouse flew right into it and dropped down dead.

Dan jumped up and said, "By the gee! Which daughter do you want? I have three." He turned to the guy sitting next to him and said, "He gets the pretty one; you'll have to take the ugly one." That fluke almost got me married!

Dan was a very good friend. There were times when he'd get me to take some of the boys from the reserve out hunting. I'd load up all the tents and grub in the grain truck, then haul them out to the end of a road we had just built, hoist the box up, and dump it all in one pile. In a week or ten days I would go back and pick them up and haul all their moose and deer back to the reserve.

That fall, my cousins Walter and Ervin Matzner (from Saskatchewan) came to Valleyview, looking for work in the oil patch. We taught them to operate the cat because we were expecting to go seventy miles into the bush to wildcat for two oil rigs in the Simonette area. We were to start the first of January, 1957.

Walter and Ervin decided to go home for Christmas and suggested I go with them. There was a slack time before we had to go to the Simonette, so I went. We had a great Christmas and I visited my old Indian friend Charlie Pissis. He'd aged a lot, and I can't say I'd have recognized him if it wasn't for my cousin. Charlie asked a lot of questions about my parents, wanting to know how their health was and what they were doing. I asked him if he was still hunting moose and bear and he said, "Just the easy ones; the young boys do most of the hunting now." That was the last time I saw Charlie; he is in that happy hunting grounds in the way and beyond now.

One thing I never forgot about that trip was visiting my Uncle John. He had his hand wrapped up in a towel that looked like a big boxing glove. I asked him if he had hurt his hand and he said, "Boy, I was chop-it the wood, and the axe she poke-it my jacket. The axe she jump- it dis way and I chop-it my thum' off." The shocking thing was he picked up his thumb, fit it back where it should have been, wrapped the hand in a bandage, cut a loaf of fresh baked bread and placed his hand in the middle of it, and had his wife bandage it real tight with a towel. And can you believe, when he died years later, his thumb was in place and functioning.

As we were coming back to Valleyview, I noticed a huge flare in the sky and I told my cousins they were going to see an oil well fire. When we got to the farm, all the machines were gone and Mom told us they were working on the fire. Guthre number three had burned to the ground.

I was back on the job the next day, operating cat and cleaning on the site wherever I was needed. The oil location was built on a muskeg and the heat from the burning well was thawing the location quickly. It took just fifteen minutes for the derrick to come crumbling down. Red Adair had been brought in from Texas to put the fire out. He was the legend in his field at the time. His specialty was putting out oil well fires.

The intense heat made it nearly impossible to get the cat close enough to the well head to place the charge of dynamite that would blow out the fire when it ignited. They modified one of our cats to do that job and Ervin operated it. Two brackets were welded on either side of the winch at the back of the cat. Two sixty-foot long drill stems were pinned to these brackets, then welded together at the far end, creating an arm and forming a place where a basket made from a forty-five-gallon barrel that had been cut open. This basket was filled with explosives and then a cable from the winch was guided through a pulley on an arch that had been welded onto the back of the cat. This cable ran down at an angle to the arm formed by the drill stems, stopping at a point where the winch could be used to raise or lower the arm. The back and sides of the cat were shielded with light metal to protect the operator from the heat.

Red Adair, dressed in fire protective gear, stood on a small platform at the front of the cat. From there he directed the operator to where he wanted him to go as he backed the cat up, moving it into position to put the explosives in place right beside the pipe that was spewing gas and oil. There was three feet of mud on the location, so it wasn't an easy job. When everything was finally in the proper position, the cat was shut off and the explosives detonated. It blew the fire out, then a special crew went in and took care of the well.

We were a few days late getting into the Simonette and the weather turned bitterly cold, 40 °F to 50 °F below. The bunkhouse that we stayed in was eight feet by sixteen feet and heated with an airtight wood heater. It had four bunks, a small table, and a small cooking stove.

Ervin Matzner got his arm pinched while angling the dozer on the cat. He was quite badly injured and was on compensation, so he did most of the cooking for us. We started out building a road along the Simonette River. There were seven cats in total working on the job.

*Ervin winding up the old phonograph—our jukebox as
we called it—in our bunkhouse at the Simonette*

The river work was dangerous because a cat could break through the ice, and in some places the river was deep. The foreman asked me to stay behind and help clear a place for the campsite. When I had it level, they moved in trailers for living quarters and a kitchen. After that, I was to go down the road the cats had roughed out and grade it as best I could, filling in the holes and smoothing it out as much as possible. The angle of the approach to the river had to be cut down, so the Bombardiers used to haul the crews and the big-rig moving trucks could drive to the river. Once on the river the plan was that they'd then drive up the river on the ice for twelve miles, using the shoreline as much as possible, trying to avoid the areas where the holes were deep under the ice.

Me sitting on the bed in the bunkhouse at the Simonette. The aprons on the wall were taken from waitresses in the cafés. From January until March there would be no hanky-panky going on! Our lives consisted of working, eating, and sleeping.

Once I had the approach to the river fixed, I was to catch up to the cats that had gone ahead. When I was following the tracks they'd made on the river, I noticed water was coming up on the ice and all the cat tracks headed for shore. I thought it would be safest for me to do the same thing, but as I turned my cat toward shore I felt the ice start to break under me. I grabbed a faster gear and said a little prayer that I'd make it, as I had no idea how deep the river was. I made it most of the way before I broke through. The water came up to the top of the tracks but I just kept on chewing my way through the ice to safety. Luckily the river was only three feet deep at that spot.

Where the ice had begun cracking, the river was seven feet deep. I was glad to catch up to the rest of the cats. Ervin came back to caution me to leave lots of space between my cat and the machine in front of me when we traveled on the ice.

We worked our way along the bank above the river, making a road so that rig trucks could move rigs in when the road was completed. When we finished that short section, we all started to move out on the ice again. I was the fourth cat in line. In front of me was a young fellow my age operating a cat for Walter Staley. All was going well until his cat simply fell through the ice.

Of course we all headed for the shore as fast as we could, then ran back to see if we could assist the operator. To our surprise there was very little water in the hole. He was so frightened that he didn't want to move off his cat. Several of us crawled down in the hole, only to realize that we'd been traveling on flood ice. At one time the river had blocked somewhere; the water built up, then froze approximately two feet thick. Later the current had cleared a path and the water disappeared down the river, leaving a hollow space of approximately four feet that we could crawl around in. The ice below his cat was only a foot thick and the water was less than two feet deep. We used one of the machines with a ripper shank to break the ice around his cat and then hooked a winch cable to the winch on it, and with the two machines connected we managed to get his cat out of the hole. I operated the machine during the process because he simply refused to go back. He quit on the spot, and when he could get a ride out, he went back home to Edmonton.

We didn't go much farther before we had a lot of debris to clear to make a road along the bank of the river. The Bombardier came to pick us up at shift change, and the nightshift finished that section of road so most of the moves on ice could be made in daylight. We had approximately fifteen miles of road to make, some of it across the ice and some of it along the bank. It was slow and very rocky, and our progress was not very fast. Our cats were a little small to rip the hard frozen ground and rock, but heavier cats were a detriment when trying to cross the river on the ice. The weather stayed miserably cold and at night you could hear the sounds of poplar trees cracking like someone was shooting a gun.

One day the temperature fell past 60 °F below. In very severe cold weather iron breaks more easily and three cats broke down during the dayshift. We moved the cats to a sandbar about six feet above the ice of the river. Ervin and I and one other operator moved our cats to the top of that sandbar and cleared snow off for the others, but they parked right on the edge of the river. The foreman insisted we shut down until the weather warmed up a bit. The next day it warmed up to about 55 °F below. We talked with the foreman, who said if it warmed up a little more we would try to start the cats. The next day he came into camp yelling, "Hurry, you guys, the river is flooding." So we all jumped into the Bombardier and headed up the river. We got about halfway there, but were unable to go any farther because there was too much ice coming down. I was afraid that we weren't going to make it off the river alive. At times the water nearly came to the top of the tracks on the Bombardier, but the foreman just kept on going and eventually we made back to higher ground. He thanked us for being such a brave crew, but we all knew we really didn't have any other choice.

We waited for the river to slow down and freeze again. When it warmed up to -35 ° F, we went back with the Bombardier, taking diesel flamethrowers, parachutes, and tarps to try to start the cats. When we got to the ones that were parked on the edge of the river, the ice was two-thirds of the way up the tracks. We got the three cats parked on top started, but only two of them had rippers, so we used them to rip as much of the ice around the machines that were frozen in as we could, then we'd hook on the winch line and try to break them loose. When we eventually worked them free, they came out in one big round chunk like a saucer. We'd drag them onto higher ground and put a parachute or tarp over them and place a flamethrower under the tarp. The tracks were frozen solid, so the nightshift had the job of thawing them out. The next day a welder came to repair the broken C-frames and other breaks that occurred in the cold weather. The cats that were in operating condition went ahead and began working on fifteen more miles of road.

We came to a natural draw where we were able to work our way up about fifty feet to the top of the riverbank. We ripped the frost and made an approach up from the river so it would not be too steep for the trucks to make it up with the rigs. From there we made about ten miles of road on land, and it sure was good to be back on solid ground.

Some of the cats continued with the road while others branched off to build an airstrip on a huge flat bench that made an ideal spot for one. The soil was sandy, and once we got the frost ripped off we made a nice level strip for planes to land on. We cleared the bush at each end of the strip to make it easier for them to land and take off.

Not far from there we made a location. We had barely finished when the trucks started moving the rig in. From there we had another twelve miles of road to build. This took us quite a while because we cleared a sixty-foot right-of-way, making the road much wider than anyplace else. All the hills had to be cut down and pushed into the hollows so the grade wouldn't be more than 10 percent. At the time that didn't make any sense to me, but I didn't know that depending on the results of that first hole, they had a second location to build just three miles away.

After we finished the three miles into the proposed drilling site, we went back to making a normal road. And sure enough, about the time they were done drilling that 7,000-foot hole at the first location, they moved some of us back to make the second location. Now the great care they'd taken when building those three miles made sense. Instead of dismantling the whole rig and moving it the way it was normally done, they laid the derrick down and took it off to move it separately. Then we skid the whole substructure of the rig along the road using several cats and trucks.

We skid this whole substructure for three miles to the new location. This was the only time I ever saw this type of rig move. We did this with cats and trucks, pulling and winching together.

Actually it moved quite well. I was surprised, as I had never seen anything like that before. In no time it was set up and they were drilling again. Meanwhile another rig was moved in to the end of the road and was drilling on that location. Around the middle of March most of the cats were sent home. The rigs would finish drilling and then they'd do all the testing, and if things turned out well there would be more work to do the following winter.

*This is a picture of a toolshed and fuel tank being
moved with one of the rig-moving trucks.*

Later a bridge was built across the river and a new road built to replace
the fifteen miles where we followed the river, and today the Simonette is
quite a large oilfield. It runs from the Valleyview field all the way to Grande
Cache, and to the foothills and watersheds of the Rocky Mountains.

Another time I was working on a D7 cat in the oil field. It had been
a desperately cold -50 ºF. We had taken a track off to repair a final drive
and the cat was still up on blocks. The tracks were stretched out under
the track frame and I was under the cat, tightening the swing frame
bolts. Because it was so cold, we had a parachute over the cat with a
flamethrower going, hoping to get the cat started. Ervin managed to get
it going after several tries.

That model of cat had an oil bath clutch, and even when the clutch
was disengaged the transmission was in gear. Because it was so cold, the
oil was thick enough that the transmission was able to turn the one track
causing the cat to spin off of the blocks. I was taking a rest when I noticed
what was happening. I rolled to the high side of the cat just as it spun off
the blocks. It pinned me to the ground about the same time my brother
got the cat stopped. They tried to pull me out by my legs, but my coat was
caught on a bolt and I was stuck. After a little maneuvering, they managed
to get me out, but that was a close call.

I remember a time when I was called to a location that had just been
drilled and the cement job didn't hold properly. The well head was shaking
back and forth and gas, water, and mud were gushing all around it. I was
told to build a berm around the well head to prevent the oil from getting
to the river. Then I was supposed to dig a hole and use the dirt to build the

berm higher. While I was working, my cat got a good whiff of the gas and started to rev up, so I grabbed a bigger gear, held my breath, and let the cat run right over the berm. I refused to go back in unless they provided a gas mask for me, but I was still concerned about the machine. They told me they would cover the cat. I guess the oil spill was a bigger concern to them than anything else. I was glad to get back to civilization and said I would rather pick fly shit out of pepper than repeat that experience. I told my dad and brothers I'd had enough of the oil patch and cat skinning; I wanted to stay home and work on the farm and ranch.

Ervin had married Joyce Horechel by then and they were living at the farm in Valleyview. Ervin began to spend less time in the field because he was married and didn't want to be gone so much.

Although I was supposed to be a fifth equal partner in Northwood Contractors, my decisions and desires seemed to fall on deaf ears. The building site that I'd picked out on my half section of homestead land had some nice spruce trees on it. They knew I wanted to preserve them, but that spot was completely cleared off. I was really upset when it happened, and little by little I could see what I hoped for was not going to materialize. So one day I called a meeting to tell the rest of the partners that unless I could work on the farm I was giving them my resignation. I had just spent thirty days working nonstop in the oil patch, very much against my will.

They seemed to ignore me, not believing that I would follow through with what I'd told them. I had half interest in a 1957 Ford Fairlane that was completely paid for. I owned two horses and had paid for things like a saddle, seed, and a fanning mill to clean the seed, a milk cow, and part of a plough. I wanted to buy out Ervin's half of the car, and I expected to get paid the money that I had put into seed, fanning mill, milk cow, and plough and saddle.

I gave them one more week to find an operator to take my place. When the week was up, I asked them if they had made their decision, and their answer was a question: where was I going to go and what was I going to do? They told me that if I was going to leave the company, I would get nothing. I told them I would catch the bus at the driveway the next day, and where I was going was only my business.

It was a big move for a young man who had grown up in the shelter of his family, but I knew the time had come for the donkey to quit chasing the carrot. From now on, I would operate under the direction of Lloyd Antypowich

Mom encouraged me to stop and see the company lawyer when I went through Edmonton. I did and told him of my decision and what I had been told before I left. I told him I felt they owed me for all the years I had worked for them for wages that had been a bare existence. He asked me if I was certain that I wouldn't go back and I said I had no doubt about that. He told me he would be getting in touch with them and was sure that a settlement would be made.

FARMING AT STETTLER, ALBERTA

1959-1970

CHAPTER 30

I'm on My Own, Following My Dream

I was beginning a brand-new venture, and believe me, I was lacking in confidence about the business aspect of things. But what I lacked in confidence, I made up for in determination. I was certain if I worked as hard for myself as I had for them, I could get on my feet financially and walk toward the dream I had held since long before I'd left school.

I needed some real experience in farming and ranching, so I caught a train and traveled to Donalda, where Shirley and her husband Ben operated a large grain farm as well as feeder steers and hogs. The summer fallow needed to be cultivated again, so I asked them if I could help them out. I needed experience in harvesting and handling livestock and farming in general. My brother-in-law told me he'd be happy to have me work for him through harvest.

I told him I'd start just as soon as I got back from Drumheller. I had a girlfriend there that I was quite serious about and I wanted to go see her before I started to work. When I got back, I did what I could around the farm. I made mistakes and hoped I'd learned from them so I wouldn't make them again. I did a lot of the summer fallow work, drove the grain truck, milked cows, fed pigs, and even learned to run a combine.

I even got in some duck hunting. It was a wet fall and the ducks were doing a lot of damage to the grain fields. The Donalda area had rolling hills with sloughs at the bottom of them, and it was a perfect haven for ducks. When I first started using the combine, as I got near the top of the hills, I wondered if there was something wrong with the machine because so little grain was coming into the hopper. It didn't take long to figure out the ducks had threshed all the hilltops. It was difficult to chase them off because they had such a great vantage point from all the small hills. If you tried to scare them away by shooting at them, they would go to another slough or another hilltop.

One day Ben asked me if I'd take the shotgun and chase the ducks out of a good barley field. He didn't want me to bring any home, just kill as many as I could and try to scare the rest away. I loaded my shotgun right to the hilt and sneaked up to some ducks that were feeding on a hillside. The field was not completely swathed, so I crawled through the standing grain. And when I was about fifty feet from them, I stood up and let them have it. A thousand ducks must have lifted off that spot.

In that volley I got twenty-eight. They were mostly mallard and pintails. The thing I remember most from that incident was the noise they made when they fed on the swathed grain. They sounded like hundreds of little combines! They walked along and clacked their beaks in a constant motion. Half the grain went in their gullet, half fell on the ground. In all I had a really fun day.

After harvest was finished, I got a job in Stettler, Alberta, driving gravel truck for Fred Kellough. I hauled cement gravel from Delburn to Stettler. Fred had a cement plant and two transit trucks. He constructed a lot of the sidewalks in the small prairie towns, where they had been made of wood in the past. I rented a small apartment upstairs in Alvin Graham's house in Stettler. I cooked my meals on a hot plate and washed my clothes at Shirley's. As soon as I had saved up some money, Ben and I went to Camrose and I bought a half-ton Ford pickup. Now I had my own wheels.

I worked into the winter months and built a stockpile of cement gravel for Fred. He had a 2U-D8 cable dozer. One day he asked me if I could operate a cat and I gave him an idea of the different jobs I'd done. He said he had enough gravel stockpiled, but if I wanted to operate his old D8 I could clear land during the winter. I took him up on the offer. I worked mostly in poplar stands and it was relatively easy clearing.

After I finished a job in the Big Valley area, a fellow came to me and asked me if I had any experience in oilfield work. I said I did and asked him what he needed done. He told me he had an oil location that had been cleaned up but hadn't met the environmental requirements. I looked at the job and realised that the operator hadn't removed all the mud, and as a result there was a big soft spot in it. I told him that I could do the job, so he gave me a go at it.

When I got in after work that evening, I told Fred I had a job to do for the oil company. He was surprised, but quite happy. When he discovered where the job was, he wasn't too sure he wanted me to do it, because he'd heard the guy who'd tried to clean up the location had made a mess of it and the oil company had paid a fine as a result. I told him not to worry, it would be a piece of cake for me and I'd get the job done without any problem.

The location was on a side hill, which made things easier. I dug a ditch in the soft bubble of mud and walked the cat back and forth over the high side, until I squeezed all the mud out of the sump. I filled the hole with dirt from the location and leveled it off, and then I spread the mud thinly so it would dry.

Two days later I was walking the cat to another clearing job, and the guy from the oil company stopped me. He asked me where I was going and I told him I had a brushing job to do for a farmer. He said he thought I was going to clean up the location for him. I told him the job was done, so he asked me to jump into his pickup and we'd have a look at it.

All the way there I was wondering if he'd be satisfied with the job or if I'd have to walk the cat back to do something else. When we got there, he drove back and forth over the location, looking for the soft spot, but he couldn't find it. He asked what I'd done and I told him, showing him where I had spread the mud on the lower side of the location. He was really impressed with the job and told me to make sure I added a few more hours to my time, and if I wanted a job he would highly recommend me to the guy that owned the cat that tried to do the job in the first place. I thought about it and told him I would let him know later.

I would have been operating a new Allis Chalmers HD16. After giving it some thought, I knew the wages would be better and it certainly would be a much better cat to work with, but I didn't want to go anywhere near the oilfield again, so my answer was no. I think he was disappointed, thinking I was crazy for running that old cable dozer when I could have been running a brand-new cat for more money. When I told Fred that I had added a few more hours to the worksheet and the guy was really happy with the job, he said he was going to go out and see it. While he was there, he met the guy from the oil company and he asked Fred what he was paying me that made me willing to keep running that old cable dozer. Fred just laughed and didn't give him an answer. He told Fred he should buy a new cat for me to operate and he would give him all the work he needed. He said, "Whatever you do, don't lose that skinner. Fred ran the offer past me and asked me what I thought. I told him my goal was to be a farmer or rancher and that I didn't want to go back into the oilfield.

I continued to clear land around the Stettler area all that winter. Early the next spring, Ole Erickson asked me if I wanted to rent a section of land seven miles from the town of Stettler. I wanted to jump at the chance, but didn't think I could put together enough equipment to get the job done. Ole was Ben's dad and he was quite capable of buying a section of land simply as an investment, so after some negotiating I took him up on his offer. I rented the land for three years before I purchased it.

I will always appreciate that he gave me a chance to get started, and my brother-in-law as well for helping me by doing my combining. That also gave me a chance to gain some important knowledge about that aspect of farming. It was a bit of a trade-off; I hauled grain for him when he combined some of his own land. My crops were probably a little below average because the land was infested with wild oats. Ben told me what he would do to clean up the wild oats. I also had a very good neighbor who was an older fellow and realized how inexperienced I was. He was always there to give me good advice.

The house on the farm that I bought from Ole Erickson at Stettler

I continued to work for Fred whenever I could during the winter months, as summers were busy on the farm. The land had a lot of weeds and wild oats, so I had a big job trying to clean it up.

The barn on the farm at Stettler

First I bought an old LA Case tractor, cultivator, some harrows, and an old John Deere press drill. I was so eager to get started on the fields that I was out scratching around before they were completely dry. I cultivated the summer fallow, harrowed it, and thought I was ready to start seeding. Ben told me not to get in too big of a hurry because he thought the wild oats would be a problem. And he sure was right. About a week later the fields started to show a green tinge. On a closer inspection, I found that something was growing, and sure enough it was wild oats. I waited for another three or four days, then went and cultivated the field again. By this time some of the neighbors were starting to do their seeding. Not wanting to be left behind, I harrowed my summer fallow fields once more with diamond harrows. Then I thought for sure it must be time to put the seed in the ground. I finished seeding all wheat, and then I started working my stubble fields into summer fallow that I would seed into barley later on that spring.

When I was going around the field, I would find duck nests and I'd stop and move the nest aside so I wouldn't destroy the eggs. My neighbor saw what I was doing as he worked in the field across the fence from me. He stopped his tractor and came over and asked what the hell I was doing. I said I was starting to cultivate my stubble land for summer fallow. He said he knew that, but what the hell was I doing with all those duck nests. I told him, and he said, "Kill them, man. If you don't, wait and see what will happen this fall and you'll wish you had." Well, I felt a little bit humiliated, but I took his advice and ran over every duck nest after that.

A few days later I began to notice the wheat coming up in nice drill rows, but a few days after that all the low spots in the fields were filling in between the rows with wild oats. So I sought some advice as to what I should do, and I was told to get a rodweeder and go over all the low spots with it. I had never used one before, so I didn't really know what I was doing, but I managed to kill a lot of wild oats, probably some wheat as well. In the end I think it was the right thing to do, because even after that when I combined I had a lot of wild oats in my grain. But that fall, it sure felt good to have some grain in the bins even if I had a lot of wild oats in it!

I borrowed Ben's small tractor and a mower to cut my hayfields that summer. I didn't have a side delivery rake, so I borrowed an old buck rake and raked my fields with it. I used a team of horses that I borrowed from Jack Bosma, another neighbor. All was going fine until I ran over a hornet nest. They stung the horses, and that started a runaway.

There wasn't much on the rake for me to hang on to and the one black horse kept kicking, not missing me by very much. To keep away, I grabbed the back of the seat to hold on, but when you were going fast with that type of rake it would automatically trip to dump the hay that the teeth had collected and they came up against the seat with a bang.

Of course my hand was in the wrong place, and as a result they whacked my fingers a good one. I dropped one line and was sure I was going to wreck everything. Then the pole came out of the neck yoke and I knew I was in trouble for sure.

I bailed off the back of the rake while hanging on to one long line. This turned the horses in a tight circle. I ran out in front of them, caught them by the bridles, and got them stopped. I managed to get them unhooked. Then I checked the rake over to see if anything was broken. Everything was OK, so I hooked them up again and carried on raking.

When Ben came to bail the next day, he wondered why I had so much hay scattered all over. I told him about my runaway and warned him to watch out for the hornets, but he just laughed and said he'd run them all into the bailer.

Now I had hay and grain. I was anxious to get some livestock, but I had no money, so I went back to work the next winter clearing land with Fred's old cat again.

The next spring I bought a disk, thinking I would get a better kill on the wild oats with it. That was partly true, but it also dried out the soil. It looked as if I was going to have to grow them out of the ground in order to get rid of them.

That summer I had planted a garden and some flowers to make my place look homier. I had some maple trees and Caragana around my yard. There was a big lilac bush by the living room window, and I could look outside and see a mallard duck sitting on her nest at the base of it. I must have been a quiet living bachelor to not disturb that duck.

The relationship with the girl that I'd been seeing at Drumheller for a couple of years dried up. She didn't think she was ready to get serious and be a wife, so it looked like I was going to be a bachelor for a little longer. I bought a few pieces of furniture and hung curtains on the windows to make the "birdcage" more attractive. The neighbor ladies would come over and comment on my garden and how I kept the house, and they'd bring cake and cookies for me.

One day Shirley asked me if I'd like to meet some of their friends. I said sure. She suggested we have a picnic and a ballgame and I told her I had a good place to do all that. I cut a ball diamond with my push lawnmower and everything was set for the weekend and the big game.

That was the first time I met Gloria, who later became my wife. We had a great day. Then everyone left to go home and I was all by my lonesome. I'll admit there were times when I felt lonely but I had lots to do to keep me busy. One weekend Shirley and Ben asked if I wanted to come with them when they went to visit Gloria's folks. I said sure. I didn't need to be asked twice.

When we got there, Gloria was going to the hospital to have her tonsils out. We didn't get to talk to each other very much, but in a joking way I told her not to bite the doctor. Her uncle, Jack Wassenaar, and I took her to the hospital in Daysland, and then we went back to Charlie and Hazel's place for supper. When we got ready to leave, Charlie told me not to get too lonesome out there by myself and that I could come and visit anytime.

I thought that was a great invitation and said I would take him up on it. Somehow I seemed to get lonesome more often and I would go there for a visit quite frequently. I would go to the barn and help Gloria milk the cows, feed the pigs, and even get in a little courting in between.

Courting days! Here I am going to help Gloria
milk the cows on her dad's farm.

I never knew that milking cows could be fun, but at that time of our lives we could have fun doing anything when we were together. I think her dad may have even kind of liked me, because he lent me his coveralls to help her do the chores.

One day Charlie and his family, along with his parents (Rachael and Oliver Little) all came to see me. Tommy, Gloria's youngest brother, was just a little tyke then and he ran to the house to see what it looked like. He came back and grabbed his mom by the arm and said, "Come see, he's even got curtains on the window." I think Hazel was a bit embarrassed.

Gloria and I went together for a few months. She was in Edmonton training as a psychiatric nurse, so we did a lot of our courting by mail.

I took her home to Valleyview to meet my family; I was so proud of her. I couldn't wait to introduce them all to the love of my life, and there was nothing that anyone there could do to interfere with my relationship now.

*The girl I chose to be my ranching partner and the love
of my life. Together we raised a wonderful family and
succeeded in making my dreams come true.*

*She started a psychiatric nursing career. After finishing
the first year, she quit to become a farmer's wife.*

On Sunday morning, I was going to bring the milk cows in for Clifford. I saddled up a young horse and headed for the pasture. The horse was cat walking and fighting the halter, so I thought a little run wouldn't hurt her. She could really get out and move, and we ate up a quarter mile in nothing flat, but we were coming up on the cows real fast. I tried to check her speed but got no response. Things were happening too fast, and I knew if I couldn't manage to get her slowed down I was in for one hell of a wreck, because a cow decided she should cross to the other side of the trail ahead of us.

The horse wouldn't slow down, the cow had her mind made up, and we all met in the middle. I squeezed the cantle and grabbed the saddle horn and hung on as tight as I could. We hit the cow in the middle, and everything seemed to explode. The saddle and I flew over the horse's head and hit the ground with such a thud that for a few seconds the lights went out. Then I sensed that the horse was going to roll over me. I reached up to grab it and must have gotten a hold of her neck because when I woke up I had a handful of mane in my hand. I tried to get up, but a lot of big lights kept flashing in my head. The horse was standing beside me. She kept on coughing. The cow was all humped up and looked like she had her ribs smashed in by the way she was breathing.

I tried to get up again, and that time I made it. I tried to put the saddle on the horse, but I realized the latego had broken upon impact. My right leg was causing me a lot of pain, so I just stood there half-leaning on the horse, waiting to clear my head. Then I limped back to the barn, leading the horse. Clifford met me at the gate, and of course he wanted to know what happened. I told him he should go and bleed the cow because she wasn't going to make it, but he was more concerned about me. He helped me to the house and I lay on the chesterfield and took a painkiller.

That was the first time Gloria met my folks and darn near had to take me home in a body bag. Some of the aches and pains that I have now probably have some connection to that episode. The horse and I both lived, but the cow was not that fortunate. It sure was a torture to drive all the way back to Stettler from Valleyview.

Gloria and I were married the following spring on April 1, 1961, April Fools' Day. That was one way I thought I could never forget our anniversary! I was twenty-two, she was seventeen.

Our wedding picture

CHAPTER 31

New Ventures

Now I was walking on cloud nine. Gloria went everywhere I went, whether it was picking rocks, making hay, milking cows, or fixing fence. Although I was young, she was younger and we learned to do everything together.

I added a new tractor and a one-way Cockshut seeder to my farm. One day she came out to the field with me and I was teaching her how to drive the new tractor. When she got close to the truck, I told her to stop. She got excited and stepped on the wheel brake instead of the clutch and ran into the back of my pickup. As a result, it pushed in the grill on my new tractor and broke a taillight on the pickup. I was sitting on the fender while she was driving, and it all happened so fast that before I knew it we were in a wreck. I think that was the first time that I spoke rough words to her. I said something to the effect that she had wrecked my new tractor.

Gloria and I also started a new venture; we were starting our family. It would be a totally new experience for both of us, but we both loved kids. Four months after we were married she was pregnant. It was no accident either, but a sincerely desired event.

That fall I was picking up stooks with my pickup one evening. Gloria drove the truck for me while I loaded the bundles, and then we both unloaded them at a stack in the barnyard. It was a beautiful fall evening and we just kept on working. The Northern Lights came out and made such a beautiful scene. The next day my neighbor's wife came over and wanted to know what we were doing driving around in the field after midnight. When I told her that we were picking up the stooks, she bawled me out for working Gloria so hard.

I fed some steers through the winter. I chopped up oat and barley straw, mixed it with some barley grain that I ground with a John Deere hammer mill, and blew it all into a self-feeder. They did quite well, and that spring I had a truckload of fat steers to ship.

As the winter months rolled on, we could see the evidence that our family was growing. It was so exciting, and the waiting was the hardest part. My anticipation of a little man looked like it may soon become a reality. But little did I know that I really didn't have anything to say about it. On May 16, 1962, a darling little baby girl was born. We named her Cindy Ellen. She was born in the hospital at Stettler. She seemed so tiny but strong, and had her mother's big eyes. She also had a lot of hair. I was so happy and proud that I must admit I forgot about a little man.

Me holding Cindy, at home when
she was a couple of months old

It was a busy time for me on the farm as I was right in the middle of seeding the crops. I would come in from the field all tuckered out and lie on the chesterfield while Gloria prepared my meal. She would lay Cindy on my chest and I would just listen to all the little noises she would make. One time, I guess I was really tired and dozed off. Gloria snapped a picture of us; Cindy was just lying there, looking at me.

Here I am enjoying my darling little daughter Cindy
on the lawn when I come in from the field.

We would take her with us wherever we went, whether it was out to the pasture to check the cows or in the truck when Gloria hauled grain from the combine.

She would pull herself up in her crib and try walking around the inside of her crib, trying to catch the budgie bird. As she got a little older and started walking around the inside of the house, she decided she would feed the fish in the tank one day. She took the fish food and dumped a whole can in. She was such a little darling, what could you really say to her? It was so interesting to watch her grow up and get her feet firmly under her.

She got into everything, and it wasn't too long before she was toddling along behind us outside. I remember the day she and I went to the chicken house to gather the eggs. The kitten decided it would come along, and when I tried to open the door to chicken house, the cat was going to go inside too. I slammed the door quickly, but caught the cat by the tail. I guess it pinched the tail pretty hard because awhile later when we were going to the chicken coop again, Cindy grabbed the cat by the tail and the tail came off. She had such a surprised look on her face, it was priceless. She looked at me and said, "Uh-oh, all broken."

During the spring of 1962, the cow that was our wedding present from Charlie and Hazel decided she was in love with the neighbors' bull or wanted to be. I was seeding crop and had a bunch of treated seed wheat in my truck, so I couldn't haul her over to the bull. She was so gentle, I thought I could lead her behind the truck, but she didn't want any part of that and pulled back and broke the halter. I made a makeshift halter with a rope and tried again. I could feel her jerking in protest behind the truck, and then everything came real easy. I stopped because I thought she had broken the rope, and when I got out to see what had happened, she was lying on the ground. I had just broken her neck. I ran to the house to get a knife to bleed her so I could butcher her. Gloria said, "You can't kill her, that's our wedding present." I told her I already had and now all I needed to do was bleed her.

I can remember Charlie and Hazel coming over to visit and asking how the cow was doing. It was hard to tell them that they were enjoying her for supper. I can still see the look on Hazel's face. Of course I had to explain what had happened, but it wasn't easy.

I always looked forward to when Grandpa and Grandma Little came along with Charlie and Hazel for a visit. Grandpa was a dedicated gopher hunter, and even at his older age he was still a very good shot. I'd drive him and Charlie around the farm and we would shoot gophers while Hazel and Grandma visited with Gloria.

One day we were driving down an old road and a gopher came running down the track toward the car. I told Grandpa to get that one, and while he was trying to get a leaning shot from the car door I kept jiggling it. Grandpa was getting a little impatient and said, "Who the sam hell keeps moving this car?" All the while I was trying to get the crosshairs right on the gopher, and about the time I thought he was ready to shoot, I touched one off and blew gopher right across the road and hung it on the fence.

I thought Grandpa was never going to stop cussing. He said, "What the sam hell kind of cannon is that?" He didn't know that I had brought my .25-06 along instead of my .22. I had a lot of fun hunting gophers with Grandpa.

He also loved to fish, and one spring we went fishing with Charlie and Hazel and Grandpa and Grandma Little. We had a lot of fun. Grandpa loved life in general and he chewed tobacco and swore like a trooper. Sometimes I think he laid it on a little heavier just for devilment, but underneath he was just a big softy. He was known to offer a helping hand more than once to people who had gotten in a bind. He loved his grandkids and was always pulling little pranks for a laugh.

He farmed right into his later years and enjoyed every minute of it. Even when his sons thought he shouldn't be out on the tractor or helping harvest because of his health, he found a way around it. He bought a piece of property and an old tractor and a disc and set about working the ground on his own. He liked nothing more than to have a crop of wheat, oats, or barley that would out-yield any of his sons'. In the end they relented, realizing that if he really wanted to help with the field work it was probably better for him to be happy rather than stress about not being allowed to do it.

Grandpa Little was very interested in my barn. It was fifty-eight feet by sixty feet. He told me I needed to fill one side up with milk cows and the other side up with pigs. Milk cows were not my favorite animal, and pigs were right next in line to them. However, I soon realized that a few milk cows would help buy household necessities. I could feed the milk to the pigs and ship the cream to the dairy co-op at Stettler. And so before too long I became a gum-boot farmer.

Gloria and I kept adding to our farm, more milk cows, pigs, chickens, turkeys, and geese.

Our first batch of chickens; we bought the chicks at the local hatchery in Stettler and set them up in an area we had prepared in the basement of our house because we had no warm place to put them otherwise

We milked the cows in the lean on the east side of the barn. That year we got a milking machine to lessen the workload. I also moved the cream separator into a small room that I built into the cow barn, so it made things easier and faster. We milked sixteen cows.

Milk cows in the corral by the barn. We milked the cows by hand. Eventually we milked as many as sixteen cows by hand, but then we got a milking machine.

The center of the barn was open hay storage from ceiling to floor. I converted that into a furrowing barn. I made sixteen stalls for the sows, and heated the barn with a Booker coal heater and forced air.

A sow and her piglets. Everyone is asleeep and all is quiet!

In the lean on the other side of the farrowing area, I built a finishing barn for the pigs I raised. It was designed so that I could start the small wiener pigs at one end and keep moving them up a pen as they grew bigger until they were ready for market. That barn would hold a total of 500 feeder pigs. I used a deep narrow gutter system to dispose of the manure, which was flushed into a covered pit at the back of the barn. I placed automatic water bowls in each pen next to the gutter. Three huge fans provided proper circulation, and the pigs would naturally keep their pen clean in the area where they lay and slept. The only place they messed in the pen was near the gutter.

I bought a "honey wagon" to suck the pig manure out and spread it on the fields; that really made things grow and helped to cut down on the fertilizer. I was becoming more of a farmer than a rancher but things just seemed to go that way, although I dreamed of ranching far more than milking cows and raising hogs. I dreamed that one day I would own a nice herd of beef cows big enough to make my living.

Horses were always a great love of mine. The first quality horse that I bought on the farm was named Bunny. She was a good horse and she had a nice little foal. I waited with great anticipation for it to be born, watching closely, hoping to witness the miracle of birth, but she fooled me. In the period of time when I ran into the house to get Gloria, she had delivered.

I was very attracted to Appaloosa horses, and I eventually began to base my horse herd on the Appaloosa breed. I bought a stud that I called Chief at the Stettler Auction Mart. He came from Onion Lake, Saskatchewan. He left me some really nice foals with a lot of color. With Appaloosas each foal is like waiting for Christmas, you never know what the package will be.

Chief, a stud colt that I bought as an unbroken two-year-old. He came from Onion Lake, Saskatchewan.

CHAPTER 32

I Might be a Farmer Now, But I'll Always be a Hunter

There wasn't much opportunity to hunt for big game around Stettler, but there were pheasants and that was a new one for me. John Pavlidge was a game warden in the Stettler area and became a good friend of mine. One day he stopped in and told me he needed to get a bunch of pheasants for the university in Edmonton because they wanted to do a mercury check on the birds. He didn't have a lot of time to get them and he wondered if I'd like to come along and help him. I jumped at the chance and told him I knew where there were quite a few. If he had a good dog, we were sure to come home with some pheasants. He said he'd bring his dog and he would supply all the shells. The next day we went pheasant hunting.

Now I had been carrying my shotgun during the harvest season, trying to scare ducks out of the field so they wouldn't do so much damage to my crops. I'd taken the plug out because the more noise I could make the better, but that morning when I went with John I hadn't thought to put it back in my gun. When we got to a place along a blind road where there usually were lots of pheasants, he stopped his truck to let the dog out and it immediately picked up their scent. John and I both began to put shells in our guns and I just kept filling my gun up.

I noticed John look at me, and then he asked if I didn't have a plug in my gun. I told him I had forgotten to put it back in, explaining that when

I was combining I took the plug out just so I could scare as many ducks away as possible.

He reminded me that we weren't scaring ducks that day, we were hunting for pheasants, but said he'd let me get away with it that time. We crawled through the fence and went to where the dog was working some buck brush. We just got there and the dog gave us his pointing signal. John asked me if I was ready, and when I told him I was, he told the dog to flush. I think there were four pheasants that came out of the buck brush and I shot three of them. John yelled "Powich, what the hell are you doing? You can't shoot those hen pheasants."

I asked him if they didn't get mercury too, and he agreed that they probably did, but the university only asked for roosters. I told him I was sorry, but he hadn't told me not to shoot a hen. As the day went on, we got six or seven more pheasants and they were all roosters. We were walking on an old road between two fields when we heard some geese honking. There was quite a lot of brush along the road, so we easily hid and we let drive at those geese and got three of them. I asked him if the geese got mercury too. He said they probably did but we weren't sending these nice fat geese to Edmonton!

When we were driving home along an oat field, a nice big deer was standing there, feeding. John stopped the truck and said, "Now, that's what I call grain-fed deer," and he asked why I didn't have that one in my freezer. I told him because the season wasn't open yet, and he asked if that mattered. Then he went on to say that was the best piece of venison I'd ever eat. I commented that was probably true, and if you had the law on your side, it didn't matter, did it? He just laughed and said he didn't have anything in his freezer either, so maybe he should come back out with his rifle and go hunting again sometime.

I did get to do some good deer hunting on and near the farm, but for moose and elk I had to go to the mountains out west, Rocky Mountain House and Caroline way. The mountains seemed to have a special calling to me, and again hunting elk was something new to me.

That fall the harvest was good, and Ben did the combining for me again. After the harvest was over, I bailed a lot of the oat and barley straw. When all of the bales were in and stacked, I decided that I would go hunting in the mountains. Ben and a mutual friend, Willie Stuart, and I went that year.

I still remember the first elk I tried to sneak up on. I was using a nice .303 that had been worked over by Ben's brother, Harry.

He'd worked on the trigger and made it quite light. When I did manage to sneak up on the bull elk, he was lying down in his bed, chewing his cud. I was not more than thirty yards from him when I touched the trigger and blew a hole in the ground three feet in front of me. Talk about being embarrassed, and to top it all off, my elk was gone. The meadow he'd been feeding in had dogleg to it. Ben and Willie heard my shot. They were at the far end of the dogleg and waited to see if anything would come by, and sure enough my elk ran across the end of the meadow. It just took one shot for Willie with his .25-06 to drop it. We got a couple more cows on that trip and saw some nice country.

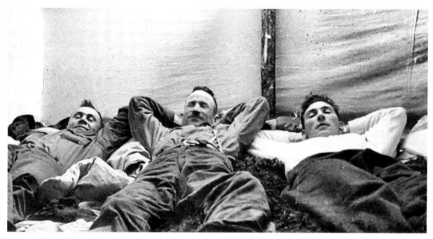

Ben Erickson, Willie Stewart, and I in our hunting tent

We had a great time hunting out there, but when I came home Gloria told me how hard it had been for her and Hazel to milk the cows, feed the pigs, separate the milk, and just keep things from freezing up because it had gotten so terribly cold. I was sure glad Hazel had decided to come and stay with her.

That winter I got Willie to ask Joe Tucker from Portage LaPrairie if he would make me a .25-06, as that was who Willie had gotten his gun from. The .25-06 is a wild-cat rifle. Joe said he was getting older and it took a lot of work to make a gun like that, so he didn't think he could make another one. But he had one that he'd made for himself that he'd sell. I ended up buying the gun and never regretted doing it. Joe was an excellent gunsmith. With a 100-grain bullet and fifty-four grains of 1148-31 powder, that bullet would travel 3,400 feet a second. And from a gun laid at 200 yards a 25-cent piece would cover three shots. It was a pleasure to shoot and I never owned another rifle with that accuracy. I have shot hundreds of gophers with that gun. I have shot moose, black bear, elk, deer, wolves, and coyotes and enjoyed it every time I put my shoulder to it.

A lot of the trophies in my den have been shot with the .25-06. I do own a 7mm magnum that I like for grizzly, but I wouldn't hesitate to take a griz with the .25-06 if I had to. Although I have left it a little too long now, I would like to get a forty-inch ram yet; and if the occasion ever does arise, I will use my .25-06.

Ben Erickson and I looking down over the Ram River areas

I went hunting every year during the next twelve years I lived at Stettler. That was my birthday treat to myself, as we were usually in the mountains on my birthday. I went with several different people through the years, some of them many times: Benny Erickson, Harry Erickson, Willie Stuart, my father-in-law Charlie Little, my brothers-in-law Tom Little and Allen McGladdery, Gerry Zuidwyck, Peter Zahacy, Garth Norman, Pat and Joe Baltimore were all among them.

Base camp while hunting with Charlie Little, Tom Little, and Gerry Zudwyck

Garth Norman and I in our hunting tent

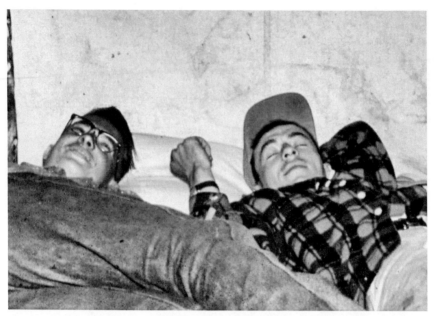

*Garth Norman and Peter Zahacy in the hunting tent when
the three of us went out west into the mountains*

Here I am hunting with the Baltimore brothers, Joe and Pat.

We stopped at the Yaha Tinda Ranch on that trip; here
I am in front of the barn with some of the crew

CHAPTER 33

My Friend, Peter Zahacy, Moves to Stettler

In 1963, Peter Zahacy and his wife and two boys moved to Stettler. Peter worked for the city and they lived in a trailer in Stettler. Peter and I did a lot of things together then, both work and play. We hunted deer and pheasants and anything else that we could. Once, late in the fall of the year, we had just gotten our first snowfall and the weather had turned quite cold, and a lot of the sloughs had a thin layer of the ice over them. There were a lot of ducks around because there were still a few fields that were not combined. It was kind of a snowy day when I got hold of Peter and asked him if he wanted to go duck hunting. He came out to the farm and we went to a field where there was a large slough with hundreds of ducks on it.

When we arrived, they all took off and some landed on the field that I had just finished combining. We picked up some bales and made a blind that we could hide in and keep out of the wet snow that was falling. We crawled into the blind and waited for the ducks to come back to the slough. It wasn't long before they came in bunches of a hundred or more. They wanted to get into the open water. I think most of the other sloughs were frozen over. We waited a little longer, and more ducks just kept on coming until that slough was simply covered with then.

As we sat there and watched them, it was interesting to see what they were doing. Bunches of them would lift a few feet off the slough a few feet and then land on the ice, breaking the ice and making a bigger area of

184

open water. I said, "Let's hope they keep breaking the ice in our direction, that way we'll get a closer shot."

We had waited quite awhile when Peter said, "I don't know about you, but I'm getting kind of cold. I think it's time we blasted a few of them." We picked the closest spots where we thought the most ducks had congregated and emptied our guns, and there were a lot of ducks falling. We reloaded our guns, and as a bunch more flew quite low over us, we emptied our guns again. By this time there were dead ducks lying all over the water and on the ice. Now we had to decide how we were going to get them out.

Peter was smaller than me, so we decided to break off a couple of small poplar trees that had died next to the slough and he used them for support to crawl out onto the thin ice and pick the ducks up that were closest to shore. He was doing really well until he got a little too far out and the whole thing fell in and he was in water up to his waist. He kept saying, "Jesus, this is really cold." I told him since he was already wet he might just as well go in and get the rest. But he didn't think that was very good idea, so he crawled back to shore, breaking the ice until he could get on top of it. I don't really know how many ducks we shot, all I know is we killed a hell of a pile of them. We picked up the nice big mallards that we could carry and headed for home.

Peter was one cold dude by the time we got to the house. I can still see him standing beside the oil heater in the living room, trying to dry his clothes and warm up. He told me that was the last time he would ever be my bird dog.

Another time Peter had come out to the farm on a nice balmy winter day. We didn't have a TV at the time and weren't listening to the weather forecast, so we had no idea that a storm was brewing. At about four in the afternoon, we decided to go over to Ralph Innocents' place (about ten miles away) and have a look at some of his horses. After that I was going to take Peter home, and I should have been back at my place in time for supper.

When we left the farm, it was a balmy -35 °F, but after we had traveled seven miles we ran into a snowstorm with about ten-mile-an-hour winds. Everything turned into a complete whiteout, and we were caught in a blizzard that made things real interesting for a little while. The wind was increasing and the road was drifting badly. Although we were nearly at Ralph's farm, we couldn't drive any farther because of the huge snowdrifts that crossed the road. We weren't prepared to spend the night in the car, but we weren't dressed to walk in a blizzard either.

Having to make a decision one way or the other, we decided that our best choice was to try to make it to Ralph's place. He was very surprised when he answered our knock on the door and saw us standing there. The first thing he asked was what we were doing out in that kind of weather. After hearing we'd hit the blizzard on our way over and our car was stranded between two snowdrifts, he said we'd better hunker down with them until the storm blew over.

Ralph didn't have a phone, so there was no way for us to let Shirley know what had happened. Of course, Gloria was frantic, wondering where we were. We didn't have a phone at home, so she couldn't call Shirley to see if we'd arrived there. Cindy was a baby and Gloria was very pregnant with Cherie. It was nice at home, so in desperation Gloria left Cindy in her crib and walked to the neighbors, Mable and Albert Watson, to phone Shirley to see if she knew anything.

Shirley called the RCMP to see if there had been an accident or if they had any information about us. All they could tell her was that we probably couldn't travel because a severe storm had blown in. It was forecasted to be short-lived and they were sure the roads would be cleared before too long.

The next morning after breakfast, the roads were plowed and we could get to the highway. When we got home to our wives, they were happy to see us but a little ticked off. They didn't realize how bad the storm was. The north and south roads had blown shut because of the way the storm was moving. When I got home around noon, the car's motor was still packed with snow that had blown in around it.

CHAPTER 34

We Complete Our Family

About eleven months after Cindy's birth, we realized that we'd dropped a little seed in places that we hadn't realized. If it is a weed you would pull it out, but if it's a flower you nurture it along and care for it in the very best way that you know how. Once again I hoped it might be a little man.

On January 27, 1964, we were blessed with another baby girl. She was the tiniest little doll you could imagine at five pounds. By the time she came home, she was only four pounds eleven ounces. But she was the feistiest little thing you ever saw.

I am the proud father, holding Cherie when we brought her home from the hospital

Cindy looking as Cherie blows out the candles on her cake

Cherie was always moving her arms and legs, and when she was a few months older she would get really excited when you went to pick her up. She sucked her two middle fingers, and even when she was older and walking around she did the same thing, only then she would hold a feather she'd found and tickle her nose with it while she sucked her fingers. She also had her favorite blanket that she would drag around everywhere. When she started to talk, she had such an English accent, everyone was surprised. We named her Cherie Lynn, but should have called her Bob because she was rough and tumble like a little boy. When she was little she was like a little pixie, and as the years passed she grew into a very pretty, feminine woman.

When Cherie was about three years old we stopped at A&W for something to eat on our way home from church. A seagull was sitting on a light pole, squawking, and Cherie would mimic that seagull to a T. It was so comical that we just sat there for a while and listened to her.

Both of the girls loved horses. When she was little, Cindy first called them "gussie," and then "kuie kuie." For Cherie a horse was an "ee he he." I wonder why they loved horses, must have been in their genes! I got them a little pony to ride. I would put the pony in the corral and set them on her and they would go round and round. That little pony was the best life insurance policy that I had on the farm.

Gloria sewed for the girls and would do such a good job of dressing up our two little dolls; they looked so cute in their little white shoes and pretty dresses. When we went to church they would sit as quiet as a mouse and not make a sound.

Eight months after Cherie's arrival, the blessings of the universe were bestowed on us again. I was really hoping for a son this time, but by now I was beginning to realize that maybe I shouldn't get my hopes too high, because it seemed that there was nothing I could do to make that decision. The months and days came and went and we began to get more excited with each passing day. On June 10, 1965, guess what? My little man arrived. We called him Murray Lloyd.

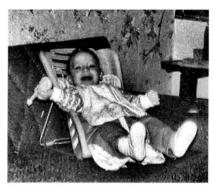

Murray, happy and smiling in his little seat; the picture is taken in the living room of our house at Stettler

Murray and Cindy riding their toy horses, a higher tech version than I used to ride when was a kid

I was so proud it was hard for me to contain myself. We had been blessed with such a lovely family that it almost scared me. Murray was such a cuddly little guy. He just loved to be held close and talked to. But it wasn't long before he tried to be just as robust as his little sisters, and he would try to copy them even when he wasn't big enough.

One day he was bouncing on the chesterfield with his sisters and bounced right off and hit his head on the coffee table before ending up on the floor. Of course, that scared the living daylights out of Gloria, because he always seemed to be banging his head or getting bumped by something. She used to say it would be a wonder if he grew up normal, but he certainly did!

We had a two-story house and the bedrooms were upstairs. As each child became mobile (crawling), they learned how to use the stairs because they were an integral part of life in our household, and with so many little ones you couldn't watch them every minute. Gloria was very careful with them and none of them ever fell, until one day when we had come home from Stettler. Gloria was making lunch and the kids were upstairs playing. Murray was pushing a toy baby carriage that the girls put their dolls in, and he managed to push it right over the top of the stairs and came somersaulting down with it.

When he hit the bottom of the stairs, he knocked himself out. I was so scared, I just grabbed him and Gloria got the girls. We put them all into the car and headed to the Stettler hospital as fast as we could go. He lay limp in Gloria's arms, and I was sure we had lost him. When we were about two miles from town, he opened his eyes and sat up, looking around like a little owl. He didn't cry or anything and didn't seem to be hurt as far as we could see, but we took him to the hospital anyway and they kept him overnight just to be sure.

He was so tiny that he could run under the kitchen table when he was two years old. But it wasn't long before he was bumping his head and seemed to always forget to duck. One day I was out fencing, and I asked Murray to bring me a fence post. He tried and tried to pick it up but could only get one end off the ground. I teasingly said, "Come on, come on, I don't want to wait all day." He was close to tears when he looked at me and said, "Dad, don't you know I am just your little man?" And that he truly was, just a little man, and I loved him so much.

After Murrays' birth, Gloria and I often talked about how lucky we were to have such a lovely family. Gloria's health had deteriorated after

Murray's birth and her doctor had cautioned her about giving birth again, but we wanted one more child, another boy. We knew we had our hands full at that time, but we were young and loved children, so we decided to adopt a little boy.

We went through all the proper procedures, and in June 1967 we went to Edmonton and picked up our ten-month-old little boy. We called him Darryl Gerry. Now we had four children, five and under, two girls and two boys. I was twenty-seven, Gloria was twenty-two.

Me holding Darryl the day we brought
him home. He was a big boy!

Darryl was a big boy compared to the other children. Like the others, he and Murray went with me whenever I could take them. Darryl never really liked to be cuddled. He was always independent. He was heavy for Gloria to carry when she did chores but he went everywhere with her.

When he started walking, he went with her in the spring of the year to collect the goose eggs so they wouldn't freeze. But when the time came to the set the eggs under the mother goose, he'd go out and take them from her. He'd stuff them in his pockets and carry more than he could manage, and as a result he would drop and break them. Sometimes his snowsuit would be covered with broken eggs. No matter how often Gloria tried to tell him not to do that because the goose had to hatch little geese out of those eggs, he couldn't seem to understand.

Darryl, looking at the candle on his first birthday cake;
Murray, Cherie, and Cindy looking on

One day while I was at the hog barn, he ventured out to steal the eggs again. This time the old gander was standing guard over the nest and it took after him. It pecked him and flapped him with both its wings. I have to tell you, that hurt! I heard him just hollering. I ran out to see what was wrong and saw the gander doing a real number on him.

I ran to his rescue and asked him what happened. He was crying and trying to tell me that the big bad gander had just "flopped on him." I told him, "See, he doesn't want you to take the eggs from the goose now. They have to stay there so that she can make some baby geese." He never took eggs away from her again.

He was such a little handful, not scared of anything. He would challenge the rooster that chased the other kids; he even tried to chase the big turkey gobbler that made a habit of terrifying the others and chased them screaming up on the barn step. One day when he was out in the barnyard, he took a little stick and walked up to the gobbler, saying, "No, no, don't you peck me." That old gobbler wasn't quite sure what to do. When Gloria noticed what he was doing, she ran to his rescue. It was hard for Gloria to keep an eye on him.

One day when I had just come in from riding and was unsaddling my horse, he came and grabbed the colt by the tail. He could have been kicked and severely injured but the colt just squatted on its hind legs a bit and stood there. Another time I rode up to the house to get my thermos of frozen semen to go out to AI (artificially inseminate) a cow that I had in the corral. Darryl came running around the house with his coat over his head and nearly ran into the hind legs of my stud horse. The horse did give a small kick because he had startled it, but it barely lifted its foot and he didn't get hurt at all.

Darryl was always trying to catch up to the three other kids. Murray was a year older than Darryl and he was much more athletic. When Darryl fell down he got up like a little linebacker; he'd come up on one hand and one knee before he stood up, and he was just as tough as the middle linebacker too. But he wanted to grow up and do everything the other kids did, and you would sometimes hear him saying, "Wait for me, you guys."

When Murray and Darryl got a little older, they became good buddies. They would fight and wrestle like two brothers often do, but as each year went by they began to stand up for each other.

CHAPTER 35

Buying the Farm

Eventually the time came when I had to buy the farm, so I decided I would sell my homestead at Valleyview and use the money to help make the down payment. I approached my dad and brothers about buying my half section. They were interested, but would only pay me $6,000. I didn't think that was a fair price, because it had two oil wells, a road, and two right-of-ways for the flow lines that came from the wells, but I needed the money, so I decided to take what they offered me.

I purchased my first combine so that I could combine my own crop the next fall. It turned out that we had a poor year as far as the crops were concerned. We got hailed out quite badly. But such is farming, and you take the good years along with the bad. The next year was much better and we had a good crop. I decided I needed more land, so I rented a quarter of land from Jess Tippy. It was quite hilly but I grew a good crop on it. I also did some custom combining for Mr. Tippy too; the crop was really heavy and my little old combine was having a hard time working through it. It was on new brakes and I plugged the cylinder many times when a root went up the rattler chain and got stuck. I baled a lot of straw that fall so I could feed some more cattle.

I knew what it meant to be in debt. But since I'd been told that I could never make it on my own, I was more determined than ever to succeed. I was proud of what I'd accomplished in just a few years, debt and all. And I was so happy to have someone like Gloria to work alongside me. And that she truly did. We had so many things to learn, but somehow with our determination we seemed to make it through everything.

Gloria's health deteriorated; she had become asthmatic. We didn't realize it, although in hindsight we should have, because her dad and Grandma Little both had severe asthma and allergies. We just didn't think of it happening to her. She went to see her doctor but he wasn't very helpful. He told her it was all in her head and she would get over it. After that she wouldn't go back to the doctor about it, and for a couple of years she just dealt with the problem as best she could. But untreated, she got much worse.

One week we branded calves and she really had trouble breathing for several days afterward. Someone mentioned it to her dad, and the next weekend they came from Daysland to visit and he let her use a "puffer" (Isrupell) that could be bought in the drugstore in those days. The results seemed miraculous to her. The relief was almost instantaneous and helped at first, but it wasn't a cure.

One day she was helping me move some of the range cows with her saddle horse. These cows were wild and would hide in the bush. She rode into the center of a dry slough that had willows growing around the edges. She was going to chase them out so I could rope them and load them onto the truck, as that seemed to be the only way I was going to get them home.

She seemed to be in there for a long time. I called to her and asked her if she was okay. She said she was having trouble breathing, and by the time she came out of the slough she could hardly breathe at all. She had lost her puffer, so I went back to the truck as fast as I could on my horse and drove it back to pick her up. We were hoping she might have had another one in the truck, but she didn't. So I just left the horses there and rushed her to town.

When we got to town the stampede parade was on and they had blocked off part of the street to the drugstore. By this time she was starting to turn a blue, so I just ran down the street into the drugstore and grabbed a puffer off the shelf, telling them I would be back later. A few inhalations of her puffer and she began to come around. She gave us a real scare. There must have been rag weed or something that she was allergic to in there. After she was breathing OK, we drove back to the field and loaded the horses, leaving the cows for another day.

Over the next while we just kept on working harder than either of us should have, especially Gloria. I added running water and a septic system to the house when we built the hog barn. That helped to make things easier for her, but still she really was working too hard.

I kept adding to the farm; first more land, then a bigger tractor, then a bigger cultivator, another truck and newer car, and on it went. With the help of Farm Credit I purchased another half section of land from Tom Taylor. It was mostly hay and pastureland. That winter I went back and rented the old D 8 from Fred Kellough and cleared a lot of the bush to make some fields and more pasture. I broke up the land and seeded some of it to barley and some of it to oats. The crops were very good that year, so I bought a brand-new self-propelled swather, but before I could even get it all swathed we got a storm that dumped four-inches of snow on us. A lot of the heavy crops just laid flat on the ground. That made swathing very difficult.

I was glad that I had bought a self-propelled swather, but even so, in order to pick up the flattened crop I had to add pick up guards to it. Somehow I managed to get all the harvesting done. The bins were all full and I had piled some feed grain right on the ground.

My cow herd feeding at the trough; view toward the barn, corrals, and the slough

I had lots of feed, so I made a deal with my neighbor, Don Lee, to take his herd of cows on shares. They were good Hereford cows; a lot of them were purebred but not registered. With a small herd of my own, I was now in the cow business as well.

That fall I baled at least 10,000 bales of the oat and barley straw and some wheat straw just to use for bedding. It was quite a job just stacking all that straw. I stacked it in such a way that it helped to make a shelter from the wind for the corrals and feed yard. I wintered my range cows on straw and oats that I hammered real coarse. The cows had free choice to salt and mineral. However, when calving time came, I was having problems with retained afterbirth. The cows were in good shape but may have been lacking in phosphorus.

The next year I dug a silage pit and seeded a lot of land in to oats and barley. I bought a silage chopper and an old Ford truck to haul silage into the pit. It was a good way to clean up a lot of the wild oat. I would take the self-propelled swather and cut a trail into areas where big patches of wild oats were just starting to head out, then make silage out of it. After the wild oats went through the silage process they wouldn't germinate. It made excellent silage for the range cows, and the next year I didn't have any problems at calving time.

CHAPTER 36

Importing My First Limousin Cattle from France

With Gloria continuing to have problems with allergies, we decided to get rid of the milk cows and added more beef cows to our existing heard, which now numbered eighty head. I also decided that I'd like to try crossing my cow herd with a Limousin bull. I had a long talk with Dr. Stothert from the Lacombe experimental farm. He had been to France to import two new breeds to Canada; one was Limousin, and the other was Simmental. I chose to go with the Limousin breed.

I made the application to import a Limousin bull. It was accepted, but as always money was tough to come by, and so I formed a partnership with three other people and we imported a bull called Edelweiss.

Edelweiss

When he arrived we put him in a bull station and drew semen from him. Each member of the partnership was supposed to put in thirty head of cows and I would artificially inseminate them with the semen from our new bull. I used thirty of my cows, the vet bought twelve black heifers, the doctor bought three Hereford cows, and I artificially inseminated and cared for all of them. The lawyer never bought a cow, but he wanted his full share of all the female offspring from my cows. I told him that he would only get them over my dead body. He didn't get any of my heifers, and we decided to dissolve the partnership and sell the bull.

One learns from his mistakes, and I learned that a partnership with a lawyer and a doctor was not the way to go. I got along good with the vet, and we remained friends for many years. He taught me how to do caesareans and put a prolapsed uterus back in place. I also learned a lot of good medical techniques from him that came in handy in my ranching venture years later. Animal husbandry is so important in the cow business; diagnosing a problem and treating it correctly can affect your profit margins.

The farm was beginning to take on the look of a ranch. The Limousin influence began to show great potential in the aspect of breeding beef cattle. I continued to AI my cows with Limousin, and sold bred half-blood Limo heifers in the first inaugural Limousin sale in Calgary. I sold a solid red heifer to Oklahoma Cattle Company for $3500.00. All the heifers sold from $2,000 to $3,500.

BOURBON FANTASY CIF-76
Born: February 28, 1970 Sire: Alaska
This French import pictured at 15 years of age is the base of this great cow family.

Bourbon Fantasy, the first heifer I imported from France in 1970

I decided I would go for a female import. I needed bank support to finance importing cattle on my own. The Royal Bank didn't think I should be meddling with imports, so I thanked them for the business I'd done with them and walked over to the Imperial Bank of Commerce. I moved my account and got all of the money I needed. I also added a new, bigger tractor and a combine to my machinery lineup, along with a baler and bale stooker. Then I rented another 160 acres of land from Martin Anderson, which I eventually bought.

My application was accepted and I got a female from the Bourbon herd in France; she was called Bourbon Fantasy.

The official permit to import a cow, Bourbon Fantasy, from France to Canada

The next fall I bought two more female imports. These females cost me a little over $12,000 a piece. The import papers for the two heifers are on the next page.

CANADA DEPARTMENT OF AGRICULTURE

PERMIT TO IMPORT ANIMALS Importation

St. Pierre November 1971

Under and by virtue of the powers vested in me by the Animal Contagious Diseases Act, and the Regulations made thereunder, I do hereby authorize and permit **MR. LLOYD ANTYPOWICH**

BOX 767

STETTLER, ALBERTA

to import into the Dominion of Canada, the following animals, subject to the conditions set forth below:

TWO (2) LIMOUSIN CATTLE

Country of Origin **FRANCE**

Date of Shipment **OCTOBER/NOVEMBER** 19 **71**

Port of Landing via St. Pierre Quarantine Station, St. Pierre

Date of Arrival **NOVEMBER** 19 **71**

In witness whereof I have hereunto set my hand at the City of Ottawa, the **8th** day of **JULY**, 19 **71**

Original Signed by

K. F. WELLS

FOR

(for)*Deputy Minister of Agriculture*

COFRANIMEX

COMPAGNIE FRANÇAISE POUR L'EXPORTATION ET L'IMPORTATION DES ANIMAUX REPRODUCTEURS

Bureau de Limoges : 11, Bd Victor-Hugo
87 - Limoges (France) - Tél. 77-53-06
       77-51-67
Adresse Télégr. : Betailimex - Limoges

Mr Lloyd ANTYPOWICH
P.O. Box 767
STETTLER – ALBERTA
Canada

LIMOGES, september 18, 1970

Ref. 269

Dear Sir,

   Please find herewith enclosed our invoice n0 5037 , corresponding to our contract n° 26

     – Total amount of invoice : Frs 20.296

     – Downpayment   : Frs 1.925

     – Balance to be paid : Frs 18.371

   We would appreciate receiving your payment by retunr mail by bank draft made to the order of COFRANIMEX, 121 Bd Haussmann – PARIS (8°).

   Of course, if one of your animals reacts to the sanitary tests to be conducted in BREST, such animal will be refunded, unless we are able to replace it by another one. In the later case, if the replacement is sold for a different price, the difference in value will be settled.

   We would like to call your attention to the fact that any animals which would not be fully settled before OCTOBER 1st will not be shipped to Canada. Therefore in your own interest, we insist on a prompt payment.

   Thanking you in advance, we are

           Yours sincerely.

           COFRANIMEX –

121 boulevard Haussmann - 75 Paris (France) - tél. 359-92-18 - télex : 29.067 Paris - cables : Betailimex-Paris
Société anonyme au capital de 2.000.000 F - R. C. Seine 68 b 627 - Mle INSEE 701 75 108 0 053

November 23, 1971

Dear Sir:

The attached slip indicates your animal arriving to Canada on the Grosse Ile Shipment. The data from left to right reads:

Name of Permit Holder//Tattoo Number//Date of Birth//Sex//Name of Animal//Herd Book No// Name and Address of Breeder

| M. | 07209 | 09 I2 70 | F | FARANDOLE | 87 70 009 793 | M. BOUTET G. BEAUNES LES MINES |
| VA | 07I05 | 05 I2 70 | F | FORNARINA | 87 70 009 7I9 | M. BOUTET M. BEAUNES LES MINES |

We wish you best of luck!!

COFRANIMEX

Anthony Stone

We wish you best of luck!!

Farandole and Fornarina, the last two heifers I imported in 1971

CHAPTER 37

Leaving Stettler

I was impatient, wanting the ranching aspect of my operation to grow quickly. And although I had a hired man, I was doing far more than I should have been and I wasn't paying enough attention to my family. Before I knew it, Gloria was in deep trouble with allergies and asthma, and although she had been going to a doctor, she couldn't seem to get the disease under control. I took her to a specialist in Edmonton and he really jumped on me, telling me she could no longer live in such an environment. That would mean selling the farm, which was devastating news for me.

I moved her and the kids into a house in Red Willow, trying to get her off the farm, but that didn't seem to help. I got a nanny to help with the kids and the housework while they were there because she was spending far too much time in the hospital, almost more than she was at home.

Finally, I took her to Calgary to see another specialist, and he was much more diplomatic but quite straightforward with me. He told me that she would have to leave the environment of the farm if she was to live. He advised me to go somewhere high up into the mountains to get rid of all the dust and pollens. Her allergies were so bad by then that she couldn't work in the garden because she was allergic to the soil. If a piece of her own hair got in her eye, she would get a reaction from it. The doctor told me she was on the verge of getting emphysema, and that the only thing that would help would be to get her away from the agricultural environment, somewhere up into the mountains.

It looked like I had come to the end of the road as far as farming and ranching were concerned. I sat down to reconsider what I had to do next. I searched my mind for anything that I could do in the mountains and came up with nothing. I then went back to look at my past experience; operating a cat was top of the list.

I called a fellow who worked for Kaiser Coal near Sparwood, British Columbia. He told me to contact a foreman at Fording Coal. I made the call and he said he would like to meet with me and there was a possibility that I could get a job. So I loaded up Gloria and the kids and we headed for British Columbia.

I went to the mine site and met with George Kalmakoff and he seemed like a nice fellow. I told him about the situation I was in and told him that while I didn't know anything about coal mining, I could guarantee that I could run a cat. I also told him I didn't want a career as cat operator, and if I liked mining I'd probably be looking at a foreman position.

He asked how soon I could start to work. That kind of surprised me. I told him that I needed enough time to sell my livestock and find someone to live in my farmhouse; I would take care of the rest of it in the spring. He told me to go back and do what I had to do, but get back to him as soon as I could.

I must say I did feel at bit relieved, but I had a very big task in front of me and time was not on my side. I don't know how I managed to get everything to come together, but in one month I sold all my hogs, all my feed grain and straw bales, and booked a livestock sale at the Stettler Auction Market, where I sold all my domestic and half-blood Limousin cattle. I also found someone to live in our house on the farm until the following spring.

Livestock dispersal notice in paper by Stettler Auction Mart

```
               DISPERSAL SALE
                      for
                Mr. Lloyd Antypowich

                December 2nd, 1971


        BRED LIMOUSIN

   Lot No. 1
       No. 51    Hereford   2 Year old      Tattoo: LAR 51B
                 Bred  May 6/71             Sire:  Eidelwiess

   Lot No. 2
       No. 18    Hereford   5 Year old      Tattoo: LAR 18B    Polled
                 Bred  Aug 22/71            Sire:  Eidelwiess

       No. 21    Hereford   6 Year old      Tattoo: LAR 21B
                 Bred  Aug 20/71            Sire:  Eidelwiess

       No. 8     Hereford   6 Year old      Tattoo: LAR 8B
                 Bred  July 11/71           Sire:  Eidelwiess

       No. 2     Hereford   6 Year old      Tattoo: LAR 2B     Polled
                 Bred  July 11/71           Sire:  Eidelwiess

       No. 7     Hereford   5 Year old      Tattoo: LAR 7B     Polled
                 Bred  July 12/71           Sire:  Eidelwiess

   Lot No. 3
       No. 29    Hereford   4 Year old      Tattoo: LAR 29B    Polled
                 Bred  Aug. 20/71           Sire:  Eidelwiess

       No. 12    Hereford   4 Year old      Tattoo: LAR 12B    Polled
                 Bred  Aug. 16/71           Sire:  Eidelwiess

       No. 13    Hereford   5 Year old      Tattoo: LAR 13B    Polled
                 Bred  Aug. 17/71           Sire:  Eidelwiess

       No. 164   Hereford   3 Year old      Tattoo: LAR 164B
                 Bred  July 11/71           Sire:  Eidelwiess

   Lot No. 4
       No. 14    Hereford   5 Year old      Tattoo: LAR 14B    Horned
                 Bred  Aug. 18/71           Sire:  Eidelwiess

       No. 3     Hereford   6 Year old      Tattoo: LAR 3B     Polled
                 Bred  Aug. 19/71           Sire:  Eidelwiess

       No. 6     Hereford   4 Year old      Tattoo: LAR 6B     Polled
                 Bred  Aug. 16/71           Sire:  Eidelwiess

       No. 36    Hereford   5 Year old      Tattoo: LAR 36B    Horned
                 Bred  Aug. 15/71           Sire:  Eidelwiess

       No. 27    Hereford   6 Year old      Tattoo: LAR 27B    Horned
                 Bred  Aug. 15/71           Sire:  Eidelwiess

       No. 38    Hereford   7 Year old      Tattoo: LAR 38B
                 Bred  Aug. 21/71           Sire:  Eidelwiess

   Lot No. 5
       No. 4     Hereford   5 Year old      Tattoo: LAR 4B     Polled
```

Livestock catalogue sheet for sale

When all that was done, I called the office at Fording Coal to tell them
I would be ready to move by the end of the month. I wanted to know if
there would be a house available for me to move into. I got the personnel

office and talked to a man by the name of Scotalaro. I told him I had been there and talked to George Kalmakoff, who had told me to get there as soon as I could. This didn't seem to make any difference to Scotalaro. He said before he hired anybody he liked to see the whites of his eyes, so I told him I would be on my way. I loaded up Gloria and the kids in the car again and made another trip to Elkford.

When I got there, a wobble (illegal work stoppage by union workers) was in progress and I had to wait several hours just to get see him. When I finally did get into his office, he wanted to go home and was quite short with me, saying, "And what do you want?"

By then I wasn't sure I wanted to work under somebody like him, but I took a good strong look at him and said, "I'm here so you can see the white of my eyes," and kept a stern face to let him know he wasn't about to intimidate me in any way. I guess he got the message and very quickly softened his approach to me and asked, "Do I know you?"

I told him what George and I had discussed earlier and that I had sold my livestock and grain and was ready to move into the valley and go to work.

"Aw yes," he said, "I remember talking with George about somebody that was coming to work for us and he seemed impressed with his résumé."

Now things were sounding more promising. However, getting a house was out of the question. He said they were building a new town and were way behind schedule on the housing. The best thing I could do was buy my own trailer with the hopes to find a place to park it.

While I was there at the office I got a look at some of the machinery. The trucks looked humongous and all I saw was D9 cats with big U-blades, canopies, and double shank rippers, but I left there knowing what I had to do.

I couldn't find a spot to park my trailer in Elkford, but I found a place twenty miles down the road in the Elk Valley Trailer Park. I went to Lethbridge and bought a new seventy by twelve foot trailer completely furnished with an eight by eight porch.

We went back to Stettler and I sold my grain truck and bought a three-quarter-ton Ford. We loaded the necessary household belongings and our personal things into the truck. Gloria drove the car and took the kids, and I drove the truck and we headed for Lethbridge.

COAL MINING AT ELKFORD, BRITISH COLUMBIA

1969-1973

CHAPTER 38

Now I'm a Coal Miner at Fording Coal

We hired a truck to move the trailer to the Elk Valley. I went ahead of it and Gloria followed behind the truck that was pulling our new home. It was an extremely windy day, and between Fort McLeod and Lundbreck I thought we were going to lose the trailer. The wind almost blew it off the road, but the driver was experienced and he got it there in one piece.

I got the trailer set up and skirted in with heat tapes on the water lines and everything was as near normal as could be expected. We had filled the last vacant spot in the trailer park. Everything happened so fast that it seemed more of a dream than a reality, and I was like a fish out of water.

Gloria enrolled the kids in school, and I drove up to the mine to see George and find out when he wanted me to start. He asked me if I could be ready to start on the graveyard shift. I said I'd be there.

I drove to the Elkford town site and caught a man bus that took the nightshift employees to work. I went to the "dry" to get my instructions from my boss; he asked me if I had ever worked in a mine before. I told him I hadn't, but I had run cat in the oil patch. He looked at me and kind of grinned, saying, "You must be a stubble jumper." I said, "You can call me that if you like, but I'm here to do whatever you want me to do."

He told me to catch the bus to the top of the mountain and he'd meet me there and show me what he wanted me to do. I began to understand the true meaning of *flatlander* as the bus wiggled its way up to the top of the mountain at 7,000 feet.

Most of the men knew what to do when they got off the bus, but I just stayed there until the foreman came and picked me up. The first thing he said was, "How does it feel to be this high up?" I looked at him and said I had no idea how high we really were. He said, well, he'd show me in just a minute. He told a few more men what he wanted them to do and then drove me down to the spoil where the waste rock was dumped over the edge of the mountain to go tumbling down more than 2,000 feet. From there I could see the plant all lit up below. I could see vehicles coming and going on the haul road. I could see the big shovels loading big rock trucks.

A rock truck dumping rock over the edge of the spoil

Looking down at the mine from up on the spoil

Then he took me to a D9 cat and told me to push rock down to a loader that looked to be as big as my cat.

This is a D9 cat at work

This is a L700 Letourneau loader loading a coal truck

Because I had gotten a late start, the loader had dug away the ramp that I needed to go up so I could push rock down to him. I was trying to build a new ramp so I could get up on top, when that big loader came up behind me. It scooped the back end of my cat up and literally pushed me up on top of an eight-foot cut. I could see someone had cut a trench, so I worked my way up it. When I got all the way to the back, I stopped the cat, got out to have a look to try to figure out where I was. Way down below, I could see lights, but they were an awful long way down. I turned around and started pushing rock down to the loader.

When morning came I couldn't believe I'd spent the night on the edge of a mountain working on a blast area, and if I'd backed up too far it would have been game over for me. It took awhile to get used to the cab on the cat because there was a lot of reflection in the windows from all of the other lights. I sure was glad to get off the graveyard shift so I could see where I was. After that it didn't seem to be so bad.

When I turned in my timecard at the end of the first shift, the foreman said, "You must have had some pretty good digging there last night."

I replied, "Well, it was all rock, but that big cat could move a lot of material." Then he told me he'd expected to have to send another cat up to help me, but I'd done all right.

I made it through the graveyard shift without falling off the mountain, and I was glad to get a couple of days off so I could get acquainted with the area. I guess my foreman told Wally Jackson, one of the shovel operators, who I was and he looked me up on my days off. It turned out that I had gone to school with him when I lived near Slave Lake, Alberta. I only went to Slave Lake for a couple of weeks and then they moved me to Widewater School. I didn't recognize him until he told me that his dad had worked for my dad on the sawmill and we'd played in the sawdust pile together. I hadn't seen him since then and that had to have been twenty-five years or more ago.

Wally became a good friend of mine and still is. His wife, Eunice, and Gloria got along really well. As couples we would visit and play cards together. In the summer we would go on picnics up the Elk River. Gloria and Eunice would go to Lethbridge to shop for groceries once a month, buying in bulk.

Usually Wally and I went up into the mountains with our snow machines, or in the summer we would take the horses and ride high up into the alpine. The Elk Valley is a very beautiful valley and if you liked the outdoors, hunting, and fishing, you had to love it there.

*I am unloading my snowmobile from my truck, getting
ready to go on a hunting adventure in the snow.*

*A cabin that we used to overnight at. First we had to chase out a porcupine
that had claimed it as its home. Then we had to clean it up. A small creek ran
though one corner of it. It was a good place to get water and to keep things cool.*

The winter was much different from what we were used to at Stettler. There always seemed to be a wind blowing one way or the other, making winter and spring days feel a lot colder. In the Elk Valley we had very little wind, but a lot more snow and it was a bit milder. We spent Christmas in the Elk Valley, and the kids had so much fun coming out and helping us get a Christmas tree. It was the first time we'd ever had one!

Gloria seemed to be doing much better in the mountains. We found that when she went to Calgary or Lethbridge the wind would give her problems. Things did change a lot for her; all she had to do was look after the children and the trailer, which was quite compact. Not saying that was nothing, but it certainly was much less than what she was used to doing on the farm.

For me, it was like a holiday. I'd come home from work and kick back in my recliner and go to sleep. I must have done that for at least two or three months before I finally caught up from all the long hours I spent working on the farm. Then I became bored. I missed my animals, and as spring was nearing, I kept thinking about what I wanted to do next.

I missed my horses so much I decided to rent some pastureland and bring the three horses I had in Alberta. Then Sparky (my big shepherd dog) and I had something to do. Sparky loved the farm as much as I did and he would go across town and down the highway to visit the horses. He would lie there and watch them for hours. A young stud that I saved from Gloria's mare was now big enough to start breaking. I called him Dally. He came along real easy and before long I was taking him up into the mountains. He was a great horse, and he gave me many years of pleasurable riding. I could pack anything on him from a weak calf to a grizzly bear hide and he never ever refused. He served me very well for thirty-three years. He sired some good colts as well. He is a horse that I'll never forget.

Then one day I was called into the personnel office and asked if I was ready to work as a lead hand with my foreman. They'd done an evaluation of my work and attitude and felt I was ready to start in the capacity a foreman. I told them that before I took that step I'd like to be able to run most of the equipment myself. They told me they'd give me all the cooperation and help I needed, and they'd like me to give it a try. They reminded me that I'd said I'd be looking for the opportunity when I first hired on and they were giving me a chance. I was not expecting something like this so soon. My foreman told me that I should go for it, that I wouldn't have any problem doing the job. I knew there would be quite an increase in pay as well, so I said I'd give it a try, but I'd need some time off in the spring to tie up all the loose ends that I had with my farm. They said they were prepared to work with me on that.

I came home and told Gloria what I'd done. I actually think she was happy; she had been afraid I would go back to the farm because it was what I loved to do so much.

I had some concerns about the reaction from the crew, but the lead hand position didn't change things a lot as far as the crew was concerned. I got ribbed a fair bit, but most of them accepted the fact that this was only going to be a tryout. However, when less than a month later I became a complete foreman over the fifty-eight-man crew and all of the equipment for eight hours of the day, that was a different story.

I got to drive a company pickup to and from work, but there was a lot more responsibility. Although I took my instructions from an instruction book that the general foreman and engineers had written up for each shift, I still had responsibility for the cooperation of the crew and the availability of the equipment. The union did not like the decision personnel made by choosing me to be a foreman. Now, I was considered part of personnel and not just a union worker. At first I got a lot of complaining and it was hard for me to get any production out of them. I am sure the union shop steward was encouraging them to slow down production.

I went to the personnel office and talked with the head guys and they told me that it was my job to find a way to get them to work better. They told me that whenever a man refused to follow instructions, I was to write a reprimand slip and hand it to him. I thought that would only create a bigger problem for me, so I took the approach of talking with my key production men, like the shovel operators. In our conversation I would tell one that in my opinion the other shovel operator could load more trucks than he could. As a result it created a little bit of a rivalry and he worked to prove that he could load more trucks than the other. I would praise them for their efforts and as a result they were starting to take more pride in their work. It wasn't long before they were starting to load five or ten minutes before the hour in order to get the jump on the other operator. I told my key cat operators that some of the operators on the other shifts were really good and could move more rock in eight hours than we could. Before long our production was starting to show an increase. I did likewise with my drillers.

It wasn't long before my general foreman noticed the increase in our production. He talked to the production engineer and they called me into the office. They asked me how many reprimands I had written out, commenting that it must have made a difference because they had noticed my production was up. I told them that I hadn't written one. George asked, "What are you doing then, because I see the shovels are swinging ten minutes before the hour? That is a first; I have *never* seen that happen before."

I told them that was my little secret. But they wouldn't accept that answer and they insisted I tell them how I managed to get more production out of my crew. I told them that I had created pride in them and got them to believe they were the best crew on the mountain. One engineer looked at the other and said, "You know, I think he even believes that."

George's response was, "He has every right to believe it too, because if you look at the timesheets they are bringing more loads off the mountain than any other shift, and some of the other shifters have been doing this work for ten years."

I guess they had a talk with the other shifters and told them that my shift was out-producing them. One shifter even promised his crew that he would buy them all a drink at the bar if they could out-produce our shift. And sure enough, they did by twenty-five loads. That really didn't bother me much, but that was the last time I would tell anyone, even my biggest boss, my secret. At a later date, Dwayne Howard, our production manager, came to me and told me the other shift had not out-produced us. They'd been making "paper" loads up and the shovels hadn't been filling up the trucks.

He forewarned me not to fall into that trap. He said that the engineers had been surveying the face the shovels and loaders had been loading and they noticed the discrepancy in the tonnage and came to that conclusion. They had also learned from other sources that the shovels were not filling the trucks properly and that paper loads had been made up to make their shift look good.

I also worked to create better communication between the repair shop and myself. When they called for a cat or a truck so they could do a PM (preventative maintenance), I encouraged them to have a machine available at the shop to replace it with. This gave me a chance to maintain better flow on my production chart. If I was down on manpower, I called the shop and asked them if we had a machine that was close to a PM. If we did, I'd make the machine available to them then. Things were going good and I had my crew really swinging.

I took time off to go back and make my farm sale and make arrangements to sell the rest of my wheat. I had prearranged a date with the auction market for the sale of my farm equipment and anything else that I needed to get rid of. I had to find a buyer for the farm as well. That was the hardest thing for me to do. I felt so empty inside when I made the final decision to sell the land. The farm sale went really well and I had no complaints. It was on a cold day in early April but in spite of that it drew a large crowd.

The Stettler auctioneers at my farm sale

We were at Stettler for less than a week, and in that short time Gloria's asthma flared up again and she stayed in the car during the sale because she couldn't breathe well enough to be out and around. When we went back to Elkford, it took antibiotics to finally get her back on her feet.

There was one thing I had not let go of and that was the full-blood Limos I had imported. I kept them on a farm in the Daysland/Strome area and paid the Houchousens to take care of them for me.

A few months after Christmas, I got a call from Houchousens. They said a fellow from Oklahoma was coming to look at the first full-blood heifer calf from my imported cow, Fantasy. They felt that I should be there because he would probably want to buy it. We packed up the family and made a quick trip back to central Alberta. When I got there, Gene Benatal from Oklahoma Cattle Company had already bought three younger Limos from the Houchousen brothers.

My little calf was just two months old and I hadn't even seen it. Gene asked me if it was for sale and I told him I everything was for sale depending on how much he wanted to pay. In one way I did not want to sell it because I was still living with the dream of raising Limousin cattle; however, I knew that I could not have someone else doing that for me forever. So I told him that for $17,000 he could have that scrappy little thing in the barn.

He said, "You Canadians sure are hard to deal with," and he went out to take a look at it again. Joe Houchousen told me I should have asked more because I had just sold my first full-blood Limousin. Gene came back into the house and wrote out a check for 60 percent of the price. The remaining 40 percent would be paid later when the heifer passed all quarantine tests. When he registered the calf, he called it *Fantasie of Antypowich*. Because of the sale of that young heifer calf, there were eventually cattle of my Limousin bloodlines in eight different states in the US. Gene Benatal put her in a multiple ovulation program, and as a result the registered offspring showed that they came from "Fantasie of Antypowich 3D."

John and Kathy Lewis, owners of Lewis Cattle Company at Kingsbury Texas, were one of the breeders who used an embryo of "Fantasie of Antypowich 3D" in their breeding program. She was registered as Pure Fantasie, J18H.

Woodhaven Limousin, owned by R. C. Loudermilk, Sr. at Coolidge, Georgia had a significant donor program that also included a heifer out of Fantasie of Antypowich 3D. That heifer was registered as Pure Lark.

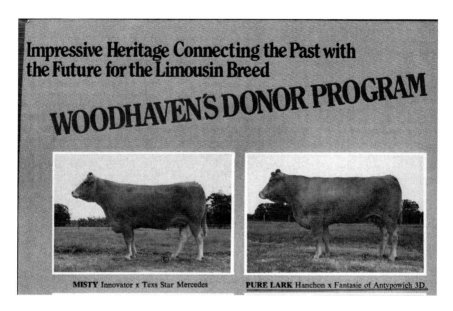

Impressive Heritage Connecting the Past with the Future for the Limousin Breed

WOODHAVEN'S DONOR PROGRAM

MISTY Innovator x Texs Star Mercedes   PURE LARK Hanchon x Fantasie of Antypowich 3D

When I went back to work, I got a big surprise. I was going to have a new crew to run. They gave me another shift with a crew of troublemakers and the union shop steward, a crew that had made things difficult for the other shift bosses. I think there was a little bit of strategy on the management's behalf.

They knew that once I had sold the farm I was not likely to quit. They took me into the personnel office and told me that they expected I'd have some problems but that they thought I would be able to handle them. I said thanks a lot and asked how much more they were going to pay me. They just laughed at me and said they were grooming me for further down the road. They me warned me to be very careful not to lose my temper and to never hit an employee no matter how badly they got under my skin. I was told to consult with them whenever I had a problem and they would help me out.

I could tell the first day when I gave the orders to the crew in the dry they were going to be a handful. To make things worse for me, my cross shift waited right until the end of shift to make their blast. That meant that my crew had to move all the equipment back into position, and that entailed a lot of cable pulling, which the men did not like to do. They all went up the mountain on the man bus and just sat there. I kept the two shovel operators in my pickup, and when I went to the man bus I walked in and handed out a bunch of brand-new gloves that I'd gotten from the warehouse. I asked them to come out to start moving the machines back into position. They threw their gloves on the floor and said their shift didn't pull cable. If I wanted somebody to pull cable, I could get another crew.

I left them there to think about it while I drove around to get a look at the situation of the blast and decided where each machine would start to work. When I went back to the bus they were still sitting there. I walked in and said, "Look, guys, there is no room on D shift for any lazy bastards." The shop steward jumped up and said, "See, I told you I'd get him!" Then he told the bus driver to turn the bus around and go back down to the dry because this was a wobble.

I jumped into my pickup, turned around, and beat them down to the dry. I informed the personnel office that we had a wobble on our hands. They asked me what happened and I told them just what I said and how I said it. They went over it again with me, making sure exactly what had happened and that I'd said exactly what I'd told them. Then the production foreman just laughed like everything and said to me, "You just might have the easiest shift of your life."

The bus came down off the mountain and the whole crew marched into the conference room. The shop steward for the union told the engineer from the personnel office that they had wobbled on the grounds I used abusive language on the crew and they wanted me relieved from my position. The staff from the personnel office went into a meeting with the men. They heard them out and then asked me to come in. They asked me what I said to make these men so upset. I told them exactly what I had said and how I said it. They then asked the shop steward if that was exactly what I said. He said, "Yes, he called us all a bunch of lazy bastards." The mine engineer asked, "Well, are you?" And the shop steward said, "Of course not." Then the engineer asked why they'd refused to go to work with the orders that I had given them.

The shop steward hemmed and hawed at bit and then the engineer said, "From what you've told me, Lloyd didn't say you were lazy bastards. He said there was no room for any lazy bastards on D shift. You have ten minutes to get on the bus to go up the mountain and go to work according to his instructions, or I will write out a three-day reprimand for every one of you."

The personnel and I left the conference room and we waited for their reply. In about five minutes the shop steward came out and said they would all go to work. It was a very long, slow shift and I was glad when it was over.

The next day before the shift left the dry, I called my crew into the conference room. The personnel people were aghast. They had no idea what I was going to do. When we all got into the room, the general foreman came in, wanting to know if I had a problem. I told him no and asked him to leave the room because what I had to say was to be just between the crew and myself.

I addressed the crew as their foreman. I told them that they may not like me but I was hired to run their crew and had no dislike for any one of them. The fact that I was in charge for eight hours of work meant I would be the only one that would be giving them instructions. If anyone else tried to tell them what to do they were to come and see me immediately. I was their foreman and I had very high regards for every one of them and their ability to do the job, and if anybody tried to interfere with my crew they were going to have to go through me first. I was there to not only give them instructions but I personally also had the attitude that I would protect and work for them to the best of my ability. With that, I asked them if they would all go to work and have a good day.

It had a good effect on at least 75 percent of the crew. But the diehard union boys were slow to come around. The shop steward for the union was the nut I had to crack. And no matter how hard I tried to show them that I was there to stand up for their rights as well, he would always try to cause a problem. He only wanted to get even with the company. He would get the truck drivers to shut their tucks down on the grounds that some mechanical device was unsafe to operate.

That only lasted a short while, because when the truck was taken down to the shop to be checked out and nothing was wrong with it, I told the driver that if he tried that again I would write him out a reprimand. It would go on his record of dependability. If he really liked his job, he should do it and not get talked into doing things by the shop steward that had no credibility. I only had to write a few reprimands out before it started to sink in that they could be demoted from truck driver to the pushing boom in the shop.

I guess it would be fair to say that I literally picked on the shop steward, and every time he made a mistake I wrote him a reprimand. Believe it or not, you might not be able to fire an employee because of the union, but you sure can demote them. The shop steward was an oiler on one of the shovels and he didn't have many man hours to go before he became a full-fledged shovel operator.

I called him on the radio and asked him to come off the shovel so I could talk to him. He came down without his hardhat or safety glasses on. He asked me what I wanted and told him that I had something to give him. Then I handed him a reprimand for not wearing his safety glasses or hardhat. He got so mad and accused me of picking on him.

He was kind of lazy, and each oiler was required to keep the inside of the shovel clean. This house cleaning was usually done just before shift change. I would go into the shovel about mid-shift and make a couple of marks in the dust on the swing motors with my finger. At shift change I would check and see if he had done his house cleaning. If he didn't have it done when he turned his timecard in, I would have a reprimand slip all ready and hand it to him. That was how I built a stack of reprimands eight inches high on him. When I asked the personnel office how big a pile they needed, they said quite few. I handed them what I had and asked if that was enough. They demoted him right down to the shop pushing a broom.

One day, Dwayne Howard called me on the radio just before a shift change and asked me to hurry and come down to the dry. I had no idea what he wanted, but seeing he was my general foreman, I went. My lead hand was quite capable of finishing the shift. When I got to the dry, Dwayne came out to meet me. He said, "You'll never guess what has just happened." I had no idea. He said, "Look around."

On the dry floor was a hardhat and a lunch kit that was open, its contents spilled on the floor. I was still puzzled. I knew that that was not what he had called me down to see. He took me in his office and told me he had been sitting there going over some paperwork when the shop steward had come in. Dwayne said he couldn't believe it. He was half crying and swearing and threw his lunch kit and hardhat on the floor, saying that he was quitting this blankedy-blank company. Then he went into the change room to shower and change.

Dwayne said, "I haven't told anyone else yet. I thought I should tell you first. I could just see the big tears rolling down your cheeks." We had a good laugh, and I asked him if he was sure. He said, "I was sitting right here listening to him talk to himself and that is what he said."

Sure enough, he did quit, and after that the crew came together much better. I defended them on several occasions and I think most of them appreciated it. It was hard to match the production that I had accomplished with my first crew, but we were never very far behind.

One day when we had just done a blast and had about half of the equipment moved back into position before shift change, my crew came down off the mountain and the oncoming crew had just gone up. I had tallied all the timecards with my lead hand and left the mine to go home. When we got down to the town site, we got word that the spoil had sloughed; in fact, it had gone all the way to the bottom, crossed the haul road, and covered two 631 Caterpillar buggies that were parked at least 200 yards below the haul road. It was a miracle that no one was killed, because shift change was a busy time on the haul road. We were off on a long change, so our crew did not get back to help clean up a lot of the mess, but it shut down production for the better part of a week until it was certain that the spoil had stabilized enough to put the equipment back on it.

When my shift came back, things were still pretty slow and there wasn't a lot that we could do. We operated the drills but the engineers didn't want to have too much traffic on the haul road until they were sure the spoil had stabilized. The engineers came up with the big idea that we might be able to slough the part that kept moving all the time, so they converted two fifty-ton rock trucks into water trucks. Their idea was that if we pumped enough water fast enough onto that part of the spoil it would probably slough by itself.

The problem was we needed to connect a twelve-inch discharge plastic pipe about 300 or 400 meters down the spoil in order to get the water in the right place. The big question was who was going down there and make that connection. It seemed no one would volunteer to do the job, so the next day, Dwayne Howard (my general foreman) asked me if I would go with him to do it. He'd asked all the other foremen and they'd refused. Big Dwayne was originally from the Lethbridge area and knew what it meant to be called a stubble jumper, but he was a good man and a good foreman, and I kind of considered him a friend.

He told me how dangerous it could be and said that he in no way was trying to twist my arm. I told him God hates a coward and we would get the job done. So when the trucks were full of water and parked at the top of the spoil, we crawled over the edge and took one section of plastic pipe, a coupler, and some tools with us. When we were about halfway through the job, we heard a strange noise that sounded like the rock was slipping; at least, in our minds that was what it sounded like.

I looked at Dwayne, and if my eyes looked like his, they must have looked like two Oreo cookies. We breathed a sigh of relief when we realized that a Canada goose had flown by and was making a weird honk. Dwayne said, "Let's get this done and get the hell out of here." We finished in no time flat and crawled back up to the top of the spoil and told the guys on the trucks to turn the water on.

As soon as one truck was empty, it would go and fill up while the other truck was unloading. They dumped out a lot of water to no avail, so the engineers gave up on that idea and devised a monitor that would tell them how fast the spoil was settling. We started to dump rock back on the area that was most stable, making sure the trucks stayed back from the edge and pushing the loads over with the cats. The spoil continued to settle all summer long. We moved from one area to the other and kept dumping rock on it. Eventually it seemed to stabilize and we didn't have any more problems.

British Columbia Department of Mines and Petroleum Resources

SURFACE MINE RESCUE WORK

This

Certificate of Competency

is awarded to

Lloyd F. Antypowich of **Elkford, B.C.**

for efficiency in Surface Mine Rescue Work, he having taken a course of training under the supervision of the Department of Mines and Petroleum Resources.

Dated this **7th** day of **February**, **19 73**.

Albert Little
INSTRUCTOR.

INSPECTOR OF MINES.

CHIEF INSPECTOR OF MINES. MINISTER OF MINES AND PETROLEUM RESOURCES.

My surface mine rescue work certificate of competency

Gloria was doing real good healthwise, having virtually no symptoms of asthma. I sold the trailer and we moved into a house in the town of Elkford. We had a nice split-level on a cul-de-sac. I went to Ferny and bought a brand-new Ford Country Squire station wagon, which gave us a lot more room than the two-door car we had. It was the first brand-new vehicle I'd owned since I left Valleyview. It cost $6,800 and was a top-of-the-line vehicle.

That fall I was given a new challenge. I was made foreman of the big Marion dragline in the Green Hills. Up until then I had been working the area known as Cload.

The Marion dragline; note the three men standing on the shoe of the dragline *The Marion dragline bucket at work*

The dragline had a sixty-five-yard bucket. It could dig eighty-five feet deep. The boom was 305 feet long, and from the ground to the top of the point chives (a pulley that the cable runs through) was 150 feet; the house was 300 feet long. It moved on two eccentric arms to which two huge shoes were attached. They were sixteen feet wide and sixty feet long. It sat on a huge round tub, and when it moved it was in steps of ten feet at a time. From dig to dump was 700 feet. The maximum grade it could crawl was 10 percent, and moving the dragline out for a blast took a full shift.

When we needed a tooth changed on the bucket, we called the blasting crew and they would blast the pins out, and a high-ab would maneuver another tooth in place.

It was totally run by electricity and it really was quiet. Inside the machine you only heard the humming noise of the big electric motors. The operator's house was fairly quiet and very stable; you could set a coffee cup on the control panel and not spill it while making a complete swing.

The bucket was big enough that the D8 could back right inside it and rip the frost that froze in it. It could also pick up that D8 with a U blade with all the heavy rock guard without any problem. I was told the machine weighed 8,000,000 pounds and that it cost a dollar a pound before it was assembled. It was clearly an amazing piece of equipment.

My job was not nearly as demanding because I only had a small crew to look after. The machine had an oiler that could operate a D8 cat to help level the pad for the dragline to sit on. It took an operator with a good eye to level an area for that machine. As well we had two electricians that stayed in the machine most of the time, along with two mechanics and the operator. That was the extent of my crew.

I enjoyed looking after the dragline. When I first went to the Green Hills, the operator on the dragline was a guy by the name of Eddie DeLauro. I believe he was of Portuguese descent and had quite an accent.

The logging company that had been hired to remove all the timber in the path of the dragline had not removed the trees yet. In my instruction book, the engineers said to work up to the timber and then shut the dragline down.

When we reached the timber, I asked Eddie what would happen if he let the bucket hit a few of the trees when he was on a backward swing. I don't know if he had done it before, but he put the bucket about forty feet above the ground and just mowed over the spruce trees like they were rhubarb. Since we were operating on nightshift, I felt quite safe harvesting a little spruce with the overburden. Eddie was having a blast knocking down some of the big trees. I told him not to knock any more down than what we could clean up before the end of our shift.

In the morning we had uncovered an area approximately 300 by 300 feet of coal. The overburden was quite soft and easy digging. Eddie would drop the bucket teeth down on the bigger trees and just chop them into pieces. He cleaned all the wood and debris off first and then piled the dirt on top of it. It looked like a real good job of stripping because you couldn't see any trees sticking out of the stripping pile. I'm not sure if the engineers ever figured out what we had done, but Kootenay Logging made sure they kept far enough ahead of us from then on.

After I was there for a while, Wally Jackson began training on the dragline. He had been a shovel operator before and caught on very fast. It wasn't very long before he operated it by himself.

Wally Jackson (in the dark hardhat), looking up, and Stan Fisher, the maintenance supervisor, on the boom of the Marion dragline

Wally and I were both on the same shift then and on days off we could go up into the mountains together. We explored a lot of country up the Elk Valley. We would go hunting or fishing on our days off. It was a good thing our wives were friends and did a lot together. They often complained, and every once in a while we were really in trouble for not doing more with them and our families

John Valentie riding the horse; Wally Jackson looking on

Packed up and moving out for a four-day adventure into the mountains. Wally is a Métis who proudly recognizes his Indian heritage and is saluting with his forbearer's stance.

One nice night in June, we were on our first nightshift and I was on the dragline with Wally, discussing the plans that were laid out for us in the instruction book, when Romeo Dosseler, the shifter from up on Cload, called for me to come to the carpenter shop. I told him I'd be there in a little while.

Wally and I were still discussing things when he called again and said, "What are you doing? Hurry up and get over here." I knew he was up to one of his tricks, and Wally said, "He's just going to con you into helping him load some standards to take back up to the top of the mountain." I told Wally I'd be back, but I'd better go and see what he needed me for. When I got there he had loaded the standards on his truck already and said to me, "Can you see him?" I said, "See what?"

He said, "Look over by the empty soap barrels behind the wash bay." And sure enough, there was about a 300-pound black bear. Since it was such a nice evening, I knew there would be some shop doors left open, and some of the mechanics would be nursing a big head after a long shift change. I told Romeo we should see if we could chase him into the shop. I parked my truck beside the barrels and Romeo bumped them with his pickup. The bear came out from behind them just scratching. I kept him right beside my door and took him around the corner, and sure enough the second bay door was open. I heard Romeo on his radio asking, "Did you get him?" I told him to hurry up, that I thought he had just gone into the shop.

I jumped out of my pickup to see how much commotion the bear was going to cause in there. By that time he'd already knocked over a couple of Snap-on toolboxes and was coming back, looking for a way to get out of the shop. Romeo and I threw our hardhats at him and he ran underneath a big rock truck, where two mechanics were working on a wheel motor. He hit their toolbox and just knocked it right over. I am sure they thought they were hallucinating because there was a black bear just scratching the cement floor, trying to get going and get out of there. He made several more rounds in the shop, and by this time all the mechanics were up on the machines.

I don't know who got word to the shop dispatcher, but he came up to the big plate-glass window of his office to see what all the commotion was. The bear spotted that big window and must've taken it for a hole in the wall. He just made for it as fast as he could go, and as he thought he was going to jump through it, he did a spread-eagle right in front of the shop dispatcher. The poor guy damn near had a heart attack.

By this time the security guard arrived. We decided it was time to step aside and let the bear go. It barrelled out the door just as fast as it had come in. We stuck around for just a little while and asked what all the commotion was. Then we got the hell out of there before anyone realized we were part of it.

When I got back into my truck, there was a lot of traffic on the radio, and it wasn't long before somebody put things together and blamed Romeo and I for all the commotion. Everybody but the security guard seemed to get a big joke out of it; he went to the personnel office first thing in the morning and told them that he thought Romeo or I had something to do with it.

In the morning, just before our shift change I was called into the personnel office to explain what all the commotion with the black bear had been about that night. I told them apparently a black bear got into the shop through one of the open doors. They wanted to know what part I had played in the situation. I asked them if they'd ever tried to get a scared black bear out of the shop. They looked at me, kind of grinned, and asked if we were trying to get him out or put him in.

I told them they could ask Romeo. Romeo said, of course, we were trying to get him out; we had even thrown our hardhats at him. And then Romeo jumped on them and said it was their responsibility to make sure the doors were kept closed so no more bears could get into the shop. The next day there was a big memo up in the shop and the dry, stating that no sandwiches could be left lying around the carpenter shop and all doors had to be closed on nightshift. We all got a big laugh out of that, except for some of the mechanics, because even when it got really warm they had to keep the doors closed. It didn't last long before they were back to leaving the doors open again and I didn't blame them.

After a while, work kind of got boring, and even the shift bosses looked for little pranks to play just to throw a bit of life into the work. For example, one day when the electricians were coming down from Cload they found a moose licking salt on the haul road. They chased it down the road, right to the grisly where the trucks dumped the raw coal. The moose got scared, jumped over the edge, and ran down to where a long conveyor belt went up to the raw coal piles. I guess it thought it could jump over the belt, but instead it landed right in the middle of the conveyor and it took the moose right up to the top of the coal pile. There were some tracks coming down the coal pile and the engineers could not figure out what made them. It was quite a while before the truth got out, and once again there was a big memo in the book. Don't ever get caught chasing moose, elk, or bear on the mine site.

In this picture the conveyer belt is seen running along the right side next to the loader beside large piles of raw coal

Some days in the middle of the summer it would get uncomfortably warm and dusty. It was wonderful to get off shift and go into the shower before we went home. As the days and months carried on it wasn't too long before I was looking for a new challenge. The work was repetitious: you drilled, filled the holes first with a detonator hooked to a primer cord that was tied in series. Next you would have the slurry truck fill the holes, and then cover them with tailings. After that you moved all the equipment out and a blaster came and detonated. After that you had to move all the equipment back in and remove the blasted rock from the coal seam. Then you would push the coal down to the shovel, and two huge front end loaders would load the coal onto the big coal trucks and they would haul it down the mountain to the grisly, where it would separate any rock from the coal. From there it went into big long coal piles and after that the plant would retrieve it and run it through, separating any small rock and debris and blended it into various ash contents to be acceptable for shipment to Japan.

Once a month the shift bosses would have to meet with the big bosses and engineers. They would tell us what they thought of how we managed all the men and equipment for them. And usually it was not good enough. They always complained about not having enough production for the amount of equipment that we were using. So I decided I'd do some homework and find out what our recovery rate was after it had gone through the plant so I'd have something to present to them at the next meeting.

Something that had been a concern to me for a while was that the settling pond looked like it was filling up too fast. I got to know the plant manager because he lived on the same street as I did. He told me they had a lot more kinks to work out of the plant. Their recovery rate was only 47 percent. That was what I was looking for. At the next meeting the big guy from Cominco at Trail, British Columbia was there to sit in on our meeting. I guess the mine production manager was trying to make a real impression on him, and was really lowering the boom on us shift bosses for not making enough production.

I resented being treated that way, so after he was done giving us a real shellacking I got up and said that I didn't appreciate being told that I didn't know what I was doing. I thought I'd been doing a reasonably good job on the production end of things; and if I wasn't, then I'd have appreciated having someone point out how I could do better. The production manager said, "All I'm telling you is that you can be doing a lot better and our production is just going to have to increase or we will have to be looking at better supervision."

Now he really got my dander up. I stood up again and said there were a few things I thought we should clarify there that day and if I was wrong, I wanted him to tell me so and find someone else to replace me. Then I asked him what the recovery rate of the plant was. He didn't reply, so I looked at the man from Trail and said, "Here's my point, it doesn't matter how much production we bring off that mountain if the recovery rate is too low."

He said, "You are making some big accusations that I am very interested in. First of all, what makes you think the recovery rate is not good enough?"

I told him I was watching the settling pond, and from my eyeball estimation it was filling up much too fast and that soon we would be looking at building up the settling pond if it continued happening at the pace it was going.

The production engineer asked me if I'd like to explain myself. He said that I had nothing to do with the plant. My job was to make more production for the company.

I stood up again and told them that I might not be considered a miner yet, but I was a farmer and I knew I could have a bumper crop of wheat. But if I didn't have my combine properly set I could be dumping 25 percent or 50 percent back on the ground. In my estimation it was clear that this mine operated very much like my farming operation.

I looked at the guy from Trail and said I hoped he could follow what I was getting at and I would like to know what the recovery rate of that plant really was as of that day. The meeting got very tense and quiet. You could have heard a pin drop. The guy from Trail turned to the production engineer and asked him what the recovery rate of the plant was. He tried to beat around the bush, but the guy from Trail would have none of it and told him point blank to just tell him what the recovery rate was. When he finally admitted that it was only 47 percent, there was quite a little stir in the room.

The shift boss that I had worked for when I started at the mine was sitting next to me. He gave me the elbow and said, "Do you kind of get the feeling there may be a holiday coming?"

I said, "So be it." He said, "I think you just stepped on somebody who has big toes, and I don't think he will appreciate that."

They were about to call a halt to the meeting when big George, our production foreman, said he had one thing that he wanted to tell all the shift bosses. According to him, we were having far too much breakage on the big truck tires. He said too often the haul road had big boulders on it that had fallen off the trucks and it was the responsibility of the shift boss to see that the haul roads were properly graded.

One of the shifters said, "What do you want us to do, shut down hauling because a grader has been taken down to the shop for an hour?" George said, "I've yet to see a shift boss get out of his truck to roll a rock off the road. In fact, I would gold plate it if I saw one." With that, the meeting came to an end.

I walked back to my office in the dry to help my lead hand tally up the timecards and make a report of our daily progress. I think the guy from Trail was putting a little pressure on the production engineer and maybe even some of the other top personnel. There is no doubt I may have overstepped my responsibility, but now that I had it off my chest I really couldn't say I felt sorry or regretted saying what I had.

We were about ready to walk out to the dry when the general foreman asked me to step into his office. He said to me, "I don't know if you were looking for a promotion or a walking ticket, but the guy from Trail was asking a few questions about you. I thought I should let you know that tomorrow after your shift is over you will probably be called into the personnel office for some kind of meeting." I asked if that was going to be good or bad and he said he wouldn't worry too much. He'd rather be in my shoes than in the production engineers.

I heard the guy from Trail probed the office all day and apparently he was not too happy with some of the things he found. After my shift was over I was asked to come to the personnel office. When I went in I asked them how long this meeting was going to take, because if it was more than just a few minutes I'd like to tell the other foreman and lead hand that they shouldn't wait for me. One of the engineers said they would see that I got a pickup truck to go home in later. When I went to tell them that they should go home, Tom asked, "What are they going to do, fire you or promote you?"

I told him I would let him know in the morning, and went back into the office. I sat down and the guy from Trail asked me how long I'd been working for this company. I told him about two and a half years. Then he asked me in what capacity. I told him, I had started as a cat skinner, and then worked as a lead hand, and for the past year and a half I'd been in the capacity of the senior shifter. He asked me what my responsibilities were and I told him that they were the same as any other shift boss, but personally I couldn't help but look beyond my eight-hour shift. I told him it wasn't my intention to create any waves or create any problems for anyone, but I had been wrongly accused of not making enough production. I assured him that I spoke strictly on my behalf and not for any of the other shifters.

He asked me if I enjoyed my work, and I told him it wasn't my first love, but yes, I did enjoy it. He asked what my first love was and I told him I would rather be a rancher somewhere in the mountains than a coal miner. He asked me how long I had been farming and ranching and I told him about twelve years. He asked me to tell him a little bit more about my combine; he had kind of found that interesting when I spoke of it earlier. So I explained the process of setting up the combine to get the maximum production out of the crop and still keep the grain as clean as possible.

After he asked me if I enjoyed my work, the thought did run through my mind that I was going to be terminated, but so be it.

He said it was quite interesting that I saw this mining operation as being similar to running my farm, because he admitted it sounded like there was a lot of similarity. He said he could tell that I had the experience of weighing profit and loss. He then asked me who told me what the recovery rate of the plant was. I told him that I wouldn't tell him; in fact, I didn't even know if it was true until yesterday. He said that I had to go out of my way a bit to gather that information, and I told him not really, I just had to ask the right people. I learned that the present settling pond was designed to last ten years under normal conditions, but at the present rate things were going, we could only have a couple of years left.

He thanked me for being so observant, and said I was the youngest personnel there and no one else had brought to his attention the fact that the settling pond was filling up too quickly. He told me he didn't mean to throw cold water on any of my ideas, but sometimes we could step over the bounds of our responsibilities and it could be very offensive to some people. However, in this situation he wanted to commend me on my alertness and sense of responsibility.

He told me that there were some big adjustments to be made and he said he could assure me that they would be made soon. Then he asked me if there is anything that he could do to make mining my first love. I told him I didn't think so at the moment, but that as long as I worked for Fording Coal my attitude would stay the same. He said, "Young feller, I think you are on the right track and don't let anybody step in your way. We are glad to have you work for us at Fording Coal."

When I went back to my office in the dry, there was no one around. Everyone else was out working and the shift boss offices were empty. I just sat there collecting my thoughts when Dwayne Howard came in. He asked, "Well, Lloyd, what did you think of the meeting?" I told him I was just trying to put some of my thoughts together and wasn't sure I had it all figured out yet. "Well," he said, "I don't think you have anything to worry about. In fact, you should be quite proud of the compliments that were given to you. But I sure wouldn't want to be in the production engineers' position."

I said I was concerned about him, because I knew I had not made a friend with him in any way shape or form and I expected he might look for reasons to relieve me of my job. Dwayne told me to just stick around awhile and I would see the day when that engineer would walk down the road. Apparently it had been discovered that he received a very large kickback for having selected the Marion Dragline for the company; not that the machine wasn't good, but it was the way that it was purchased that was so wrong.

He told me that some of the truck drivers on other shifts had been running over big stones and were breaking the cords in the tires. Each tire cost over $6,000 apiece. He warned me to make sure I kept the corners clean because that's where the trucks were spilling the rocks, and that if I needed to I should put a cat or a loader on to clean the rocks off the road.

Well, guess what? One day, even though I had a grader on the road, a truck spilled some rocks before the grader could get there and clean them off, and who should come along but big George. He got on the radio where everyone could hear, even down in the personnel office, and he asked me to get them big "donikers" off the haul road before a truck ran them over and wrecked the tires. That was the only place on the haul road that there was a rock. I drove there with my pickup and was so pissed off that I got out, picked up the rock, and loaded it into the back of my truck. Tom, my lead hand asked me where the rocks were, because he had just come up the road and there was nothing on it. I told him that the truck was loaded a little bit to one side and lost the rock.

Tom said he would call the grader and make sure that it cleaned off the road. I told him not to bother because I had already removed it. He asked how I did that, and I told him I threw the damn thing in my truck. He looked at it and said he could never have picked that rock up. I told him he'd never seen me mad before. He asked what I was going to do with it and I said, "This one is for George." At the change of shift I backed my pickup to the side door. Seeing that George was not in his office, I carried that big dirty old rock inside and sat it right on top of all the papers and stuff on his desk. Then I grabbed a notepad and wrote, "George, please gold-plate this one for me. Lloyd."

The damn thing was so heavy it almost gave me a rupture. I honestly don't know how I managed to pick it up off the ground and put it in the truck. I went into my office to help Tom do up cards and write in the instruction book about our daily happenings. I hoped that George would soon come along, but he was in the personnel office, and so we just showered and went home.

The next day Dwayne Howard told me that George got two guys to try to carry out the rock, but they dropped it on the floor and it broke in several pieces. He didn't believe that I carried it in myself. George took it all in good stride. The next day, he said to me, "Jesus, man, did you have to get such a big one." I told him the next time to be more careful what he said on that damn radio. He never gold-plated a rock for me, not even a small one.

Everything seemed to carry on as normal as could be expected at the mine. Gradually the plant maintained a better recovery rate, and as a result of us moving down the mountain with every blast, the pit floors became larger, the seams bigger, and the haul became shorter. The number four seam that we had found near the top of the mountain was picked up again at the 5,400-foot level. We had started at 7,000 feet and run into a major fault in the number four seam. It was quite interesting to eventually prove that it was the same seam of coal. The ash content was exactly the same and the depth of the seam was very much the same as up near the top of the mountain. Interestingly, you could find small fossils embedded in black shale that lay between the coal and the bedrock.

The dragline continued to keep swinging; first, stripping overburden, and then digging out the coal seams and stockpiling them in a huge pile of a hundred feet or more. Then a Latternau L700 with a sixteen-yard bucket would load the 150-ton trucks so they could haul it to the plant.

Every now and again we would run into a water seam, where the water would come gushing in. It was important to keep the coal dry so we would use big flight pumps mounted on a steel platform with four forty-five-gallon drums used as pontoons. Actually I thought the pumps were a real pain in the butt.

One day we hit a real gusher. The dragline operator had just uncovered a huge seam sixty feet thick when the water came gushing into the pit. We were just finishing dayshift and were going on our three-day break. The engineers were going to figure out a way to get the flight pumps down into a pit that was approximately seventy feet deep and 350 feet wide and at least 400 or 500 hundred feet long.

When I came back on graveyard shift, the instructions in our book were to keep the dragline shut down until the engineers figured a way to get the water pumped out. I have a hard time just sitting around and doing nothing, so I had my operator walk the dragline back 300 feet, dig a ramp down to the water, and use the material to build a dam across the pit about 100 feet from the coal seam.

We put the D8 cat in the bucket and lowered it into the pit so the cat operator could spread the material to make the dam. Once I had a dam about twenty feet high, I brought the cat back up out of the pit. Then I had the dragline operator move ahead a few hundred feet and start bailing out the water with the dragline. A sixty-yard bucket makes for a pretty big dipper, and before long we had a dry coal seam again. Then we moved ahead a little more and started digging coal. We had a pile about forty feet high by the end of the nightshift. I guess when the big brass came into the mine site and saw the dragline swinging they had a real conniption fit. I was in the dragline talking to Wally when the radio called for me. I said go ahead. There was a long pause, and then they asked if I had read my instructions. I said, "Yes, sir, I sure did." They said I seemed to be bailing coal and I said, "Yes, sir, I sure am." Then they asked if I didn't know that the coal couldn't be mixed with the water. I said, "Yes, sir, I sure do."

There was another long pause and then they asked how I could keep the coal dry with all the water that was coming into the pit. I said, "Maybe you better come and have a look." Right shortly there were two engineers and the production foreman at the dragline. I saw them coming, so I went out to meet them at my pickup.

The first thing the production engineer said to me was, "You know that the coal must be kept dry at all times." I said, "I sure do." He asked, "Well, how the hell can it be dry if you are digging it out of the water?" I walked to my pickup and called my dragline operator on the radio and asked him to stop his swing so that the engineers could go in and check the coal. They did and the engineers both said there was nothing wrong with the coal. They then walked over to the pit and saw what I had done.

The production engineer asked me how long I thought the dam was going to hold. I told him that all depended on how long it took them to get that water out. The engineers said it was not that simple. When they had a sixty-foot seam of coal, they didn't want to ramp through it. So I took them to the ramp that I had instructed the dragline to dig and showed them that they could run right down the ramp.

He said, "But first you've got to get the pumps in the water." I told him that that wasn't a problem at all, that he could put the pumps in the dragline bucket and they could be put whatever he wanted. He asked me how I was going to get someone down to man them. My reply was that was a problem that they were going to have to solve because I had a shift change to look after right then, and I left them there.

I was in my office at the dry doing the timecards and making up my shift report when I was called into the personnel office. The production manager asked me when I was going to learn to follow instructions. I just looked at him for a bit and then said, "I guess when they make common sense." I knew the fight would be on, and he would be looking for every opportunity that he could to fire me.

He said, "I had plans to do a PM (preventative maintenance) on the dragline and now you have put it to work." I told him he had three days and nights to do the PM, and if he was planning to do a complete PM he needed a pile of coal or a berm to set the boom on, so I thought the pile that we had dug the previous night should be just about right.

He said, "That's not the point; you are to follow my instructions." I told him there was nothing in the book about doing a PM on the dragline. In the past we had always had a week's notice when we were going to do one.

Right about then big George came in. He had also seen the pile and drove right down to it before stopping at the office. When he came in he looked at me with kind of crazy grin and said, "Who engineered that for you?" I told him I had. He asked if I had read the instruction book. I told him I had, but I didn't know they were planning to do a PM on the dragline. He said "Oh no, we won't be doing a PM for at least two weeks."

I looked at him and said, "Thanks, George, you'll never know how big a favor you just did me." I told them that I couldn't keep the shifter truck waiting any longer and unless they had something more important to say I was going to have to leave. The next day Dwayne Howard came to me and asked how the cat tracks had gotten on the dam that I had built to keep the water from mixing in with the coal. I grinned and told him that that was going to have to be my secret.

He said, "Look, Lloyd. I have a pretty good idea but I'm not going to say a thing. I just want to warn you that Bob would sure like to pin something on you and that might be his ace. He will try to get you for unsafe working practices. You know you made a few people look a bit dumb when that the dragline had been sitting for three days and you put it to work on one graveyard shift. That will show up at Trail unless Bob can fudge those three days."

I thanked him and he said, "I owe you one, buddy." He was referring to the fact that I had crawled over the edge of the spoil and connected that water pipe for the engineers with him.

A few months later there was a shakeup in personnel. The production engineer was relieved of his duties, not that it really made a lot of difference to me. I got along real good with all the rest of the personnel and things just kept a rolling on.

CHAPTER 39

I Buy Some Cattle

Every month I would get the *Limousin Journal* and I yearned to get back into the cattle business more with each one that arrived. There was a sale coming up in Airdrie, Alberta of half-and-three-quarter blood Limousin heifers. I rented forty acres of good pastureland from Mike Barr. I told him that I had plans to buy a few cross-bred Limousin heifers and that I needed a place to keep them. I also told him that I might need some hay if I didn't find a bigger place to rent and he said he would have lots of hay if I needed it.

I went to the sale and bought fourteen head. Most of them were three-quarter blood Limos. Mike came to look at them as soon as they arrived. His comments were, "By the GD, them sure have a nice big hindquarter." Mike had a small herd of Hereford cows and was a pretty good judge of cattle.

Now I had something to do. I built a loading chute and the small corral. My big German shepherd Sparky almost loved me to death. He had never left the yard until I brought my horses and cows into the valley. Then I had to tie him at the house, because he would go down to where the animals were and he would just kind of herd them all day. He had a real desire to work livestock. He was very intelligent when it had anything to do with animals but he was as gentle as a teddy bear with anybody who came to my house.

Some of the cattle that I brought home from the sale

Eunice and Wally Jackson lived across the street from us. Eunice would call, "Sparky, I have a cookie for you," and he would go over and get it. It wasn't too long before he would go over on his own and scratch at the door. Then she would let him in and give him a cookie or a wiener. And one day she called me and told me she wanted me to see how smart my dog was. I went over and there was Sparky sitting in her kitchen. She asked him what he would like, a cookie or a wiener. He got up and went to the fridge, where she kept at package of wieners, and she said, "Oh, you want a wiener today," and he sat and begged her for it. She said sometimes he would decide he wanted a cookie and he would go to the cupboard where the cookies were. She had previously owned a German shepherd dog, and when she saw Sparky she just fell in love with him and spoiled him rotten.

Now I was a miner/rancher. I had my little herd of cows and my horses right in the valley next to Elkford town site. A few people bought their mares over to my stud to have them bred. There didn't seem to be any Appaloosas in the valley, and because both of my horses had good coloring, they were a conversation piece. I fed my cows that winter, and in the spring the heifers were heavy with calf. A lot of people wanted to go down and see the animals but I wasn't too comfortable with that idea because they knew nothing about cows or horses, and those Limos can be very protective mothers when their babies arrive.

Gloria had been going down to check on the heifers when I was at work. One night she got between a heifer and her calf while she was walking with a flashlight on and the heifer charged her and knocked her down. She rolled her around and beat her up quite badly. Luckily, her younger brother, Tommy, had gone with her that night. That cow was very determined. She could have killed Gloria had Tom not been there. After a lot of struggle he finally managed to beat the cow off with a fence post and help Gloria get to her feet and into the car.

Eunice Jackson called the mine and they called me on the radio and told me that I had an emergency at home. Tom, my lead hand, finished the rest of the shift for me. I went home as fast as I could and when I got there I immediately took Gloria to the Michelle Hospital near Fernie. When they saw her, they asked me if she had been in bar fight because she had cuts and scratches and bruises on her body and her coat was all dirty and torn. They kept her in overnight to just keep an eye on her.

That put an end to her checking the heifers. I was quite lucky and didn't have any calving problems. However, tagging and banding the little calves was a bigger job than I expected. First of all, I didn't have a very good setup and then I found out that those Limousin cows where very, very protective of their babies. There was no way that I could just go in and grab one and tag it without that mama trying to eat me. So I would rope a calf and drag it under the coral, tag, and vaccinate it and then push it back. Once the calves got a little older and the cows settled down, I could walk among them without any problem. The next big job that I had to do was to AI them, as I didn't have a bull. This was a real point of interest to a lot of people; they had never heard of doing that before. I think I made true believers out of a lot of them that I really was a rancher.

Wally and I spent a lot of time going up into the mountains. When hunting season opened, we knew just where to go to get our elk. One day we took my truck out to Little Weary Mountain and set up camp. We had planned to go right back home and pick up the horses but we decided to have a look for the elk we knew were there. Sure enough, there was a herd of seven cows and three bulls. We were looking for young animals, not big horns. There was a young spike bull, a four, and a five-point. So we decided to sneak up on them and take the spike and four-point.

By the time we got to where they were, they had moved into some thicker jack pine trees. Wally circled down a little lower and I stayed up above in case the elk decided to run back up the mountain. It wasn't long before Wally fired a shot. When I heard him chirp like a bird and I knew he had got one. I waited for a little while, and when nothing seemed to be coming my way, I started down to him. It was quite thick with small re-gen, and all of a sudden there was a lot of commotion. I stopped to listen, thinking it may have been an elk but instead I could smell some freshly digested huckleberries. I had flushed out a grizzly.

I quietly backed out of there and worked down toward Wally another way. He had shot a spike bull and was just starting to dress it out when I arrived. He asked what had taken me so long. I told him I had run into a grizzly. We finished dressing out the elk and looked up, and there on the side of the mountain was a five-point with the cows trailing behind him. He was a long ways away, so I aimed at a big rock in front of him and fired. I hit the rock and it scared them; they came running down the hill toward us. They came down a couple of hundred yards and stopped. I fired another shot and broke his neck. Even though we knew there were grizzly bears in the area near the kill, Wally was quite sure that they wouldn't touch our elk because of all the fresh scent of us being around. I wasn't so sure, but all we took was the heart and liver. We put it into our lunch bags and headed back to get the horses.

When we got back the next morning the horses did not want to go anywhere near where we had left the elk, so we tied them and slowly walked in. Sure enough, the spike bull was gone. We saw where the bear had covered up the elk, but then I guess he thought better and uncovered it and carried it up into the thick willows. Then we went to the five-point, and sure enough a grizzly had covered it with a huge pile of logs, grass, and dirt, and then he crapped on the pile and probably urinated on it as well.

Don't let anyone tell you that a grizzly won't try to steal a fresh kill from you. There were a lot of grizzlies in that area. I counted as many as nine from one spotting site. Although they are nice to see, they also make hunting a much bigger challenge, especially when you can't kill them. We had just fed two real good elk to the bears. If we hadn't taken the heart and liver off, no one would have believed that we had even shot those elk. But now we could get a chance to try and do it all over again.

The mine continued to operate fairly smoothly. Little things popped up from time to time but we took them all in stride and worked through them. There was talk that when the union contract was up at the end of the year, there would be a complete shutdown of the mine. I have to admit that although I am not a union man, I did have to join the steelworkers union in order to work there and the first contract that the union signed with the mine was a company contract. But I could never see the benefit of just wage increases. That was only going to put a lot of the employees into a higher tax bracket, and as a result they would take home very little more than what they were making before.

Since Elkford was a brand-new town situated in a very beautiful valley, I was much more inclined to bargain with the company for better recreational facilities and other facilities in general that would make the town more compact and complete. A minimal increase in wages would most likely be acceptable to the company and would mean there would be no big shutdown and loss of work time. Most of the employees were not in a position to be without work for very long and the company could surely force them into a situation where they would have to go back to work or look for work elsewhere. Better facilitates for their town would not be money out of pocket, and they would reap the benefit of having the convenience that would make it even more pleasurable to live in the valley. For myself, I would not be in the same situation as the average employee because I was considered personnel and was not governed by the union. It never failed to amaze me how badly employees wanted to bite the hand that literally fed them.

In the spring I decided I was going to look for a piece of property where I could run my import cows and a few crossbreds, even if it meant that I would have to work at another job besides. When my holidays came, we traveled throughout British Columbia looking for a piece of property. I can remember being at Jackson's house one evening and we were looking at a map and different places of interest to me. Eunice saw a place called Horsefly, and she laughed and said, "That probably is where Lloyd will end up." I had never even heard of the place before.

We looked at the Creston Valley and liked it enough to put a deposit on a hundred acres of hay land without any power or facilities. The asking price was $1,000 an acre. But we continued to look and got as far west as Cache Creek, but it seemed too much like a desert to me. I was not into irrigation. I had only been to Williams Lake once and I thought it would be nice just to go and see it again. I really didn't have any intentions of going that far north to live, but the big hype of the famous Williams Lake stampede was kind of a drawing card to me.

There was a real estate office right along the highway that went through a little village called Clinton. I stopped there to see what price land was going for in the area. The guy in the office said he had a piece

of property at Horsefly that we should have a look at. We laughed at the
fact that there was really even such place, let alone a small ranch. He told
me the guy wanted to sell it quite badly, and seeing that we were going to
Williams Lake, it didn't seem that far to go and check it out.

When we left the highway at the 150 mile, the road was only paved
a few miles. After that it was gravel all the way and very crooked. The
road did not impress Gloria and it really didn't impress me much either.
When we got to the ranch I was much more impressed than Gloria was.
The surrounding area was nice, no big mountains close, but yet not too
far away. The Horsefly River ran along one side of the property. There
was a small creek that ran through the property from a small lake above.
There were a lot of lakes in the area. There was a lot of logging activity also.
The price of the ranch certainly was reasonable, and something we could
afford without being in debt right up to our eyeballs. There was a lot of
hunting and fishing in the immediate area as well. I was beginning to like
it more and more all the time and that was beginning to scare Gloria.

There was not much on the ranch as far as buildings were concerned.
The house was a double wide, quite liveable but not as large as we would
have liked and not very clean. The rest of the buildings were old and
mostly made of logs. When I made the decision that I would purchase
the place, it was a disappointing day for Gloria. It is quite easy for me to
see that now. We had a new home situated in a beautiful valley, a good
income, and within driving distance of big shopping centers. But as the
saying goes you can take the boy from the farm but not the farm from
the boy. The kids were quite excited about being on a farm again. So I
finally made the decision to buy the ranch with all the hay that was in the
sheds. I would take possession of the ranch by the end of September 1973,
because I had to give my resignation to Fording Coal.

While I had been away, Wally Jackson had told a few people that
I was looking for a ranch and he wouldn't be surprised to see me leave
Fording Coal. I handed in my resignation after the first shift when I
got back to the work. I don't think anyone in the personnel office really
believed I would quit and go back to ranching. When Trail heard that
I was leaving Fording, they offered me a position of straight days as a
general foreman. That would put me in charge of all the shift bosses. I told
them that I appreciated their offer and the increase in pay that it would

mean, but I had put a fairly heavy deposit on the ranch at Horsefly, British Columbia.

It was really interesting to see what happened with the men that had worked for me over the years and even some who did not agree with me on certain issues. They would come and wish me well and some of them would bring me little gifts like welding rods, scaling bars, a sixteen-pound hammer, gloves, and other small items. I knew that they had all come from Fording Coal originally. It was hard to say no, because I am sure they meant well. Some even said when their holidays came next summer they would come and see me on my ranch. And some did. One of the mechanics that worked at Detroit Diesel said he was going to leave Fording. He was going to Kamloops and he would be coming to the ranch to see us. And he did.

It was a busy time for me, I had to sell my house, make arrangements for a moving van, a cattle liner to haul my cattle and horses, and have that all happen on the same day.

RANCHING AT HORSEFLY, BRITISH COLUMBIA

1973-2006

CHAPTER 40

Headed for Horsefly, British Columbia: I'm Going back to the Land

A friend of mine drove the moving van to Horsefly because we also had a pickup and a station wagon to bring at the same time. The move went well, except that when we turned onto Horsefly Road it was raining and the road was full of potholes. There were a lot of logging trucks heading for Williams Lake as well. It took us about a week to get settled in, the kids in school and all the other normal things that go with a move.

We had barely settled in, when a fellow came over to see the new people in the district. He asked me if I would be interested in working on a small sawmill. I asked him what kind of mill it was and he said it was a tie mill. They sawed two-by-fours and ties. He asked me if I could operate a cat, and I told him I could. He said that they needed someone to skid logs to the mill as well as scale the logs. So I went to the mill to meet his boss. It was not very much of a mill but it was a job and it was right close to home, so I took it.

Whoopeedee! I was operating a TD 14 cat, skidding logs and scaling them for the mill. When I filled up the yard, I would grab a power saw and do some bucking. I was having a lot of fun because it reminded me of when I lived at Lesser Slave Lake and my dad owned a sawmill. There really wasn't anything on that little mill that I couldn't do. Sometimes I would cant for the sawyer or run the edger. The pay was about a quarter of what I'd been making at the mine.

One day, I got a call from Wally Jackson. He told me that they were going to go on strike at Fording and that he thought it would be a long one. He asked me if there was any work he could get for a month or so at Horsefly. He said he and his oiler would come up if I could find them a job. I talked to my boss and told him that I could get him two good men to work for him. He thought about it for a while and then said he didn't think he really needed them. I told him one could operate the cat and skid, the other one could run the edger, and we could increase production by at least 50 percent. If I had to I would take a power saw and help do some of the falling. He said he'd give it a try, so I called Wally and told him if he didn't mind living in a little old house on the farm, he had a job and the cabin wouldn't cost him at thing. They came and brought their wives with them. We had a great time that winter. We would play canasta nearly every night. On Saturday and Sunday we would go snow machining out behind the ranch to the small lakes and even did some ice fishing. It was kind of a sad time when Wally and Dwayne had to go back to the mine.

The machinery on the ranch was quite old but still usable. I had an old two-lunger John Deere 534 tractor with hand clutch. My harrows consisted of four chain harrows on a twelve-foot draw bar. When I went out to harrow the field, I didn't want anyone to see me because I felt foolish. In Alberta I had 125 hp tractors with sixty feet of harrows on a rolling drawbar. But this was not farming country; it was strictly ranching.

I bought a couple of milk cows, some laying hens, ducks, geese, and a few pigs, and of course I had my horses as well as my Limousin herd. I had a real "old MacDonald's farm" like the one in the nursery rhyme.

Shelly Nichols gave me a Muscovy duck. The next time he saw me he laughed like everything and asked me how I liked the duck. That Muscovy was the craziest duck I had ever seen. Its libido was in overdrive all the time and it took on anything it could nail, anywhere. One time I was milking the cow in the stall and it nailed a chicken right in the gutter behind the cow. Talk about a commotion! The poor chicken was squawking and fighting like crazy, but the duck didn't pay any attention. He just went ahead and finished the job, then strutted off looking very proud and satisfied, leaving the poor chicken flattened in the gutter.

This is the famous Muscovy duck on the ranch

At one time, when we had pigs, one of the piglets discovered that he could slip in between Cherie's 4-H cow's hind legs and grab a teat and she would stand and let him suck, and he took advantage of it every chance he got.

A piglet sucking my daughter's 4-H cow;
if it is free, why not take it?

I always loved my horses. I bought a mare called Holly's Angel from Wyalta Appaloosas at High River. I bred her to my stud, Dally. They produced a beautifully colored foal. Later, a cougar killed it in the pasture. He ate it completely. The only way I knew what happened was I found the hide in the cougar's dung. What a disappointment.

The author standing with a beautiful Appaloosa
foal and its dam, called Holly's Angel

I was kept quite busy around the farm that summer. It was so nice to be able to work with my kids again, especially the girls, who were a little older and were a lot of help. We fixed a lot of fences, built some new ones, and did the haying. My kids really liked the farm.

They had a few chores to do, and could go out with the snow machines on the hayfields. In the spring the Horsefly River flooded into the field and they would go down into the field and play in the water.

I had a seventy-five head permit for my cows to graze on open range. I didn't have enough commercial cows to fill my permit, so I had to buy some more or lose a portion of my permit. I kept my full-blood Limos and crossbreds on the ranch, and just ran the commercial cows on open range. I bought a horse for each of my daughters and they would ride with me to check the cows. You would see moose, deer, and black bears every time we went out riding.

That fall the girls and I went to the Kamloops Winter Show.

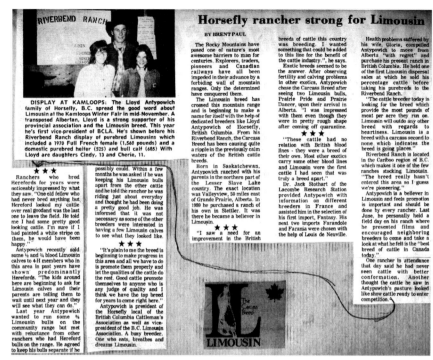

This was my first venture into showing in British Columbia

At that time I called my ranch Riverbend Ranch, but later I found that I couldn't register my Limousin cattle under that name because someone else was already using it, so I chose Black Mountain Limousin as my ranch name.

Sign posted on the main road

This is a carved wooden sign for the ranch

I had a painted sign posted along the main Horsefly Lake Road by Jim and Ellie Veninga's place across from the turn onto the road that I lived on. My ranch was about two kilometers in on what was then called Gardner Road and was later changed to Little Horsefly Road.

At first, I got into showing my animals slowly; it was a new experience for me. After going to Armstrong with Cherie and Cindy, I went to Kamloops; Cindy and Murray went with me. My kids were a lot of help to me.

Showing my Limousin cattle in the Kamloops show
with Cindy and Murray, my helpers

That summer, Gary Negrin, the friend who helped me move from Elkford, got transferred from Kamloops to Williams Lake, so we saw a lot more of them. My lead hand, Tom, and his wife stopped in that summer when they were on their holidays. Tom had gotten a promotion to become a shift boss. He filled me in on all the happenings at the mine, but for the most of it things were pretty much the same. I got a call from John Low; he operated the L700 Leturno loader. He also operated the

631 Caterpillar buggy at the mine. He was working near Kamloops on a construction crew, operating a buggy. He called to tell me that I really was a pretty good foreman, that he regretted never telling me that while he worked for me at the mine. Now that he was working on the highway in the Caribou, he decided to call me and wanted to know how things were going on the ranch. I thanked him and said it was real nice of him to call and he could stop in any time.

Gloria went to work at the Forest Service in Horsefly. That helped out a lot because it was a government job and she had medical and dental benefits for the entire family as well as making a good wage. It brought in income for our living expenses and a few extras that we wouldn't have had otherwise. She started in the office filing and then moved into drafting. She learned to do the mapping for Horsefly District.

She was very busy because at home she was still a wife, the mother of four, cooking and cleaning, sewing clothes for the kids, as well as doing the numerous household chores. She looked after a big garden from which she canned and froze a lot of the vegetables from the garden. She did chores with the kids when I was working away from home, catching the milk cow and milking her and making sure that kids had fed the pigs and chickens every morning before they left for the day and when they got home after school.

She also looked after any daily things that cropped up on the ranch if I was working away from home, like when my stud, Dally, got out of the corral and ended up on the main road two miles from home at the Wynstra place. A neighbor called the office and she had to leave work and go catch him and take him home; keep in mind that she was extremely allergic to horses.

She was my secretary, did the bookwork for the ranch, and ran errands for me. She also did a lot of remodelling in the house, painting and papering, changing walls and rooms by herself. I was too busy to help with those things.

She loved her job and it was good for her because she got to meet a lot of people. It took quite awhile, but in the end working helped get her over being pissed off at me for taking her away out in the bush and back to the financial hardships that came with ranching!

I did a little work for the Forest Service on a cedar project that the forest ranger had set up. I also worked doing quality control for tree planting, but it looked more and more like I was going to have to get a good job somewhere if I wanted to upgrade things on the ranch. The cattle prices dropped off a lot that fall, so as a result I butchered the cull cows to help generate a little better cash flow, but that was a lot of extra work as well.

Later that fall a fellow came and asked me if I was interested in falling timber for them that winter. He said it would be an all-winter job. He was going to hire my neighbor, Jack Gardner, and his D7 cat to do the skidding and would like to hire as many people from the community as possible. He said they would have a first-class camp set up in the valley and would work ten days on and two days off. He made it quite clear to me that he was expecting production and didn't want anyone just wanting to put in time and get paid. He asked me if I had a preference for how I wanted to get paid for the falling. I told him I would prefer to get paid by the tree or the cubic meter, but that I would like to see the timber first. He said that was fine with him because he liked people that wanted to be paid by piece work instead of by the hour. I told him that I would be looking to make as much money as I possibly could because I had a place to put it all and I wouldn't be out there just for the good of my health. He said he would talk with my neighbor again, and if it was okay with him if the two of us worked together and they would keep our logs separate from the rest of his crew.

They were logging on two sides; one at Walker Mountain, and the other in the McClusky Creek Valley. We ended up working in the McClusky Creek Valley and I was sure glad we did. Although there was some smaller wood to start with because we were logging right of way into the main block, the rest of the timber was excellent. I had to get a bigger bar for my power saw. I was using at 2100 Husqvarna with a thirty-two-inch bar.

In a lot of the bigger timber, I had to make a double cut just to get a proper undercut, and sometimes I would have to use three wedges just to get the trees started in the right direction so that the top would hit the skid trail. My bar was not long enough to reach all the way through the tree. At times Jack was only able to pull three or four trees at a time. Some of the nice big fir would be 160 to 170 feet tall.

Jack was a good cat operator, so we did real good that winter. I averaged $300 a day, and our daily average from November 15 till March 15 was 5.4 loads per day. The camp was really nice.

Large timber on the Monkman landing in the McClusky Creek Valley that I had fell for the cat to skid

Jack Gardner's cat on the landing with wood that I fell and he had skidded

My boss, Gordon Swanky, would come to my room in camp just to visit and ask a lot of questions. He was really interested to know why I was trying to ranch when I could be out making a lot more money working in the bush. I told him I had a dream to raise purebred Limousin cattle and that I had already had some imports from France. He was real interested when I told him all about them, especially when I said I had sold my first heifer's calf for $17,000. I gave him some of my magazines so he could read up on them.

When we were just about finished for the winter, Gordon came to me and asked me if I would be interested in putting a new D8 cat to work with them on another logging show. I told him that I could not afford to buy a D8 because I had just bought the ranch. He said, "Don't worry about that. I would get one delivered right to where you would start working on the road." All he needed was for me to say that I would come and work for them until they had finished the three blocks that Weldwood had given them to log in the Mathew area.

It was a very generous offer, but I told him that I didn't think I could run the ranch and the cat at the same time. I don't know where I would be today if I had taken him up on his offer. They were very good people to work with and had a reputation of being good loggers, but once again, that strong desire that I had right from when I was a young boy won out. I'm not saying it was right, but that's the way it turned out. Ranching was a good way of life at one time and one could make a reasonable living doing it. Today we are controlled by so many bureaucratic decisions and regulations, there is little left for the person who is doing all the work and having all the headaches, trying to figure out how to follow all the rules and regulations that have been imposed upon us.

I continued to work on my small ranch, and I managed to sell a few Limousin crossbred bulls, but it was hard to convince a lot of a commercial cattleman that they should use anything other than their traditional British breeds. I will admit that when I first came to Horsefly I realized I had basically stepped back about thirty years in time.

When some of the neighbors saw me AI my cows, they were very critical and said they didn't think that those homemade bulls would work. I got a real big laugh one day when the bus depot sent a message out on the radio station for me. At twelve noon every day they would broadcast on the radio station for people that lived way out in the boonies. Anyway, my message was, "Lloyd, please come to the bus depot and pick up your semen." I got a lot of ribbing from people who heard that. Many wondered what the bus depot was doing with my semen. They didn't realize that I had a tank that I had sent to Milliner, British Columbia to be charged with nitrogen, which kept the vials of bull semen stored in it frozen.

I served as president of the Horsefly Cattlemen's Association for seven years. While I was president of the Horsefly Cattleman's Association, I was approached by the district agriculturist, Peter Poffenoff, to start up a Horsefly 4-H Club. I gave it some thought and decided it would be a good way to spend more time with my children, who all became 4-H club members. I told him that I had never done that before but I would give it a try. It taught me a lot and was a good learning experience. I led the Horsefly Club for seven years. It was strictly a beef club, and with the assistance of a neighbor, Babs Augustine, we led the club to be a club of champions.

The last two years the club members won all but one championship. They excelled in public speaking, judging, best groomed, best heifer, best steer, grand champion steer, grand champion heifer, reserve grand champion cow /calf pair.

*Me, receiving leadership trophies as
leader of the Horsefly Beef Club*

*Me and the members of my 4-H club; left to right: Kenny
Walters, Darryl, and Cindy (hidden), Lori Walters, Cherie,
Sahara Best, Murray, Chad Ridley, and Debbie Walker*

My kids were active in the 4-H Beef Club, and they were required to do everything on their own: feeding, grooming, training, showing, and recordkeeping. For one thing, it is the true way 4-H should work, but also, I was so busy with my work that I didn't have time to help them. Cindy won grand champion heifer and grand champion steer. Cherie won reserve champion cow/calf pair. Murray and Darryle, both had steers that won in their weight classes. Mathew Powel and Debbie Walker both won grand champion steer. All these cattle carried the Limousin influence.

Babs Augustine and I and our club members in front of the tack barn in our stall

I am still interested in 4-H. Two of my grandchildren belong to the Horsefly 4-H Club today. In 2011, one took a market lamb, the other had turkeys. In 2012 they both did sheep projects, so Grandpa and Grandma spent the week at the 4-H show and sale once again.

I still sponsor the grand aggregate trophy and the best heifer trophy for the Horsefly Club.

I enjoy going to the 4-H banquet to help them raise money for their next year. They have a cake, cookie, and pie auction. It is a good way to help them raise money. Now the club is run under different leadership and is still doing very well. They have diversified, and along with the help of assistant leaders, they do mechanics, horse, beef, sheep, rabbits, turkeys, and dogs.

*I am presenting Jennifer Heidle with a trophy
for the best heifer, which I still sponsor*

CHAPTER 41

Black Creek Ranch

In the early 1970s, the Black Creek Ranch sold to an investment company owned by a wealthy Italian by the name of Eduardo Visconti from Milan, Italy. He was a man of great wealth. The Visconti estate was involved in pharmaceutical industry in Italy. He was involved in many businesses there and he owned farms and vineyards in the northern part of Italy. Generally it seemed that he was treated and greeted with great patronage and respect there.

In time I realised that Black Creek Ranch was just another place to invest some of the money that he was trying to get out of Italy because of the Socialist threat to that country at the time. He had other investments in North America that were quite large also. I knew of ones that were in Calgary, California, Vancouver, and Manitoba. In Vancouver, he had an investment company called Farland Investments. He owned a thirty-seven story highrise on Robson Street, which I visited several times. The Black Creek Ranch was a rather large ranch that got its name from the famous Gold Rush days. It is situated in the watershed of the Caribou Mountains that formed the Horsefly River that runs into Quesnel Lake and then on into the Fraser River, which eventually runs into the Pacific Ocean on the West Coast.

The valley was first opened up by gold mining in the 1800s. There are stories told about gold that was found, and apparently a miner by the name of Black found some large gold nuggets up Black Creek, which runs into the Horsefly River. In the early '70s, descendants of Black still owned that claim and worked on it occasionally, but to my knowledge they never found the mother lode! It was located just up the creek behind the ranch and we went through there when riding on the range.

There were a few small sawmills operating in the valley during the 1950s, and in 1961 the Vunder fire burned uncontrolled through the area, over several mountains, jumping Horsefly Lake before it finally burned itself out.

Dan Gunderson and his two sons operated one of the many sawmills in the valley. After the big fire they were able to log a lot of the burned timber at a reduced stumpage rate. Gunderson developed the Black Creek Ranch. He had his sights set on ranching and let it be known that he would like to own the entire valley. It is quite fair to say that he almost succeeded in doing that. There were only a few pieces of land that he was unable to add to his ranch.

The barn at Black Creek Ranch as it was when we lived there

When Eduardo Visconti bought the ranch, he hired a man that used to play football to be his ranch manager. He may have been a good football player but he knew nothing about ranching, and that spring he was losing a lot cows. The cattle were dying like flies because of lack of nutrition. It really was a pathetic sight.

One day when Visconti had come from Vancouver, he sent word to me, asking me to come and look at his cows. After looking the situation over, I told him that the hay they were feeding didn't have very much nutrition and they needed to get some high protein into them as soon as they could or they would lose a lot more. I also thought they had a lot of old cows that didn't have any bottom teeth. Eduardo asked me to come to his house for a coffee, and then he asked me if I would be interested in looking after his cowherd for him,

He was a very interesting man. He told me he knew he had the wrong man to run his ranch and if I'd come and look after his cows my wages would be $2,000 a month after tax. He'd provide a house to live in and I could use his equipment to hay my own property. I could bring my Limousin cows to the ranch and he wouldn't charge me to keep them there. He had owned Limousin cattle in Italy and he indicated that he would be interested in using Limousin bulls on his cowherd at Black Creek. I guess you could say I kind of took the bait, because I accepted the job and we moved up to the Black Creek Ranch.

We lived at the "white house," locally known as Duffer's Dip. This was another one of the houses on the ranch. It was located about a quarter of a mile down the road toward Horsefly from the main ranch buildings, and below the road was an old barn and wooden corrals.

*Eduardo Visconti walking beside
the corrals at the ranch*

Gloria continued to work at the forestry in Horsefly. I bought her a JC5 Jeep with a nice canvas top to drive back and forth to work. She had twenty miles to drive, and there were quite a few logging trucks on that road. They all looked out for her because they knew when she would be on the road. She was a bit of a speed ball and they used to say, "She drives that Jeep on a wing and a prayer, with God on her shoulder."

Running the Black Creek Ranch was a bigger job than I expected. It was a real learning experience for me. I came to realise that it had been bought strictly as an investment. The ranch consisted of approximately 5,000 acres. The Horsefly River ran through the ranch property for approximately ten miles and the river-bottom land was very fertile but was prone to flooding in the spring and during the summer months when heavy rains happened. This created a real problem in haying season.

The facilities on the ranch included three houses. Two were quite nice; the other one was a huge roughly-finished wooden house. There was a nice barn with a tack room and hayloft. At the back of the barn there was a small corral that had seen its better days. There were several hay sheds and a shop with a Caterpillar generator that we used for power as BC Hydro hadn't come into the valley yet. As well, there was an airport and a small hangar for a single engine plane.

Across McKinley Creek there were 280 acres of deeded land that could be developed into good hayfields. There was another 160 acres of the same kind of land that needed to be cleared so that we could make hay on it. All this added up to a mountain of work that I eventually accomplished. Besides that, I had my small ranch at Horsefly to hay, as well as another 800 acres known as the Wynstra Place, which was located near my ranch at Horsefly. Visconte had bought the Wynstra place for his friend in Italy.

The ranch held a 300-head grazing permit on crown range that consisted of mainly bush land, and managing cattle on that kind of range was more difficult than I expected. I realised that I needed a plan of my own to manage it properly.

The land that was fenced near the ranch was used for my Limousin cattle. Very little of the ranch property was fenced, so new fencing was needed. After calving, the cows were allowed to pasture the hay land, and from my experience that was not an acceptable management practice. I needed to make some changes, but I had to meet with the owner and discuss what needed to be done and what the priorities were.

Stopping the cows from dying was top priority, so I ordered a load of barley from Alberta and started to slowly work this into their diet; still, many died because they were too far gone.

I needed help to make the necessary changes and Visconti agreed to hire a native (Indian) fencing crew that would start building temporary corrals to facilitate the calving, which would start soon. After the corrals were in place, they would fence other areas of the property to facilitate better movement of the cattle.

It was difficult to deal with all this while trying to get things turned around. There were other issues that needed to be dealt with; I needed to have full control of the management of the ranch if I was to make it work, which was impossible when the previous manager was still involved. I called Visconti and discussed my concerns with him.

Once those problems were settled, things started to work more smoothly, and I hired two ranch hands to help with the cattle. This took some of the pressure off me. Jim Walls was the first hand that I hired and he was the best all-around ranch hand that I ever had at Black Creek Ranch.

Jim and Joanne Walls; they looked like two
kids when he came to apply for the job

The house where the ranch hands lived burned down several years after I left the ranch. At the time Eduardo Visconti owned the ranch, he lived in this house at first and he brought some very old, antique-type furniture from Italy.

Even though he had a large modern home that he called the "California" house across the road, he really didn't want to move into it, and at one point he even suggested that the families that we hired should share the big house with him as they would have been happy to do in Italy.

The house at Black Creek Ranch where the hired men with families lived

The house had many rooms and logistically this could have happened, but realistically this was Canada not Italy, and Mr. Viconti was not revered by his employees here as he apparently was in Italy. A Canadian family would have been very uncomfortable with that arrangement, so Eduardo and his furniture moved into the "California" house.

Raymond Ross was the second man I hired. Raymond was a very likeable native guy, and he was quite handy around the ranch. He could drive tractor, help do the fencing, and liked to ride range. One time after I had given the men their paychecks, Raymond asked if he could go to Horsefly as he had some things that he wanted to get, so I gave him the ranch truck. On his way back home he noticed some cows had come in off the range and gotten into the hayfield. He saddled up his horse, gathered up the cows, and pushed them back up the mountain. On his way back home he realized he'd lost his wallet.

Raymond Ross, sitting in the big chair with my son, Darryl,
beside him down at the big house on the ranch

When I got home he was at the barn unsaddling his horse, and he said, "I did a very foolish thing." The first thing I thought was he might have dinged the ranch truck but then he told me that he had left his wallet in his hip pocket, and when he was chasing the cows, he lost it. He had $500 in his wallet, so I told him to saddle up a fresh horse and try to backtrack the stock trail he had taken to see if he could find it. He saddled up and went, returning in about half an hour. I thought he must have found it. When I asked, he said, "No, if him wants to be lost, him can be lost." That fall, when I was making hay I thought I might find his wallet, but never did.

That fall I had to buy more cows to fill our range permit, so I took Raymond with me and we headed into the Chilcotin country looking for some. Let me tell you, that was a real learning experience for me. The roads to some of those ranches were something else. We weren't having much luck finding good cows, so we decided to visit a fellow who lived in the area for quite a while, thinking he'd have some idea who might have cows for sale. He took us in, sat us down and offered us a cup of coffee. He said his wife didn't make the best coffee, but he had a bottle of whiskey that would fix it up and he poured a good shot into the cup.

After chatting for a while, he said he didn't think I'd find any cows in that country that I'd want to buy right then. They'd had a bad winter the year before and there were a lot of cows that had just barely made it through the winter. In his opinion, those cows wouldn't be bred or if they were, they'd be very late. I thanked him for his frankness and asked him a few more questions about the Chilcotin area, but didn't want to spend too much time for fear he would want to give us another cup of coffee.

He sat in a big armchair that seemed to be moulded just to fit him. Right beside the chair, hanging on the wall, was a .45 pistol in the cartridge belt. He asked me if I was any good with a gun like that. I said not really because I didn't make a habit of using one. He said he used to be pretty good with one when he was younger.

Now, the door of his house was open and out in front of the door was a pile of cans that I'm sure must have been there from the time the house was built. He took that pistol out of the holster and took aim and blew a can off the pile. There were some young kids, about six or eight years old, running back and forth in front of the door. He took aim and blew another can off the pile and then a kid ran across the open door again. I don't know if they were used to playing that game or what, but it seemed awfully dangerous to me. After a few more shots and seeing a kid passing in front of the door again, I thought it was time for us to hit the road and look for some more cows, because I was sure I was going to witness the shooting of a young child. We spent two days in the Chilcotin and never bought a cow.

One day I got a call from a cattle buyer in Kamloops and he said he had a nice herd of fifty cows, all from one owner, and I should come down and take a look at them. I called Sharp Wings in Williams Lake and talked to Gideon.

I told him I needed to make a quick trip to Kamloops and asked him if he could fly out to the ranch and pick me up. I'd wait for him at the airstrip.

He asked me what the weather was like in the Black Creek Valley. I told him it wasn't ideal for flying but I didn't have time to drive all the way to Kamloops. He said it was kind of socked in at Williams Lake, but he'd give it a try and see what it looked like once he got up in the air.

About fifteen minutes later the ceiling came down to about 500 feet and I was sure he wouldn't show up. I was just leaving our airstrip when a plane came out of the clouds and landed. I drove back and he taxied up to me and asked if I was ready to go. I thought he was joking, and asked him if he was really seriously thinking of flying in that kind of weather. He said that at about 7,000 feet the sun was shining. I decided if he wasn't afraid of dying, I shouldn't be either, so I jumped in the plane and off we went. It seemed like we were barely off the ground when we were into the clouds, and it wasn't until we reached 7,000 feet that we found the sunshine.

Now, it was nice flying up there, but when I asked Gideon how the hell we were going to get back down on the ground, he said that Kamloops country was nothing but a desert. There wouldn't be any clouds when we got there.

When we were somewhere above Canim Lake, there were a few breaks in the clouds, and he pointed out a little patch of blue that was the lake. We flew a little farther, and then he said we might have to go down to get under the clouds and then we should be able to fly into the Kamloops Valley via Dead Man Creek. I don't know how he knew where he was, but I guess that was why he was the pilot and I wasn't. He found Dead Man Creek and flew just above the tips of some of the trees, and once we got into the valley it wasn't too bad. When he radioed the tower in Kamloops for landing, they asked him where he'd come from. When he said Williams Lake, they told him he couldn't have come from Williams Lake because they were all socked in. He asked if they were going to talk about it or if they were going to let him land, and of course they gave him the okay to land.

The cattle buyer met me at the airport and took me out to see the cows. They were what I was looking for, so I bought them. When we were ready to leave, the airport told Gideon that the weather had improved some, but there was still only a 1,000-foot ceiling. Gideon said it would be all right; he had found his way through it on the way down, so he should be able to find his way back, and he did.

After the cows were calved out and the branding and vaccinating was done, it was time to put them onto the crown range. The cows didn't like to stay on the range when they could find better grazing on the hay lands, so I needed a rider to work the cattle and keep them from coming back into the valley. I hired an experienced range rider named Ulrich, and it was a full-time job for him, riding six days a week.

Gideon, the pilot from Sharp Wings

But I needed a better plan. There were no roads or trails even suitable for a four-wheel-drive pickup on the range, only cattle trails that we could access with horses. I needed a way to get the salt higher up the mountain without packing it on a packhorse. I got permission from the Forest Service to make approximately twelve miles of stock trail. Then I could move the salt to different locations and all the rider had to do was keep pushing the cattle higher up the mountain. Since Gloria worked for the Forest Service and was the mapping technician, I was able to get a map of our crown range. I marked all the trails and the locations where I wanted the salt to be put and tacked the map on the wall of Ulrich's little house, and together we worked the system by using different colored pins to mark where we put the salt and where we wanted to make the next move. Things were starting to come together much better and we were able to manage the range in a way that it hadn't been done before.

When I explained our system to the Forest Service and Fish and Wildlife, they gave me more cooperation. When it came time to bring the cows down in the fall, we'd move the salt down ahead of the cows and they'd follow it back down toward the main ranch. Managing cows in heavy bush was a very difficult job, and from time to time I'd have to help the range rider.

Keeping the bulls from bunching up was a problem. At times like that I'd help, and sometimes even another rider would go out with the range rider. Also there were times when a bull got foot rot and needed to be treated with antibiotics. It is very difficult to rope an animal in heavy bush, and when you had a bull that was a little cranky to start with it could be a little dangerous, so I would work with the range rider.

I have to admit there were times when he clearly amazed me with what he could accomplish with a horse and rope and those two dogs. He had three different horses to ride and he rode enough that I was having a hard time keeping shoes on them. He would wear them out faster than the horse's feet would grow, which made it difficult to reshoe, so I welded small toe and heel plates that I made from a grade-twelve bolt to the horseshoe. That lasted a lot longer than a basic shoe. I got an older pickup truck that he could haul his horse with and that saved him quite a few miles of riding to where the cattle were. It also allowed him better traveling time to different parts of the range.

Rod and Chester, my two German shepherd cattle dogs
that helped the rider to move cattle on the range

The watershed to the Horsefly River is quite large, and when the mountain snow melted the river overflowed its banks and flooded the whole river valley. When we had a lot of rain it could also cause the river to flood. If that happened during haying time it was impossible to make hay on the low ground. One year we had just nicely started haying when it rained for three days. That was on the first of July and the river bottom flooded with three feet of water. I had some large three-ton stacks and about a thousand small square bales still on the field. What a mess! I called Visconti in Vancouver and asked him if he had any suggestions about what I should do. He came down to have a look. And when he saw the situation, he said he thought he had bought a ranch but it looked like he had bought a lake instead.

That year was the most difficult time I ever had trying to make hay. It was a rainy summer and the bottom land never really got dry. We finished making hay in October—if you could call it hay. When the ground froze I would swath the hay and Jim would run the three-ton stacker right behind me. I think he thought that I was crazy, because he thought nothing would eat it. But that winter we fed 400 head of cows range cubes and used that hay for roughage.

Jim was good with a rope, a good horseman, and good with equipment. One day, while we were repairing the swather in the field, I looked up and saw a bull moose walking across the field. I asked him if he had his gun and said, "I don't like this mechanic work. Why don't we go hunting?"

He looked at me as much as to say, "What do you mean? It's haying time." I said, "There's a bull moose over there in the field." He grinned and replied, "Well, in that case, let's go get him." So that's what we did, but how we did it, I'm sure not many will ever duplicate. I drove the truck down the road and told Jim to jump out when I slowed down and I'd just keep driving. The moose would watch the truck and he could get a good shot at him.

All went as planned, except he shot it in the front foot. That moose hopped around on three legs like a dog. Jim shot him again, and that time he went down. We started across the field toward it, but as we got closer I noticed he was still very much alive. I told Jim to shoot him in the head. He did, but his shot was way too low. The moose just did a shiver. I wasn't sure if he was going to get up or not, so I ran around behind him and was going to grab him by the horns. I thought I might be able to hold him down while Jim cut his throat. But no sooner had I grabbed his horns than

he tried to get up and he would have taken me with him. That's when Jim
came to my rescue or I may have had my first moose ride. Jim grabbed his
horns and we rolled him back on his side. The problem was, he was doing
so much kicking and striking that it was very difficult to get a knife into
him. By ducking and dodging, we finally got his jugular cut. When all was
quiet and the animal was just lying there, Jim said, "*Whewwee!* Is that the
way you always kill them? Hell, I'm going to take you steer dogging with
me the next time I go to town."

I laughed and said, "No, only when you're not a good shot! What the
hell is the matter with your gun?" He said he didn't know, but it sure didn't
shoot where he was aiming. After we took care of the moose, we tried his
gun at a target, and it was shooting almost three feet low. The scope must
have gotten bumped when he was carrying it around in the truck.

We finished cutting the bottom fields and stacked the hay in three-ton
stacks. We had a three-ton stack mover with a feeder head on it. It would
cut the stack and auger it out the side as we drove the tractor along, and
the cows would eat it all. We bought some good hay to go along with all
that poor stuff during calving time.

The forestry said that we had to fill our range permit, so that meant
we had to buy some more cows. The owner did not want to pay as much as
was required to buy good cows, so we bought 150 head of first-calf heifers
instead. They were all supposed to be bred to black angus bulls, but it was
a different story come calving time.

CHAPTER 42

I Become My Own Veterinarian

When you work in the beef industry it is important to learn how to read symptoms in order to diagnose properly what the cause or injury to an animal is. This is why veterinarians go to school for seven years to become a vet. But as producers, we have to learn on the go. Sometimes we are too far from the vet or need to act immediately to correct a problem. In life you really learn to appreciate your friends. Some of my friends have been doctors, carpenters, salesmen, cowboys, politicians, ranchers, loggers, managers in various businesses, and veterinarians. I have called on them and their expertise to show me how I could increase my knowledge in various ways. When I lived at Stettler, my veterinarian friend encouraged me to come to the clinic, especially late at night in calving season, to give him a hand during some of these operations. I had done this enough times I thought that I could do one of them if I had to; not as well as he could, but maybe I could squeak through and save a calf or a cow.

When I was on the Black Creek Ranch, I needed to do my own veterinary work. We were quite a ways out of Williams Lake, where our nearest vet office was, and we were running 650 head of cattle. There always seemed to be something to treat for various problems, so I went to the Williams Lake Vet Clinic and asked the vet that owned the practice if I could buy some equipment from him so I could sew up an animal or do a caesarean or repair a prolapsed cow. He looked at me as if I'd just fallen off the turnip truck.

I told him I'd learned to do a lot of those things from my veterinary friend in Alberta, but the problem I had right now was I needed some of the necessary equipment to do the job. He stood there and looked at me for a while, then turned and walked back into his operating room without saying a word to me. I paid the clerk for some product that I had bought and was about to turn and walk out the door, when he came back and asked me to come into his surgery room and show him just what I needed.

I went to the backroom with him and told him it wasn't necessary for everything to be new. He picked up a tray and started to put a bunch of tools in it, scalpels, scissors, crimpers, syringes with a four-inch long needles, and anything else that he thought I might need. Then he told me to go to the desk and get a couple of bottles of Lidocaine, three or four bottles of penicillin and some cat gut for stitching, half a dozen needles of various sizes, a bottle of cloth sutures and a bottle of Fuerisan, and some wound dressing to put on the incision after I sewed up the cow. He looked at me and said, "Good luck. Let me know how you make out with them."

That spring we had a lot of heifers to calve out. I did twelve caesareans and only lost one calf. I also did three prolapses. At turnout time I lopped off the bottom part of the tail on all the caesareans, as well as the prolapsed cows. The ranch sold that fall, so I told the guy that bought the cows that the ones with lopped tails should be culled. He looked at me as if I didn't know what I was saying. When he did the pregnancy test, he kept eight of the twelve that had bobbed tails.

Gloria came to the barn and took pictures while I was doing a caesarean. In all there are about seventeen different steps you take, and she had taken all but one of them. She missed the one where I was doing a spinal. I put them all into a little folder and took them in to show the vet. That spring Jim and Joanne had a baby boy and we had taken some pictures of him, so when they turned the last page in the folder, there was a picture of the baby. We had a good laugh. He asked me how I made out with the cows and if I lost any. When I told him, he just looked at me and said if I kept doing that I could get good at it. I promised him that I would not do his work for other people. We became good friends, and I bought most of my supplies from his vet office.

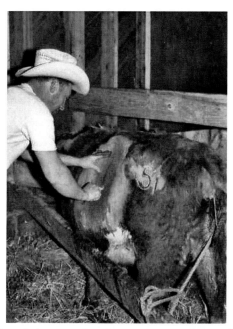

After he had shaved the animal and given it a spinal shot of Lidocaine, the author is reaching in to find the hind legs of the calf. He will then make an incision on the calf bed or uterus big enough to get the calf through.

I am delivering the calf through the incision.

Here, the author is sewing up the incision after doing a caesarean

The baby calf

CHAPTER 43

Bringing in the Cattle in the Fall

I hired Sharp Wings to help me find cows on the range when we were rounding up in the fall, and I learned to really appreciate Gideon's flying skills. We would fly over meadows, cut blocks, and even logging roads. When saw some tracks in the snow, he got right down low, just over the treetops, and asked me if I could tell the difference between moose tracks and cow tracks. He said, "I don't want to be wasting your time flying around looking at moose tracks."

When we found some cows, I made note of where they were, and then Jim and I would take the dogs and ride into the area on horses and bring them home. One has to appreciate how difficult it was to round up the cattle in the fall when they were scattered over thousands of acres that were mainly covered with bush.

One time, late in the fall, I was flying with Gideon and found twelve head near McKinley Lake, so Jim and I saddled up and rode out to gather them in. One was really wild and made a run for the lake. I shook a loop as quickly as I could and tried to catch her before she got to the shore. The lake had a thin layer of ice covering it and I knew it would not hold her up. My horse did the best he could to put me on her, but he came up just a little short. As he slid to a stop at the edge of the lake, I reached as far as I could with my loop and about that time she went through the ice. I guess I was really lucky, because that loop landed right around her horns, which were only about eight inches long. I tried to pull her back to shore, but I couldn't get her up onto the ice, so I just held her there to keep her head from going under the water and drowning.

I kept calling Jim to come and help me. When he got there he managed to get his rope on her too and the two of us dragged her out of the lake. I am sure we stretched her neck a little but she was still alive and madder than a hornet. We kept both our loops on her, and while I dragged her back to where the other animals were, Jim helped steer her around the trees. When we got to them they were very curious about her, probably because she had fallen in the lake and was soaking wet. When she got her strength back, we shook our loops off and herded the bunch to the ranch

Still, we missed a few. In February, a logger, George Campbell, stopped in to tell us there were some cattle where they were logging and he wondered if they were ours. I went and took a look and sure enough they carried the reverse six brands. There was a cow and calf and a yearling. Jim and I loaded two horses on my one-ton truck, and at the end of the logging crew's working day we went out to attempt to rope them one at a time and drag them into the back of the truck. The loggers really enjoyed this; they said not every logging show has its own rodeo. But for Jim and me it was all in a day's work.

Later in March that same winter, three steers wandered onto the haul road about two miles from the ranch. They were thin and as wild as a March hare. I fed them some hay thinking we could quiet them, but they only ate the hay at night. Finally, Jim and I decided we would have to try to rope them. I am sure I could have caught a moose on the rope easier than I could catch those wild steers. We finally had to admit that our plan was not working, so as a last resort we took the two dogs with us. We sent the dogs on the steers, and it wasn't long before they had them all tuckered out and we were able to catch up to them.

Then they charged the horses. As they ran by, I snagged one with my rope, dallied him short, and dragged him back to the road. It became plain to us that he wasn't going to go any farther, so Jim caught a ride back to the ranch and brought back the three-quarter-ton pickup with a sheet of one-inch plywood. We use a sheet of plywood for a loading ramp and after tying the front and back legs together we dragged the steer up the plywood sheet into the pickup. Then Jim drove to the ranch, backed into the corral, untied the ropes, and the steer literally jumped out.

I went back into the bush with the dogs and snared another one. We loaded him the same way and I went back to catch the last one, which proved to be much more difficult. Not only was he the wildest one, but he had also gotten a bit of a rest and the dogs had a hard time cornering him.

I finally managed to catch him and maneuver him back to the road, but Jim didn't come, so I attempted to lead him down the road. After choking him down a few times, I guess he decided it was easier to follow, so down the road we went, but it wasn't long before he thought he could run away again. He ran past my horse, and then it was my turn to follow him as long as he stayed on the road. When he tried to leave the road, the dogs would bring him back on it. He was beginning to look a pitiful sight as the dogs had worked his legs over pretty good.

Near the ranch there was a log-sorting yard, and he decided instead of staying on the main haul road he would go through the log-sorting yard. As long as he kept going in front of me, I followed. We went right through the log-sorting yard and I'm not sure he saw too much of what was there, because nothing seemed to bother him. As I was going past one of the drivers yelled, "Jesus, Lloyd, you got that critter half-butchered already."

Jim had a flat tire on the truck and that's why he didn't come back, so I followed that steer all the way to the ranch. By the time I got home with him he was halter broke, ready for a 4-H project.

One day while I was away in Kamloops attending a cattlemen's meeting, Jim called me and said he thought I had better hurry up and get back home. I asked him what was the matter and he said that the wolves had killed seven head of cows that had crossed the Horsefly River to graze on the flats. We had less than a foot of snow and it was quite mild. The river was shallow and hadn't frozen yet, so the cattle could walk across. So I told him to bring as many of them back as he could. I had one more day of important business and then I would come home.

When I got home there were still some cows that he couldn't chase back, so the first thing I did was help him get them. After that I took a look at what had happened to the dead cattle. In my estimation there were twelve or thirteen wolves in a pack and that was enough of them to pull down and kill good healthy cattle as they chose.

Jim was determined that he was going to shoot some wolves, so we set up a blind 200 yards from the dead cows. He took his sleeping bag out into the field late one afternoon, hoping that he would get a shot at some of them as they came back to feed on the cows. When they came back it was dark and he could not see to shoot. He said there were a lot of snapping, snarling, and howling going on all night.

The next night we set up a battery with a spotlight that would shine on the carcasses in hopes that when they came back he could get a shot at some of them. Well, they came back all right, but it was after dark. And when they began to howl, snap, and snarl, he thought for sure they were feeding on the carcasses. When he snapped the light on them, they were at the edge of the bush, about seventy-five yards from the dead cows. He fired a couple of shots, but they disappeared into the bush so fast he didn't manage to hit any of them. The weather had turned cold, and he said he'd had enough of that kind of wolf hunting.

That spring Jim left to ranch with his father at Quesnel, British Columbia. I didn't blame him for going to work with his dad, as it was his opportunity to work in the ranching business and it was a good move for him. But I sure did miss his help and companionship. We worked so well together and had fun doing it.

While I ran Black Creek ranch, several men worked for me. After Jim left, I hired Bob Miles and his son, Robert Jr., who also worked on the ranch.

Bob Miles, at the corrals
at Black Creek Ranch.

Robert Miles Jr. branding a calf

That spring, when we were calving we did a midnight check, and every now and then a wolf would let out an eerie howl that stood your hair on end and stopped you dead in your tracks. Those wolves were real close to the calving yard.

I had my .25-06 gun with me every day when we worked around the calving yard. One day early in May, I saw one going across a field to an island of bush that was only a few acres in size, but quite long.

My dog Chester and I with the wolf after I shot it

I sent the hired man ahead of me and told him to take my two German shepherd dogs and walk from the far end of the island toward me. I snuck out to a little clump of brush on the edge of the field and waited for the wolf to come back, which he did as soon as he realized there was somebody coming toward him from the island. He came back into the meadow and was about 400 yards from me when he stopped and looked back. The dogs had picked up his trail and were in hot pursuit.

He was a fairly large wolf, and I was sure he was capable of doing serious damage to either one of my dogs. I could see he intended to take them on, so I made a quick calculation of the distance, aimed high on the wolf to allow for the drop of the bullet and pulled the trigger. To my surprise, it went down. I had broken his hip as he was walking away from me. I shot again and got him through the ribs, but that didn't completely kill him, so I ran to stop my dogs from chewing him up. He still had enough life to try to get hold of one of the dogs, but Chester got him by the throat and managed to choke the last bit of life out of him. That was small revenge for all the damage his kind had done to the cows, but at least he now hangs on my wall in the den and I can feel a sense of satisfaction when I look at him.

Around that time the Horsefly Parade Committee asked if Black Creek Ranch would put some horses in the May Day parade. When I talked to the cowboys, they thought it would be fun to do. I decided to dress up like an Indian and ride Dally, my Appaloosa horse. I made a headdress out of chicken and turkey feathers, and used food coloring to dye them different colors. Then I took some of the horsehair we'd pulled from the horses' tails when we trimmed them in the spring and fastened it to the head dress. I used brown shoe polish on my face and arms and any part of my body that was exposed. I wore a long-haired lama vest that Mrs. Visconti had given me, my buckskin chaps, and a pair of beaded moccasins from my younger years.

Judging was done before the parade and I was awarded first prize in the equestrian lineup. They said I needed an entry number so they would know whom to give the trophy to, but they could find no place to pin it on me. Manual LaFlamme recognized who I was, and he cut a poplar sapling and made it look like a spear. He stuck the spear though the cardboard that the number was written on and handed it to me. I carried on like this was what had been planned all along.

Me, riding Dally in my Indian costume;
Bob Miles on horseback behind me

Once the parade got underway, I was quite vocal throughout it. I did a lot of whooping and hollering. I charged my horse up to bystanders watching the parade, let out a yell, and threatened them with my spear, then rushed back to the horse section and threatened a few cowboys before I fell into line. I did not use a bridle; instead, I put the rein line around Dally's lower jaw and tied it tight enough that he could not slip it over his bridle teeth. Because he was a stud, I put Vicks ointment in his nose so he couldn't smell the mares that were in estrous (heat). He was very well broken and responded to my commands with very little effort, so I felt confident that I could do anything I wanted with him.

He was a perfect gentleman throughout the parade and I was disguised so well that most people didn't recognize me. It was threatening rain and everyone was hoping to finish the parade before it started to pour. When the prizes were being handed out after the parade, the announcer didn't mention my name, but asked for the Indian on the Appaloosa horse to come and receive his trophy. I galloped my horse right up to the small stage, slid to a stop throwing dirt and gravel in every direction, got off and did a little dance, and let out a whoop and holler that startled a lot of folks. I was about to get back on my horse when the announcer asked me if I could do anything to stop the rain. I did another little dance around my horse and said, "I talked to my friend Thunder, told him no rain parade today." I then did a little whoop and holler and jumped on Dally and galloped away. I spoke very little to anyone, mainly using "ugh" and "how," which confused a lot of people all the more.

Me, in my Indian costume, riding my horse called Dally

CHAPTER 44

Hunting up Black Creek

There have been a lot of interesting moments in my life, which include encounters with bull moose in the fall, black bears, and wolves. A lot of my knowledge of hunting came from the many years that I spent hunting with my dad. One day he phoned and said he had a friend that wanted to go moose hunting. He wondered if I had time to take him out and call a moose for him. My dad had lost his eyesight to glaucoma by then and was living in the Okanogan on the same property as my younger brother Clifford.

I was still running the Black Creek Ranch at that time and it was the fall of the year. I was busy making sure that all the cattle got off the range, but I told him to come and I would see what I could do for him. The morning after they arrived at the ranch, I took Dad and his friend Herb Grey with me to pick up some salt blocks and move them down closer to the ranch so the cows would work their way down off the mountain in their search for them. On our way up to the last salt block, which was quite high up on the mountain, there was a good spot to make a moose call.

Dad said he would just sit in the truck and Herb could go with me. I called and didn't get an answer. After several more calls without an answer, I decided to go up and get the last salt block and try a call from somewhere else. When we returned to the spot where I'd made the first calls, there were three moose standing there looking at us.

I told Herb to get out and shoot his moose. He got out and slammed the door shut; of course, the moose took off. They were running up a cow trail, one behind the other. I don't know what Herb was waiting for. Possibly he thought they would stop so he could shoot at them. The moose were quite close (less than 100 yards), so I stepped out of the pickup and shot all three.

What surprised me was that Dad knew I had shot three of them. I asked him how he could have known that; I might have missed one. He said, "No, I heard the bullet hit every time you shot." It was then I realized I was hunting with a very wise old hunter. He asked what I was going to do with the third one. I told him that one was for Clifford. I did a quick job of dressing them and we went back down to the ranch. I asked the hired men if they would bring the moose back down to the ranch. That was the last time that I hunted moose with my dad.

Wayne Randall, a friend of mine, wanted me to call a moose for him. So one day I took him with me when I was out on the range and called a bull moose within fifty yards for him. His first shot killed it. He was excited and he asked me how come other guys didn't do that when they hunted moose. He said it was so easy, they just came out and looked at you. I told him it wasn't just every day that it happened that way, and besides, when you called a moose, you had to be sure you knew what to tell them.

He said he was going to tell his brother, Gene, to get me to teach him how to call moose. Wayne just lived up the road from the ranch. One day he got hold of me again and said Gene wanted to come out and have me call a moose for him. I told them it was the wrong kind of day. It was a little too windy and the conditions weren't good to call moose. He said Gene was on his way from Williams Lake, so we should just try one or two calls.

I was reluctant to go because I was busy, but I had to check a waterhole on the side of a mountain, so I told him they could come with me and somewhere along the way we'd make a couple of moose calls. There was a brisk wind and I told them it was a waste of time, but Wayne wanted me to just try once.

I left them in the pickup and walked down the mountain for ten minutes and made a call. A few minutes later, when Wayne and Gene drove down to where I was waiting for them, I asked if they could hear me and they said they hadn't heard a thing. I couldn't help it. I said, "I told you, it's not a good time."

The author calling a moose

Me, in the foreground, holding my .25-06 rifle; Wayne Randall walking away down the trail

We jumped in the truck and started down off the mountain. We hadn't gone 100 yards when the trail took a sharp turn to the left, and as we turned the corner there was a young bull moose running up the trail toward us.

I told Wayne and Gene to go get him but not to shoot him in the hindquarter; instead, they should wait until he turned off the trail and then poke one right behind the front shoulder. The moose ran down the trail quite a ways and was about to turn off when they both cut loose on him. At first I didn't think they hit him but I hated to leave a wounded animal in the bush, so I told them to walk down the trail very slowly while I made a circle around to see how badly it was hit. I didn't go more than 200 yards when I found their moose. He was standing with his head down and all four feet together like a tired old pony. I thought it was odd, as I had never seen anything quite like that before.

He was facing away from me, so I sneaked up a little closer. At first I thought they must have gut shot him as I could see something hanging down between his hind legs. Then I realized they had shot him right through the knackers and one nut was hanging down on about ten inches of cord. He lifted his head to look back at me and I shot him right behind the ear.

I called to Gene and Wayne and told them I had found their moose. When they arrived, I asked them where they thought they hit him, and they both said they had aimed right behind his front shoulder. I pulled his hind leg up and spread it so they could see where they'd hit him. I told them if they were always so good at doing that I could use them in the spring of the year when it was time to castrate the calves!

On one occasion I took Bob Miles with me to help Ulrich move some persistent cows back up the mountain and we ran into a sow bear with two cubs. The dogs took after the bear and the cubs went up trees. The range rider thought it'd be nice to have a little bear for a pet; one of the cubs climbed up a tree that was not very big.

Although Ulrich really wanted the cub, he wasn't brave enough to crawl up the tree after it, so I agreed to be the monkey. They promised they'd make sure the old mama bear didn't come after me, so up the tree I went. But I found it was more difficult to climb a tree wearing a cowboy hat, a pair of spurs, and a pair of chaps than I thought. The first thing that had to go was the hat, and when I was about fifteen feet up the tree, I saw the old mama bear coming back for her cubs. I yelled at the boys to chase her away again, but they ran to their horses, where they thought they would be safer. There I was up the tree and I could just see that mama bear pulling the spurs right off of my boots.

I don't remember exactly what I said, but both my dogs came to my rescue and took her for a good long run. I was unable to go high enough to catch the little bear, because he could just stay out of my reach and the top of the tree was getting so small I was afraid it would break and I would go crashing to the ground. So I crawled back down near the bottom of the tree and Bob handed me the end of his lariat, and I crawled halfway up again and tied it there. I came down and tied my lariat to the ground end of Bob's. I told Bob and Ulrich that when I jerked the tree back toward me with my horse they were to catch the little bear when he came down.

Well, I did a lot of jerking, but the little fellow hung on like he was glued to the tree, and he started to cry. That was when the mama bear showed up again and there I was, dallied fast to the tree that the cub was in. This time she was more determined to get her cub and she was prepared to fight if she had to. Bob and the two dogs managed to chase her back into the bush. Then Bob and Ulrich got off their horses again, planning to catch the little guy when I jerked him out of the tree. The little bear must have relaxed a bit, because that time I jerked him free and he came tumbling down. Ulrich was determined to catch it, but when he jumped on it, it scratched and bit him until he let it go. Needless to say, Ulrich didn't get his pet bear.

Another time Ulrich asked me to ride out with him and see what was tearing some of the smaller calves up. I thought a bear was probably the culprit, and sure enough, it was a mother bear with three cubs. The cubs would start playing with the calves and then the mama bear would come, and in defence of her cubs, would slap the calves around, leaving large deep cuts on them. I quietly disposed of the three cubs and the problem was solved.

By now the routine of the ranch operation ran smoother for me than it had ever done before. I had convinced the owner we most definitely needed higher ground for hay land and we also needed to start clearing land immediately so we could get it into production as soon as possible. I cleared approximately 250 acres, bought a big heavy breaking disc to work the newly cleared land, and another field disc to follow up on the breaking. I thought that things were going good and I was making good progress in making his investment into a working ranch, but when I asked him for a root rake, he thought I was spending too much.

He also told me to stop clearing land. This was all a big letdown for me. I asked him to buy a combine so I could combine the barley that I'd grown on the McKinley land, but he didn't favor that idea either. I took him and showed him the barley and asked him what he wanted me to do with it. He said to put the cows in it. I could not convince him otherwise.

I knew Italians had a reputation for being stubborn, but I couldn't believe that they could be that stubborn. That crop of barley would have produced more than enough grain to feed the cows and yearlings all winter.

CHAPTER 45

The Irwin Brothers

Larry and Kenny Irwin were the last two hands that I hired at Black Creek. They were brothers and both had long beards and wore cowboy hats. They both had "wives" and there were children involved also. They both liked their beer and wine, or *grog*, as Kenny called it.

*Ken, giving a needle to an animal
in the chute at branding time*

Larry liked to grow those plants that could be mistaken for tomatoes to the uneducated eye when they are little!

Larry, who was a good range rider,
both were fun and good entertainment!

Not long after they came to the ranch, they decided to take a trip down the river in a canoe. They had a gallon of wine and a tippy canoe, but they were doing okay until the wine jug got below the halfway mark. Now, neither one could swim a stroke, nor did they have any lifejackets on. It was a total recipe for a disaster.

They came around a corner in the river and there was a brood of young Canada geese. They tried to catch some, and that's when they tipped the canoe. They came up coughing and gagging, and Kenny was telling Larry, "For god's sake, don't lose that wine." They didn't catch any geese, but they did manage to hang on to the wine.

Somehow they managed to get everything under control again. But they had one problem: the wine jug. They didn't want to chance loosing that jug again, so they decided to drink it. Larry said it was the only sensible thing they could do.

Now the canoe really became tippy. I don't know many times they dumped it. They finally gave up and dragged it up onto shore. They were walking back to the road when I found them. They were good workers, but when they played, they really played hard. They were totally crazy (wild and humorous, not mentally) and you never could guess what they might do next.

One day in the fall, we were starting to gather up cows on the day before moose season opened. Larry and his two cousins took my two German shepherd dogs and went up the back of Black Mountain to gather up any strays that might have been left behind. On their way up they met a yellow car with two guys in it. They had been chasing a cow moose down the road. When they met the ranch truck, the moose stopped and turned back around and started running back up road in front of the ranch truck. She didn't go too far before she was tuckered out. Larry bumped her with the truck and she fell down. Those two Shepherds had her, one by the ear and the other by the leg, so the boys thought that they might as well cut her throat. You couldn't ask for anything easier.

Before they had the moose dressed out, the little yellow car came back again. I imagine they were hoping to find their moose and must have been upset when they realised they had been beaten to it. They turned around and went down to the ranch to phone the cops. They reported that someone had shot a moose and loaded it into a truck. When Larry and his cousins came back to the ranch with their trophy, the mechanic that was doing the service on the light plant told them they had better get rid of her because they had been reported and the cops were on their way. They got rid of the body, but they left a lot of evidence behind.

That day I was at the Wynstra Place near Horsefly, moving hay stacks with Ken. We had just come home for supper when the cops and a conservation officer arrived. At that point I didn't know anything about what had happened. The CO asked what I knew about a moose being shot on the ranch. I imagine I looked a bit surprised. I told him I knew nothing. He said that a moose had been shot, and looking at Ken, he said the guy that was with me fit the description of one of the people involved. I could make things easier for myself by telling them where the moose was.

I told them that their "suspect" and I had been moving hay all day. We'd had nothing to do with a moose and I was going to sit down and have my supper. If they wanted to, they could go and have a look around. After I finished supper I drove down to the barn.

Without a doubt, there had been a moose in the truck box. There was hair and blood all over. The cop came to me and said, "You told me that you didn't know anything about this." I said, "I didn't until you showed up. You tell me who shot the moose."

The other boys had gone home to Williams Lake, but Larry was sitting in his bunkhouse, having a beer. There was hair and blood on his boots and pants. The cop and the CO were rattling questions at him right and left. All he seemed to say was, "Don't know, can't tell you." Finally, the cop said, "You know, Larry, confession is good for the soul." Larry just sat stoking his long beard and said, "You know, you are right. They taught me that in Sunday school." He was one cool dude.

The cop and the CO looked all over and couldn't find anything more. They decided they would take the .30-30 rifle that I lent Larry for when he was out riding, his pants, and his boots. When the CO asked him for his pants, he refused to give them to him. The cop said, "We will take them if you don't give them to us."

Larry just sat there sipping on his beer. Then the cop walked around behind him and put a bear hug on him and the chair, while the CO took his pants and boots off. They told me that they would be back later. They sort of admitted they didn't think I had anything to do with it, but they would be back to find the moose and then they'd be laying charges. I asked them to make sure they returned the gun to me, and they said I'd get my gun back but it might be awhile.

They never did find the moose. I eventually got my gun back, and Larry got his boots and pants back too. No charges were ever laid.

About five years later, I was in a café in Williams Lake and two cops came in. One of them had come out to the ranch with the CO over the moose episode. I was hauling logs then, so I was sitting at the truckers' table. The cop recognized me and said, "Powich will buy the coffee." We shot the breeze for a while, and then I asked him if they ever solved the crime that was committed up Black Creek. He just grinned at me and said they knew the guys had shot the moose, but they couldn't find the evidence. He said I probably knew the whole story by then. I laughed and told him they were not even close to knowing what had happened and thanked him for returning my gun.

What actually happened was those cowboys took the moose out to the range and buried it. To this day I really don't know where. I tried to get Larry to tell me, but all he would say was, "You know, boss, if you don't ask too many questions I won't have to tell you any lies."

The ranch owned 650 head of cattle and I knew that unless I was able to put more land into production for hay and pasture we couldn't continue to run that many cattle. The land was there and the ranch could have been very productive. When we were discussing some of the things that would help bring the ranch into better production, clearing the land for hayfields was just one of them. The Wynstra Ranch, which I thought he owned at Horsefly, was actually one that he had given to his friend, who was a bridge engineer and doing a rather large job at Montréal, Québec. He called his friend and said he must come to Black Creek Ranch because some bigger decisions had to be made concerning these properties. When his friend arrived, he told him that he was planning to clear a bunch of bush land and put it into hayfields.

His friend said to me, "I have such a good friend. He bought me a ranch, and now he wants me to pay for clearing the land. But I don't think I want to do that. He can have everything off of the land, but he must clear it himself if he wants to make more hayfields. I just own the land, and he looks after it for me."

I was somewhat disappointed that the Limousin cattle were an aspect that had not materialized as he had promised. He seemed to be juggling things around far too much for my liking. I got the feeling he did not really want to make the ranch into a profitable operation. When the books of the ranch showed that I had been in the black for more than three months, he immediately called me to Vancouver to meet with him and his accountant. I was reprimanded for making decisions without his consent to put the ranch back in the black rather than showing a loss. He told me that he did not want me to put the ranch too far in the red, but when it came to making decisions as to whether or not it was going to make money, he would decide that and not me.

I was upset with his intentions for the ranch, and after he had gone with two of his Italian friends to find a shoe store that he was going to buy for them, I talked some more with his accountant. I told him I didn't know if I could continue to run the ranch under those circumstances. I had never worked for anyone that didn't want me to make a profit for them. He told me that if I was happy working the ranch, I should not worry so much about the financial end of it. He said the ranch was used as a tax dodge. I told him I realized that he was a wealthy man, but I could not understand his kind of thinking. He looked at me and kind of grinned, and I knew that he knew a lot more than he was going to tell me. He said people could do things differently when they're worth more than 200 million.

I learned later that his wealth had come to him through family businesses in northern Italy, and that he was trying to move his money out of Italy because of the Socialist threat to the government at the time. I regret that I didn't learn to understand him before I decided I could no longer ranch like that for him. I had worked just as hard and gave as much of myself to him as I would have if the ranch was mine and I got the feeling that my efforts were not appreciated. So at the next meeting at the ranch, we had a man-to-man talk and I told him I was no longer prepared to run the ranch for him under those conditions. I think he was quite shocked that I would make a decision like that.

He asked me if I would go to Manitoba and manage the farm there for him and he would sell Black Creek Ranch. He had bought 16,000 acres in southern Manitoba, and although I never saw it, he told me it was light sandy soil and very prone to drought conditions. However, he did manage to clear a large portion of it and raised corn, fava beans, and alfalfa

My answer was I wasn't interested in going to Manitoba. I told him I would see that all the cows were brought off the range in the fall, but after that he had to find someone else to run his ranch. He told me I could not leave until he sold the ranch. I told him I'd no plans to stay that long, because I didn't know how long it would take to sell the ranch. I wanted to go back to my little ranch and continue raising my Limousin cattle.

He looked at me in a way I never saw him look before and he said he would no longer be my friend, and turned and walked away. I didn't intend to end our friendship, but I didn't intend to work for someone that didn't show more enthusiasm and appreciation for what I'd done. If that meant that he was no longer my friend, so be it.

CHAPTER 46

Leaving Black Creek to Go back Home

That fall, after roundup I moved back to my little ranch, where I belonged. I could now concentrate on developing my purebred Limousin operation.

The Black Creek Valley is very beautiful. The mountains and rivers and lakes make it a place where one can really enjoy the beauty of Mother Nature. My kids enjoyed being there on the ranch. They all helped with the labor that it took to run the place. They would help during calving time, tagging and vaccinating the calves, and at branding time they would help with anything they were asked to do. I can say now, when all those things are behind me, that I probably was not very fair to them, because I became too involved in trying to run the ranch. I regret now that I did not take special time just to play and work with them.

Cherie bottle feeding an orphan calf while Cindy holds it

Me holding a calf while Cindy gives it a shot; Cherie watching

Darryl shovelling pellets; Murray driving the truck

Murray in the alleyway at the corrals

Darryl standing in the alleyway in the corrals

Loading the bales into the old barn

CHAPTER 47

The Rancher Becomes a Trucker

When we moved back to Horsefly from Black Creek Ranch, I knew I had to have another job to create enough finances to build my ranch quickly. The following spring I was approached by Larry Ross, who was hauling off-highway from the bush to the reload at Black Creek. He was looking for a truck driver, and I decided to give it a try. Although I'd driven truck before, I had never driven one quite as big or hauled any loads as long as those trucks did.

The truck I drove was a PT 510 Pacific with extra heavy transmission, rear-ends, and frame rails. We used twelve-foot bunks and the loads where at least one and a half highway loads, which was approximately 200,000 pound. The trailer was extra heavy duty, with a gross weight of sixty tons and twenty-four-inch rubber on it. The logs we hauled were full tree-length and the longest ones were 170 feet. The loader operator ran an American heel boom machine, and would put the shorter trees on the bunk to start with in order to keep the long ones from dragging on the road. But sometimes they were so long they would drag anyway.

From the bush to the reload was approximately twenty to twenty-five kilometers. At the reload we would trip our stakes and then a 966 Loader would push the load off onto a set of brow logs. The trailer was so heavy, it was all the 966 could do to set it back on the rider bar on the truck.

I enjoyed being up in the mountains where the air was fresh and the fragrance of the newly-cut timber was like sweet perfume to inhale. The method of logging was hand felling with a yarding system that skid the trees to a deck next to a haul road. There, a heel boom would load them onto our trucks. This was high mountainous country, beautiful, steep, and very rugged. In the summer time we would often watch moose browsing in the cut blocks while we were being loaded high up on the mountain.

Me standing by one of Larry Ross's off-highway trucks

After that, the challenge was to maneuver a loaded truck out of the high-cut blocks, down the narrow, winding logging road to the main haul road below. I liked to say that it took nerves of steel and a brain the size of a pea to do a job like that. But you know, by the time I had worked there for the first month, I enjoyed it so much I actually made plans to buy two of the trucks.

I sold my commercial herd of cows to raise the down payment and the rest I would borrow from the bank. Everything was approved and all the finances were in place, and the bank was just waiting for me to sign the papers. The day we were supposed to go to town and sign them, Dave Kerens, a Jacobson Brothers bush supervisor, phoned Gloria at work and asked her if we had made the deal. She told him we were going in to sign the papers that day, and he told her not to do it until I talked to the mill again, because the mill was changing its operations. I was grateful to him for the heads-up.

The mill said they were not going to log white wood anymore but I could haul cedar. I decided not to go ahead with the deal. I was afraid that the cedar haul wouldn't last very long, and I would be stuck with those heavy trucks and trailers that I couldn't use on a highway.

After negotiating with the mill in town, I was given a promise that if I put a regular highway truck on the road I would be given a position to haul logs for them from up the Black Creek Valley into Williams Lake. On the strength of this promise, I bought a brand-new White Western Star and an Artic trailer and went to work hauling logs. Now I was a fully equipped log hauler. I made two trips a day into Williams Lake, five days a week. The haul was good and easy on fuel and brakes. The truck was new, so there was little or no repair work to be done, and if any major thing happened it was covered on warranty.

I thought I'd found the job I needed to go along with my small ranching operations. Pay was good. At the end of every month I made $25,000. But the next year was a totally different story. I no longer could haul from the Black Creek Valley. I was told by the mill that I would have to haul from three or four other locations, some of which were not very good at all. I stayed with that until I could find something better.

I negotiated with Ainsworth lumber company in 100 Mile House, British Columbia to do an off-highway haul, but it required four trucks, two of which had to be mine. So after signing a contract, I purchased the second truck and equipped both of them with ten-foot bunks, and hired two more trucks to work with me.

My logging trucks on the landing

Ainsworth's off-highway haul was quite different from the first haul that I had been on in the Black Creek Valley. This was strictly in jack pine timber and the haul was closer to eight to ten kilometers. It was relatively flat land and we never even loaded our trailers to return to the bush. We were loaded with a Barko loader, branches and all. At the reload they spread the timber out and would flail the branches off the trees. Then they bucked them into highway lengths and delivered it to the mill with highway trucks.

There were things about the job that I didn't like. One was that I was away from home, living in a trailer, batching or eating in a café. It was too much for Gloria and the kids to manage the ranch without me being there, but they did the best they could. The money was good, but I wanted to be able to spend more time on the ranch.

I could not believe my ears the day I was told they were going to shut down the off-highway haul. Although I had a contract that guaranteed I would be able to haul logs to the Ainsworth mill as long as they were in operation, it didn't say which mill or where. Now I would have to move even farther away from home and rerig my trucks for highway hauling if I wanted to continue to work for Ainsworth. I was deeper into the log hauling business than I'd ever intended to get. I liked it less and less every day, but because of all the money that I'd invested into the trucking operation, I was compelled to keep hauling logs until I could find some way out of the mess that I had gotten into.

I finally ended up hauling logs for Lignum Lumber Company in Williams Lake, and I moved my trailer back into Williams Lake. At least then I was only fifty miles from home and could spend most of the weekend at home on the ranch. This still was not to my liking but both my daughters were in high school in Williams Lake by then, so they were able to stay in the trailer with me and work in the café after school.

As the trucks got older, there was more and more maintenance and repair work to be done on them. If I hired the truck shop to do repairs for me instead of doing it myself, my paycheck was not very big at the end of the month. I was getting desperate to find a way out of this trucking business that I disliked more and more every day.

I was beginning to understand the logging industry a little better. I realized that I could bid on small timber sales and sell the logs to the mills in Williams Lake. If I hired another driver, I could manage my logging operation right from home at the ranch. That meant I would have to purchase a cat, a skidder, and a loader and several power saws to become a logger, but they could be utilized on the ranch, clearing land when I was not working in the bush. I made a decision to do that. I didn't buy new equipment, but it worked and I had the trucks to haul my own logs, which was helpful.

A 1700 Timberjack loader decking wood on the landing

I am repairing a hydraulic hose behind the grille guard in front of the rad on my TD15

I used a 450 Timberjack skidder

Me with a load of firewood that I salvaged out of the slash pile

Me standing on a landing with some logs ready to ship

My loaded logging truck coming out on a snowy day

* * *

There are times in life when we have no control over the circumstances that come into our lives. That became such a reality early in the morning of April 5, 1985, when an RCMP officer knocked on our door to tell us that our youngest child, Darryl, had been killed in a motor vehicle accident. Now, I only have my memories of him to cherish and the privilege of having had him in our family for eighteen years.

The truck Darryl was driving when he was hit by a drunk driver,
right in front of the hospital in Valleyview, Alberta

Darryl at about seventeen
years, coming out of the
river after having a dip

Bow, my constant companion
wherever I went, in the
bush or on the ranch

Darryl's funeral was held in Valleyview, where he had been living and had died. He was buried there. When we came back home, I had to pick up the pieces and continue on even though my heart was breaking.

By now I was much more a logger/trucker than a rancher, with really no idea how I could spend more time being a rancher. With more equipment to repair and keep running, logging had basically become a full-time job. And hiring drivers to drive my trucks and look after them was not such a great idea. Maintenance, such as the fuel costs and tires, increased every year, along with insurance. Ultimately, I decided it was cheaper for me to hire trucks than to own them, so I sold my trucks and concentrated more on my logging.

While I was logging, I kept adding to my cowherd, buying heifers of good quality, as well as a few outstanding bulls. It was tough because the logging took most of my time, but it did provide the money to make those things possible. I had to buy most of my hay and I worked late evenings in the cold, feeding the animals after I got in from the bush. Weekends were spent doing whatever I had to do on the ranch so I could go back logging on Monday. In those days we could get a lot of snow in Horsefly and that made things more difficult in the bush and on the ranch.

A load of bales; through the years I bought thousands of dollars of hay

The loader doing double duty, unloading hay when not working in the bush

During the first few years we had a lot of years with heavy snowfalls

*Murray and Circle 4 Friday, one of my herd sires that
produced correct calves with good disposition*

This was part of my Limousin cowherd

CHAPTER 48

I Become the President of the BC Limousin Association

For several years, the BC Limousin Association had wanted me to get involved in their directorship, and finally I decided to do it. The BC Limousin Association was pretty dormant when I took over the presidency. I talked to the secretary manager of the Canadian Limousin Association, which I was a member of, and asked him for a few pointers. Harvey Tedford was a great help to me as I struggled to develop the BC Association. The first thing I did was try to get a more active membership. I personally absorbed most of the costs and gave all of my time with no compensation, trying to get the people who were using Limousin to participate in the BC Association.

I called for a membership meeting and we established a new board of directors, of which I was president. Ann Qusenell was the secretary. That first year, with the help of my wife Gloria, we pretty much ran the association. I can remember when our stationery budget was larger than the budget of the whole association the previous year. Gloria and I acted as the advertising committee. We also did a newsletter that was sent to every member and anyone else we thought might be interested in Limousin. The newsletter was a lot of work because putting it together was done by hand.

It wasn't long before talk started to circulate about the revitalized BC Limousin Association, or maybe I should say the new president. When my stationery budget was larger than the operating budget for the previous year, some of the old members started to get a little concerned that I was going to bankrupt their association. That summer I made it a point to take cattle to several cattle shows in the province and encouraged every other breeder to come along. We didn't have enough Limousin at any one show to make a class, so we were put into what was called the "others." But they couldn't ignore the fact that we were there with our cattle and we got all the promotion that I could muster. And I got to talk to a lot of the members and some not yet members who were interested in Limousin cattle.

By the end of show season, we had quite a few more people interested not only in the breed, but also in the association as well. I lobbied with the Canadian Association to get a two-dollar kickback on every registered animal from British Columbia to help the young and struggling association get on its feet. That was passed along and with the increased membership, and our association was starting to look better and better.

The annual meeting was held in September, and I had heard through moccasin telegraph that I was going to have to be removed before I bankrupted the association. I contacted an auctioneer that was interested in Limousin cattle and I asked him if he would auction some pies as a fundraiser at the annual meeting. He said he would, and so I got twenty ladies to bake pies for the auction.

I gave the president's report and had the secretary read the minutes of the last meeting. Then I gave a report about where I thought the association was going and what progress we had made during the year. It was quite clear that our membership had increased, that some of us breeders had been to three or four different cattle shows throughout the province, and we had created a presence in the British Columbia cattle industry. A lot of people had gotten their first good look at Limousin cattle.

I made it clear that the association would go nowhere without the cooperation of the members and we needed dollars to operate and to be half-respectable in the cattle business. I introduced the auctioneer and told the people at the meeting that we were going to do a little fundraiser to help kick the association into higher gear. When first pie was auctioned, the auctioneer started at $5 and ran it to $50, and then said it had sold to his ranch name. There were a lot of surprised faces. I bought the next pie for $50. That was all it took to get the ball rolling, and after the twenty pies were sold we had made a little over $450.

Then I called the meeting to order for the election of officers. I explained how important it was that we have a membership committee and an advertising committee to advertise that we had Limousin cattle for sale. I also explained that it was the responsibility of every member to try and do the best they could to help carry this association along. I told them I believed if we could succeed in doing this for a year it would pay great dividends to each and every member. When the new board of directors was nominated, Ann Quenelle was still the secretary and I was still the president.

At the annual meeting in Prince George, Gloria and I were presented with the Limousin Leader of the Year Award from the Limousin Leader

For the next seven years the BC Limousin Association grew bigger every year. We had Limousin at six different shows every year. The Limousin breed had the largest representation of any breed at several different shows. In 1991 we hosted the annual meeting for the Canadian Limousin Association at the Prince George Fair. There were over a hundred head of Limousin cattle at the show and sale. The sale was held right after the show, and although it was not a complete barnburner we had an average of approximately $1,800 a head, that included cows, calves, yearlings, and bulls. Cattle came from as far away as Lloydminster, Saskatchewan, and some from Alberta as well. I am sure many members realized the benefit this effort had made to their operation. I have been called many things in the past, but the thing that I remember the most is being called a mover and shaker for the breed.

I was a director on the board of the Canadian Limousin Association for seven years. During that time I gained a lot of experience about different breed associations and the functions that were required to not only build but also maintain a profitable organization. I worked on different committees advertising and promoting the Limousin breed. It was an incredible experience to make so many different friends across Canada and from other countries, and to work with them to organize, shows, sales, and inaugural meetings. Our head office was in Calgary, Alberta and just to work with the functions and operation of that office alone was quite a job. It gave me a lot to draw from when it came to running the BC Association.

This is a picture of the members of the Canadian Limousin board in my first year

for the Limousin Assoc

Members of the new board, front row from left, include: Gloria Antypowicl President, Canadian Limoselles, Horsefly, BC; Harvey Tedford, Secretar Manager, Calgary, AB; Mark Cressman, President, Waterloo, ON; Bill Scrive Vice-President, Ayton, ON; Gerry Good, past President, Carstairs, AB ar Henry Hays, Treasurer, Hardisty, AB.

Back row: Rob Garner, Simpson, SK; Lloyd Antypowich, Hosefly, BC; Marv Latimer, Innisfail, AB; Michael Horsnell, Aylesford, NS; Kelly Yorga, Flintoʻ SK and Lawrence Daniels, Kenton, NA.

A newspaper clipping of the Canadian Limousin board members

Harvey Tedford was the secretary manager of the Canadian Limousin Association. Harvey worked tirelessly at promoting the Limousin breed; his knowledge of the cattle industry across Canada and the USA, as well as France, where the Limousin breed came from, was highly looked upon by other associations. From time to time he had chances to work for other associations because of his ability to manage the functions of a breed association and to make it excel.

His job didn't come without problems, but problems are meant to be solved and in my estimation he did a very good job at doing that. The registration of cattle between Canada, USA, France, and England and other countries could present unique problems. To be able to set up a system where registrations could be transferred smoothly between various countries was no small task and required someone with very good public relations and the knowledge with which to make all these functions work smoothly.

Management of the office and staff required Harvey to be a step ahead of the rest in order to meet all the various challenges and have a solution for everyone's problem, whether it was to do with importations, exportations, or embryo transplants. I can remember the day when our office had to become bilingual and one of the girls in our staff was required to speak French. The marketing aspect could be very challenging and competitive in the cattle industry. Breeds watched what the others associations did very closely, and if an association was going to remain competitive and stay on top, it required sharp, knowledgeable judgment.

The call to rent or to own a building became the responsibility of the directors. This was never taken lightly without consultation of the membership at an annual meeting. Then the directors were called upon to make the best possible decision on behalf of the membership. It required information from real estate and the legal advice of lawyers. There were times when I wondered what the hell a rancher from Horsefly, British Columbia was doing there, but it was a learning experience for me, and I enjoyed it very much.

The time came when I was asked if I would let my name stand for president of the Canadian Limousin Association as the constitution stated that no director could run more than two terms on the board. I didn't feel that I had the time to spend doing all that was required to become a president. I knew it would require a lot of time traveling from one end of Canada to the other and attending on special occasions at meetings between other association representatives discussing the business of various upcoming problems.

I can't say that I didn't look at it as a challenge and I'm sure it would have been a tremendous learning experience, but I decided I'd better look after Black Mountain Limousin and the BC Association. When I left the directorship I was given a nicely engraved plaque that read "Presented to Lloyd Antypowich, in recognition of your years of service on the Canadian Limousin Association, from the board of directors, November 30, 1993." That was a very special birthday present for me that year as my birthday is on November 29.

I continued to concentrate my efforts on promoting the Limousin breed in British Columbia. I hosted a field day at the ranch each year around the end of May for many years. Some years there were over a hundred people present at this event. I tried to make the day educational for everyone, from 4-H members to anyone else who was interested in the cattle industry.

I brought in guest speakers and had demonstrations presented by a variety of people. The intent of the field days was strictly to show the producers in the beef industry some of the changes that were taking place in marketing and grading in the feedlots and in the breeding of cattle. I invited people like agriculturalists, people involved in marketing and grading, people involved in feedlots, and people involved in crossbreeding of cattle. I also invited editors of magazines like our local *Beef in BC* and the *Limousin Journal*, which was a national magazine. The editor of that magazine was Mr. Randy Bolum. Gerry Good, the president of the Canadian Limousin Association, and Harvey Tedford, the secretary manager of the Canadian Limousin Association, came several times.

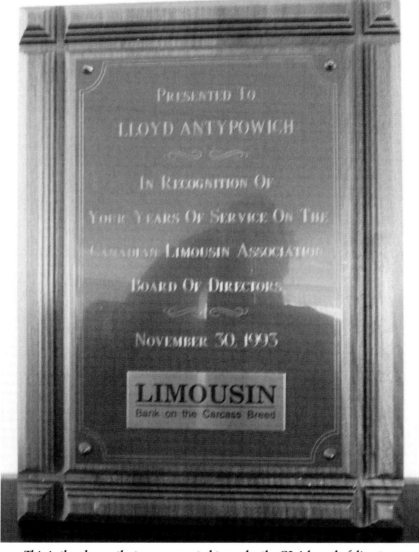

This is the plaque that was presented to me by the CLA board of directors

The people from BCAI supplied me with the nitrogen for the tank in which I stored the semen from different bulls that I used in my AI program over a period of ten or twelve years. I invited them to come and explain what all was involved if someone was interested in venturing into this type of program. They also brought their van out to demonstrate to the people the technique of flushing embryos from a donor cow.

I had also been dealing with the people from Bovatec from the Calgary area in Alberta and I invited Darrell DeGraft to give everyone a more detailed look at what took place when they did embryo transplants. He brought a complete reproductive tract of a cow and demonstrated with a pipette and iodine. That made it possible for the people to see what the pipette was doing, where the embryos were placed, and then he went on to explain that a donor cow that was stimulated with the necessary hormones could produce a multitude of good live embryos. The embryos would later be flushed out of the donor cow, screened for defects, and then put into recipient cows that would carry an embryo for nine months and produce a full-blood animal. This enabled a purebred breeder to select a specific bloodline and get into the business much quicker.

Some of the people that I invited were from Alberta and Saskatchewan and were reputable breeders in the purebred industry. They would mingle with the crowd and the people had an opportunity to ask them questions about their operations.

I even had our local MLA, Mr Alex Fraser, come one year to talk to us about the happenings within the province. Another year I had an older couple from Vancouver Island demonstrate a small portable sawmill they had designed to cut timber that was logged right off the farm.

I invited the local 4-H leader, Mr. Tim Rolf. He was a purebred Herford breeder in the area. I asked him to be a judge and instructor to the 4-H students. I had a pen of heifers and bulls for them to judge. They had judging cards to fill out for their placements and the reasons why they had made their decisions. They did a very good job and Tim explained fully how he saw their reasons for judging to be correct or faulty. At the end of the day, I gave Black Mountain Limousin T-shirts to all the 4-H kids who had participated.

A couple of times the whole field day was videoed by Channel 10 Television. Their commentator was Doug Johnson, who had been a truck driver for me at one time. He talked to a lot of people during the day and interviewed them. This was seen on Channel 10 Television, and it gave the people an opportunity to take in the field day without actually being there.

One of the guests that I invited was Lorne Bodel from Alberta. I asked him to come and demonstrate to the 4-H group how to fit and clip an animal for show. After he had explained and shown the group what to do, he proceeded to clip just one-half of the animal. Lorne was well known for his ability to clip and fit animals for show. After he was done, he told them that was pretty much what they needed to know about clipping and fitting an animal. He then handed me the mic. I thanked him for the demonstration and told him I didn't think he was done yet, because he had only clipped and fitted one-half of the animal. His reply was the other half was mine to do and he was sure the kids would like to see how I did it.

My field day sign

Me speaking as I opened my first field day

Part f the group of people who attended my field day at the corals

Here I am pointing out different things to look for
when examining prospective herd sires

BLACK MOUNTAIN LIMOUSIN
1ST PRODUCTION SALE
Saturday, October 27th, 1990—1:00 p.m.

BLACK MOUNTAIN LIMOUSIN
Box 131, Horsefly, B.C. VOL 1L0
Lloyd and Gloria Antypowich (604) 620-3567
Herdsman: (604) 620-3516

at the ranch
Horsefly, British Columbia

The cover of my first production sale catalogue

BLACK MOUNTAIN LIMOUSIN
1 ST PRODUCTION SALE

AUCTIONEER AND SALE MANAGER'S COMMENTS

 Don Savage Auctions

108 Flett Drive Airdrie, Alberta T4B 1N2 (403) 948-3520

Welcome to Black Mountain Limousin's 1st Production Sale in beautiful and scenic British Columbia. Lloyd and Gloria Antypowich have been, and continue to be, very active in the promotion of the Limousin breed throughout the Province of British Columbia. Their tireless efforts have not only succeeded into developing a strong Limousin industry within the province, but also the development of a very strong, well managed herd at Black Mountain Limousin.

Their herd has been cultivated around a nucleus of very feminine, solid producing females coupled with the additions of some very outstanding herd sires; herd sires that give their females the traits that are demanded in today's beef industry. The latest herd sire added to the Black Mountain herd was the record high selling Circle T Wrangler at the 1988 CLA National Bull Test Sale. Wrangler adds to their program the highly inheritable performance trait that is so evident in his pedigree.

The cattle on offer, we give you the buyer, are a good cross section of the Black Mountain herd from bred females, 1990 calves and a reliable set of yearling fullblood and purebred bulls.

If you require further information please contact Lloyd and Gloria, or myself. If you are unable to attend the Sale but wish to make a purchase, please contact Randy Bollum or me and your order will be handled in a professional manner.

Yours truly,
DON SAVAGE

BLACK MOUNTAIN LIMOUSIN WELCOME

We at Black Mountain Limousin would like to welcome you to our First Annual Production Sale. We believe that we have selected good, sound useable cattle. All cows have been preg tested and have been found safe in calf to the dates mentioned. All bulls have been semen tested, and found to be healthy and sound, ready to go to work. We take great pleasure in serving our customers, we welcome you to become another one.

Sincerely,
Lloyd and Gloria

Cattleman's Draw!

Be sure to enter your name in the draw for the Limousin calf Black Mountain Limousin is giving away to some lucky cattleman attending the sale.

SPECIAL REVRESENTATIVES

Bill Scriven, Prseident, CLA
Harvey Tedford, Secretary Manager
                Canadian Limousin Association
Anne Quennell, Secretary, BCLA

SALE DAY PHONE (604)-620-3567

Join us for lunch prior to the sale

SALES STAFF
Don Savage, Auctioneer (403) 948-3520
Randy Bollum, Limousin Leader (403) 248-6760

OFFERING
55 Head—51 Lots

12 Fullbloods Bred	2 88% Pairs
2 Fullbloods Open	6 Fullblood Yearling Bulls
2 Purebred Pairs	7 Purebred Yearling Bulls
20 Purebreds Bred	

* All Females Pregnancy Tested   * All Bulls Semen Tested

BLACK MOUNTAIN LIMOUSIN
Box 131, Horsefly, B.C. V0L 1L0
Lloyd and Gloria Antypowich (604) 620-3567
Herdsman (604) 620-3516

1

The first page of my first production sale catalogue

*   *   *

Preparing cattle for the show circuit required a lot of the halter breaking, and believe me, I had many a blisters on my hands before I could get those critters to follow me around without trying to pull away. One day when

I was at the auction market, I was talking to another rancher and telling him how much work it was to halter break my show string. He asked me why I didn't get myself a donkey. I told him I didn't think I needed any more donkeys; I had enough stubbornness to deal with from the show cattle, especially when it came to leading them. He told me all I would have to do was tie them to a donkey and the donkey would drag them around until they were completely halter broke.

Well, that sure sounded good to me, so I asked him where I could get a couple of donkeys. He said he knew someone in the Chilcotin who had two of them that he had used to halter break his young colts and he thought he wanted to sell them. However, I would have to take both of them, because the fellow didn't want to split them up.

He gave me a phone number, and I called the man who had the donkeys. He did want to sell them. He wanted $100 apiece. He told me where he lived and said he would put the donkeys in a pen and I could come and pick them up, because he was going away to a rodeo. I had never met this man before, so I asked him how I was going to pay him if he wasn't going to be there. He told me to put the cheque under the door and he would get it when he got back home.

So I made the trip and the donkeys were in the corral as he said they would be. I slipped the cheque under the door and took them home. I tied one of the yearling heifers to the strap that he had left on the donkey's neck. The donkey dragged that yearling around the corral and I just sat there, totally amazed. You would think the donkey would slip the leather strap off from around its neck and let the yearling go, but no matter how hard the yearling tried to get the strap off of the donkey's neck it was never successful. If it tried to run ahead, the donkey would turn around and go back the other way.

I got a coffee and watched the little 500-pound donkey train a 1,000-pound heifer to lead. In about a half an hour, the donkey had the heifer following it around the corral on slack rope. I just sat there and said, "Thank you."

"Thank you," because that was the slickest way to halter break a cow. Later I made a little harness that had a breast strap on it and a cinch with a big ring attached to it. That made it much easier on the donkey. I had an area about three acres in size. I could open the corral gate and the donkeys would follow me through into that area, each had a cow tied to it. I could sit in the house and have coffee and watch the donkeys halter break my show cattle.

They became great conversation pieces when people came to purchase cattle. On field days, I put them in a pen and kids would crawl on them. Sometimes there would be three or four kids on one donkey. They never seemed to get tired of playing with the kids and never once did they kick or bite any of them.

Children playing on the donkeys during the field day

I continued to show cattle at seven different fairs each year throughout British Columbia. I sat on several different fair boards to encourage not only the Limousin breed, but steer shows as well. At the Armstrong Show and Fair they held a steer show that had a $5,000 prize for the grand champion steer. The steer that won was from Lloydminster, Saskatchewan.

I needed a stock trailer to haul my cattle when I was showing them at the fairs (it worked great for hauling horses and supplies when I went hunting too). I bought one that was built in Manitoba. It was twenty-eight-foot long and had a tack room and sleeping quarters in the front. I used it for many years, showing and hauling cattle that I sold.

A picture of the stock trailer taken while I was on a hunting trip into the mountains

Several years later I had an unfortunate incident when I was moving some horses from Horsefly to Miocene. I had four teenagers that were helping me pick rocks and roots, and they had finished doing their job. I was taking them back home at the same time as I was delivering the horses. I stopped at Clarkes General Store in Horsefly to buy them each a chocolate bar and a bottle of pop. It was about six miles to Gravel Creek Hill from Clarkes. I was about two-thirds of the way up the hill when my truck sputtered and coughed. Thinking that my fuel tank was empty, I switched over to the other one, which I knew was full. The truck picked up the fuel and returned to operating normally, but I had lost a lot of momentum on the hill.

As I got to the top of the hill and was shifting into a higher gear, the truck backfired. This was not normal and the truck had never done it before. We went about a quarter of a mile and I noticed something red flopping at the back of the tail gate. Thinking it may have been a jacket that belonged to one of the kids, I kept watching to see if I would see it again. That was when I realized what I had seen was a flame, and as I slowed down it became very visible.

I told the kids the truck was on fire, and when I stopped I wanted them to open their door and jump out and run away from the truck. I had a Tidy Tank in the box, which was about a quarter full, and I was afraid it might catch fire and blow up. What I didn't realize was how big the fire was under my truck. As I was coming to a stop, they quickly opened their door and I opened mine so we could jump out. As soon as we stopped, the flame came right up to the back of the cab. By opening the doors the way we did, a vacuum was created and the flames were sucked right into the cab. The kids managed to get out okay and so did I with a few skin burns and a lot of singed hair. They ran back up out of the ditch and stood on the road with me, a couple of hundred feet from the truck. I could see there was gas leaking out from under my truck, running under the trailer, which of course was going to set my trailer floor on fire.

I ran around the back of the trailer to get into the living quarters, because I had a fire extinguisher mounted on the wall by the door. But there was too much flame burning along the side of the trailer and the grass on the side of the road was also on fire. I realized I had to get the horses out of the trailer quickly. I had one tied and two lose because there were two compartments in the trailer.

When I opened the door on the back, it was full of smoke, so I just kicked the two loose horses out onto the road and untied the horse that was in the front compartment. Believe me, it didn't take long for it to come out of there. I took it away from the trailer and tied it to a fence post beside the road.

There were several large explosions and I assumed it was my tires blowing. Then there was just a big gush and roar as the bungs on the Tidy Tank melted and the gas caught fire. There were two torches of flame shooting into the air about twenty feet out of the tank. It didn't take long to burn off the excess gas. I was still anticipating an explosion, but it never really did happen. There wasn't a tire left on the truck. The glass had popped out of all the doors and windows and I couldn't believe what I was seeing.

My trailer was on fire. I carried a lot of show equipment in the living quarters: halters, brushes, buckets, feed tubs, bedding for the sleeping bunks, my pack board for hunting, several boxes of shells, two spare tires, a set of tools, and a set of truck chains. It was a total disaster. Believe me, it did not take very long, only about fifteen minutes from start to finish.

A vehicle came along and I asked them if they would go back to Horsefly and call the fire department because there was a considerable amount of grass burning in the ditch. It wasn't long before the fire truck arrived. They put out the grass fire and then the trailer fire, but everything inside had pretty much burned by that time. Then they worked on putting out what was left of the truck fire. There were a few anxious moments when all those shells started exploding. I'd had enough excitement for one day.

The Horsefly volunteer firefighters at the scene when my truck and trailer burned

My vehicle insurance covered the truck, but the trailer insurance would not cover the trailer because it was registered in my name and pulled by a vehicle registered in my name as well. They said I couldn't sue myself to get payment. It cost over $9,000 to repair the trailer. Then I put it in Gloria's name so nothing like that could happen again insurancewise.

I used that trailer to haul my show cattle to many shows over the years. On a few occasions we even slept in it if my show helpers were all male. I had nice big foam mattresses, and there really was a lot of room in the sleeping area. It wasn't a like a motel, but we were right on the site with the animals and most show grounds had showers. It was certainly less expensive.

The Black Mountain Limousin stall when showing cattle in Prince George

Here I am showing one of my animals at the Smithers Fall Fair

Another way I promoted Black Mountain Limousin was by sponsoring a pony chuck wagon. I paid Marcel Ruthier $1,200 a season to carry the

Black Mountain Limousin logo on his chuck wagon tarp. Marcel ran at twelve or more shows a year, and that put my name out in front of the public. I was fortunate enough to have sponsored a driver who won a lot of races.

My Black Mountain Limousin canvas on Marcel Ruthier's chuck wagon

While I was on the board of the Canadian Limousin Association, I worked with others on the bull test committee. Our bull test station was at Strathmore, Alberta. All the bulls were indexed for rate of gain, ease of calving, milk production, and disposition. At the end of the test the top of the bulls were sold and buyers would come from every province and quite a few other countries like Britain, United States, Mexico, and South America. One year I took a liking to a bull named Wrangler and paid $18,000 for a half-interest. The Tedfords from Circle T Limousin, were the breeders. The half-share they retained only applied to semen drawn from the bull.

Before I paid for the bull, people from England and Australia wanted to buy semen from him. We put him in a bull stud and drew semen. We sold $40,000 worth of semen the first year.

That deal proved to be one of my better judgment calls. A number of years later, when I was dispersing of my heard of full-blooded cows, I sold him to a fellow at Dawson Creek, British Columbia for $12,000. He sired many good calves for me. His steer calves were always in high demand for 4-H projects.

An advertisement in the Limousin Leader *with a picture of*
Ernie Tedford and I when I bought Circle T Wrangler

At the show and sale in Prince George, British Columbia, I had a group of heifers that were like peas in a pod. I sold them to one person. His name was Ross Roach. He was a logger, but like me he was a rancher at heart. Ross bought several more animals from me later. His wife would jokingly tell me that I couldn't sell him any more. Ross and I have stayed friends through the years.

Through the years I kept logging and building my herd, purchasing some outstanding animals to base my herd on. I purchased a young bull named 747 from Baltimore's at Stettler. He became a terrific herd sire.

Herd sire 747 that I purchased from Baltimore's at Stettler, Alberta

*LBC Unthinkable, an incredible heifer that I bought
from Lorne and Flossie Bodel's herd*

*I bought an "embryo flush" from LBC, which resulted in six fertilized eggs out
of their heifer, Nordic Prudence. These eggs were put into six Holstein surrogate
cows, which were brought to my ranch in Horsefly and I calved them out.*

Reaching The Peaks of Perfection

Bulls at
Vanderhoof
Bull Sale
Apr. 11&12

Black Mountain has
purchased the first Apollo
heifer in Canada - sired by
YKCC Apollo 243R
and out of a
BVF High Fashion R34M
cow.
Apollo is a full brother to
Spitz Navaho -
the 1985-86 American
Triple Crown Winner.

Class of '86

Another First For Black Mountain Limousin

BLACK MOUNTAIN LIMOUSIN
Box 131, Horsefly, B.C. V0L 1L0   -   620-3567

*Another excellent heifer that I added to my herd. She was the first
heifer to be offered for sale in Canada that was sired by Apollo.*

A few of the black Limousin crossbreds that I bred

Part of my Limousin herd in the field

*   *   *

The Limousin breed is very competitive in carcass competitions. They won the steer show at the Agrabition in Regina, Saskatchewan for over twenty years in a row. I must say now that when I made the decision to import a Limousin heifer from France in 1967 it was a good one. The breed did me very well through all the years that I raised them. Now that I have retired from raising cattle, I can look back with fond memories at all the people I have met and all the places that I have been because of the cattle.

Antypowich never quits

"Ranchers are being limited to the size of their operations."

By DANIELLE HARDER

Lloyd Antypowich is a rancher at heart. He's concerned daily with the progress of his herd, the prices he will fetch at the next sale and getting the hay up on time. However, Lloyd is also a business man who is concerned not only with ranching as a way to earn a living, but also as an industry facing a tough future.

He began ranching in Valleyview, Alberta when he was 18 years old. He married Gloria in 1960 and continued to ranch 1,300 acres in Stettler, Alberta.

The couple moved to Elkford, British Columbia in 1970 on the advice of her doctor. Lloyd worked as a shift boss at Fording Coal but soon realized his heart was with ranching and than prompted their move to Horsefly in 1973.

Lloyd was initially amazed that "so many cattle could run in the bush country and do well at it." This set him to work improving range conditions during his second year as president of the Horsefly Cattleman's Association.

Working with other ranchers, Lloyd implemented extra stock trails that were bulldozed and seeded to give cattle better access to salt blocks and water. They also made small, seeded pastures in the bush that made it easier to rope a cow and examine the animals for diseases.

In the mid-'70s he and Jack Lynn developed 160-acre coordinated management units that were cleared, seeded and cross-fenced into several sections. These areas provided ranchers with early turnout breeding pastures.

Lloyd says he has seen many changes in ranching in the past 20 years, most of which benefit the industry. He says more exotic breeds are being used now with increased cross-breeding helping the Cariboo to keep up with the rest of the cattle industry.

Marketing trends are also changing, he says, with more ranchers opting for a cow/calf rather than finishing operation. He says this is mainly because in an area such as the Cariboo where little grain is grown, it is cheaper to move the cattle to feed than the feed to cattle.

However, Lloyd says he is disappointed with the lack of available agricultural ground for expansion.

"I'm not in favor of opening forests but they should grant use of them to established ranchers to allow them to keep up with the times. Ranchers are being limited to the size of their operation."

Lloyd has also been a very active community member. He was president of the Horsefly Cattleman's Association for five years, Horsefly 4-H leader for five years, and vice-president of the Cariboo Fall Fair at one time.

He is also past-president of the B.C. Limousin Association and is a director of the Canadian Limousin Association.

"I'm not that active now, though. I just got to the burnout stage."

However, Lloyd has no plans to fully retire yet — especially from ranching.

"I'll probably spend another 10 to 15 years involved in some aspect of the business. Retirement is admitting defeat and giving up. I still have a lot to contribute."

A rancher he may be at heart, but a businessman he is in mind.

Lloyd Antypowich works with his cattle

This was a write-up in the local paper

Over time, I applied for and was able to obtain a few agriculture leases that had a lot of timber on them. I would then log them, clear the land, and put it into pasture. Although this was a lot of work, I felt that I would eventually increase my ranch base and looked forward to the day that I would be able to ranch full-time. I never could get quite the amount of acres that I needed. My neighbor got a 400-acre agricultural lease in one block that was good soil. Somehow I always got shut down by politics on anything very big. So while I obtained several leases, they didn't total 400 acres, and in many cases the soil was poor and rocky. The ranching industry has a lot of ups and downs, and maybe more downs than up, so it seemed I was going to have to hang on to my logging a little longer. I really looked forward to the day when I could work with just one or two men, shut down when I wanted to, and not be under the pressure of someone telling me what I had to do all the time.

Logging was good to me. It was a good cash flow and allowed me to establish my ranch. But then government and politics came into play, and I was not able to acquire any more agriculture leases, so I fine-tuned my ranching operation and did less and less logging.

CHAPTER 49

Leo, My Friend and Partner

A fellow just a few years older than me stayed on with me from my logging operation to help me do the odd small-timber sale and work on the ranch. Leo Morrisette became a very close friend of mine. He was an excellent man with a power saw and he would do the falling and help do the bucking while I did the skidding and loading. He was French and I am Polish, and he would often say, "Lloyd, this is one hell of an outfit and only a Frenchman or Polack could work for an outfit like this." He had a lighthearted way about him and he always had a joke or a prank to lighten the day.

He lived in the house with us and was part of our family. When Gloria came home from town, he was out the door right away, helping her bring everything into the house. He was quick to help her any way he could around the house, and she liked him and appreciated his consideration for her.

Leo Morrisette, my friend, hunting partner, and employee for ten years

He worked for me for ten years, and during that time we not only logged, but we also went fishing for spring salmon at Bella Coola and went hunting west of McKenzie in the Johansson/ Lay Creek and Sustut areas. We shot moose, caribou, grizzly bears, mountain goats, and deer. There was never a job so important to Leo that he couldn't stop for a week and go fishing or hunting. On one of our hunting expeditions we spent twenty-one days in the mountains with horses. Another time, my brother-in-law, Tom, came with us too. We were far enough back off the beaten trail that we never saw anyone until we came out. And we enjoyed every day of it.

Tom Little and Leo Morrisette in our hunting tent. Notice all the light in the tent, because we used clear plastic for the front of it. I made a door that would swing real nicely and we had ourselves a real cosy camp.

I am bringing in my caribou

Me with my grizzly bear

The author in front of his spike camp, in the mountain

*Taken at Sustut Lake, about 300 kilometers north
and west of McKenzie, British Columbia*

Taken in the David Keys, southwest of Fort Nelson

Leo had four daughters and all were avid fisherman. Diane could catch a fish when no one else could. She had won quite a few fishing derbies in the Caribou. I will never forget the ribbing she gave me one day while we were fishing on the Adnarko River near Bella Coola for spring salmon. We weren't standing very far apart and I was teasing her that I was going to catch the biggest fish first. She hooked a twenty-five-pound spring, and said, "See, Lloyd, this is how it is done." On my next cast I caught a little six-inch bull trout. She never ever let me live that down. I got ribbed at the campfire all the time.

One time, while Leo and I were packing into the mountains on horses, we had to cross several swampy areas. Leo's horse got a bit excited and started jumping, trying to find better footing. Leo was trying to get off his horse before it bogged down. When he had one foot out of the stirrup and the other leg halfway over horse's back, it catapulted him right into the swamp. When all the cussing in French was over and it seemed that he wasn't really hurt that bad, I said, "Leo, just because you're French, when you get to a swamp you don't have to play the frog and jump in." He said, "Yeah, yeah, that's all right for you to say because your horse has longer legs, but I tell you, this horse is dangerous to ride in a swamp."

What I didn't realise was when the back of the saddle came up, it caught him right between the legs and broken his tailbone. That made it very difficult for him to ride, so when we reached the spot where we were going to make our camp, I cut a chair out of an old dry tree and put a pillow on it for him. Of course, this was all done in fun. At the time I didn't realize what the situation really was. When we got back from hunting, Leo went to Vancouver and found out that his tailbone was broken. They operated and put a plate in.

Leo was quite a joker and I had to be on my toes and be alert all the time or he would pull the darndest tricks on me that you could imagine. So early one morning when we were hunting, I got out of bed before he did. I took my video camera and set it on a log facing our tent. Then I went back to the tent and asked him what the hell was taking him so long to get out of bed. Leo always slept with his long johns on and a red toque to keep his head warm. That morning he came out of the tent dressed in his toque and a sweater, his long johns, and a pair of running shoes. I conned him into a conversation about whether we should go up the mountain to look for some big rams. He assured me that was the wrong area and let me know in no uncertain terms there was no way he was going to crawl up the mountain, because there weren't going to be any sheep up there anyway.

What he didn't know was the video camera was recording not only our conversation but also all his movements and what he wore. I didn't let on what I had done and I didn't retrieve the camera until he was busy making breakfast. One evening after we were home at the ranch, he suggested that we look at our hunting pictures. I thought that was a good idea, so as we sat on the couch watching the TV Leo saw himself in an unexpected situation. He said, "What the hell is this?" And I said, "Be damned if I know, it must have been some kind of sasquatch up in the mountains." He said, "You know, Lloyd, it's my turn now and you can be sure I will get you for this one day."

The last trip we made, Leo and I packed up two packhorses and two saddle horses and headed for the mountains again. We enjoyed the outdoors, the beautiful scenery, and the fresh air of the mountains more than anything else. Hunting was secondary on our priority list. We took a small boat and motor along with us and traveled up and back down Thutade Lake. That in itself was a wonderful experience. We watched caribou swim across the lake in front of our boat but we didn't shoot them.

We managed to shoot two goats that year. One was an exceptionally large Billy with a set of horns that measured 11 3/8; the other one was just 9 ¼. The day before we left for home, we went and shot a nice trophy caribou. We tried for sheep but were unable to find any larger rams, and so left them to grow for another couple years.

The weather was near perfect and in the evening we sat around our campfire and talked about life in general, all the things that we had done, where we had been, and what we would change if we had to do it all over again. It was on a night like that when he told me how thankful he was I had taken him back into his old hunting grounds. He said he had enjoyed the trip so much and he didn't think he would be making another one.

I sensed there was something wrong with him healthwise but didn't know exactly what it was. The next spring, I pressured him to go to Vancouver to the cancer clinic and have a complete checkup. The diagnosis was not what I or his family wanted to hear. Leo had cancer in three different spots in his body and they gave him four months to live. He spent some of those four months with us at the ranch, but he also spent a lot of time in Quesnel with his daughter, Diane.

It was a very sad day for me when we celebrated his life. To this day I still miss him and I feel so very privileged to have gotten to know him, and become he was such a good friend for all the time we spent together. And whenever I go out hunting and sit around the campfire at night, I have a feeling that his presence is there in the shadows.

The next year was a real trying time for me. I had a checkup because I was having problems with my waterworks, as well as feeling tired a lot. After the test, I was sent to the Quesnel Hospital and had my prostrate reamed out. It was much enlarged and Dr. Thomas removed thirty-five grams of tissue that was sent away for a biopsy. When the results came back I was diagnosed with prostate cancer. It was a shocking thing for us and the treatment they prescribed was more than what I would have done to my horse, so I declined it. I decided I would see if there was anything that I could do for myself. I talked to friends in Alberta that I knew had dealt with prostate cancer. Joe Baltimore, a long-time friend of mine, had taken the traditional treatment and was still dealing with the side effects. To be fair, in spite of all the side effects he said he would choose the same route again. I contacted Bryce Mailer, who lived in the same town as Joe. I knew he'd had prostate cancer, and although I wasn't sure just what he had done, I knew he was still up and going and doing quite well.

Bryce told me he had undergone the surgery, and in spite of that, had been told to go home and put his affairs in order, that he had three months to live. He said he took 35 percent food-grade hydrogen peroxide and he swore by it. He started with three drops in a glass of water and drank it three times a day. Every day he added one more drop to the glass. He gave me lots of information to read and Gloria and I researched on the Internet. I decided to go the hydrogen peroxide route. I bought 35 percent food-grade hydrogen peroxide and started taking the drops. When I was up to twenty-one drops a day, I found out that I could have it injected intravenously. We researched and found a naturopathic doctor in Williams Lake. He was also an MD, and would give me hydrogen peroxide intravenously. We set up a program alternating food-grade hydrogen peroxide and vitamin C one day and chelation the next. I did that five days a week for eleven weeks then I had another PSA test. I wasn't sure if their machine was working as the tests come back .03. My doctor suggested I go to the cancer clinic in Vancouver for a checkup just for my own peace of mind and I agreed to go.

Gloria and I went and they checked me out and could find nothing. They told me that my cancer had somehow gone into remission, but that I should have another PSA in thirty days. I did that and still it remained at .03. After another trip to Vancouver, the oncologist at the clinic told me it wasn't necessary to come back again because I could have the checks done in Williams Lake. He said go home and continue to eat my tomatoes and do whatever it was I was doing, because he felt the cancer was no longer active.

That was sixteen years ago. I don't know how many more there are in store for me, but I am very thankful for those I've had. I still use hydrogen peroxide drops in water periodically. I often get calls from people who want to know what I did and I tell them. At times I refer them to Bryce. I spoke to Bryce a year or so ago. He was still doing well twenty years after he was supposed to die and he was still taking his hydrogen peroxide drops. He absolutely swears by them! So do I!

CHAPTER 50

Because I Love Horses So Much,
I Made Them My Retirement Project

There are more things in life we don't know than we do know, and it's interesting to look back on your life and try to understand why you chose to go down the path that you did.

Animals were always a large part of my life, and I can say that horses were probably at the top of the list. In order to fully understand and communicate with them, one must learn their language. You might say a horse will never learn to speak the English language, and you are probably right. So you need to learn how to understand the horse's language, and when you do, he will respond to you in a way that tells you that he understands you.

Have you ever watched a little child that is learning to talk? One of the words they repeat so often is *why*, and that is because they have not yet fully learned the meaning behind the words that we speak to them. A horse is no different. From the day he is a born, he learns the horse language and that teaches him fear, how to communicate with other horses, to hear, to see, and to smell, to taste, to understand harsh from kind and softness. Although somewhat curious, the horse's natural instinct is to run away from things he does not understand. So you might say that his first instinct with man is to run away from them, unless, that is, we have learned how to speak their language.

First you have to learn how to read the signs, and the signs the horse gives you tell you what he is thinking. If he pins his ears back and turns his rump to you, he is telling you that you are encroaching on his space and that if you continue to crowd him he will kick you. Then you must communicate with him to show him that it's all right for you to be in his space and he in yours. Because he does not yet understand what you are trying to do, you must convince him that you are not about to hurt him. When you can do that, you have overcome your first hurdle and the horse loses the fear that he has of you. Then he becomes more curious about who and what you really are and responds to gentleness and kindness. You will be able to reinforce these ideas in his head.

Go slow. Remember he is learning a new language. And when you think you have gone too slow, just cut that time in half again and you will probably be right on target. His curiosity will make him reach out and smell you. That will tell him a whole lot about you. Very slowly reach out to him, and when you can finally touch him, scratch him very lightly. You may want to reward him with a little nibble of a grain or fresh green grass and then step back and give him the opportunity to follow you. If he doesn't follow, let him watch you. He is trying to understand what you are about; you must be patient. Do these things over and over until his response is, "Okay, I know who you are, and I now understand that." Then you can proceed to go a little further. Scratch him where it is difficult for him to scratch himself. That will feel good to him and he will like you for it. When you are able to rub your hands over his entire body to lift up his feet without him resisting, you have just completed grade one.

Remember, a horse learns to respond to you by the release of the pressure. Have you ever seen someone trying to lead a horse and they are pulling on the halter shank one way and the horse is pulling the other way? And guess who will win, the horse will. He is much larger and stronger than you. You must learn to use psychology. Remember, everything that you do must go through the horse's mind for approval or disapproval. When you first start to lead a horse, it is important to be very gentle with the pressure and step to the side. Create a little pressure to get his attention, and as soon as he responds to it release it and reward him. If you do this, it will not be long before he is following you around and learning what you are showing him. He is responding to your commands. If your commands are incorrect or harsh, that is how he will respond to you. Always try to remember to read the signs; that is how he is talking back to you. Licking his lips tells you he is saying everything is okay. When the ears are tipped forward, he is listening to you for your commands. When he is stiff and rigid, he is telling you he doesn't understand. When he is relaxed and calm he is saying, "Okay, now I am ready for the next lesson."

Horses are very intelligent animals but a person must remember they are animals and their sense of reasoning is different from ours. Their playful ways can be hurtful to us because they don't realize how fragile we really are. When we work with them, we need to be very observant and always discourage the least desirable habits and encourage the good ones by rewarding the horse for what he does.

I love to work with young colts. They are so inquisitive and open to learning that it makes doing things with them very interesting. When they are little they like to nibble on your fingers, but as they get a little older the pulls become a little stronger and before you know it they are biting. To them it's just another way of communicating with their siblings, and they don't realize there is any harm in it, it is just their way of being playful. I learned how to deter this undesirable habit by presenting my hand to them with my thumb and forefinger about two inches apart. When they try to bite it, I close my fingers on their whiskers. They will immediately draw back, and sometimes shake their head. The next time they try to do it, you will notice they come up very tentatively. If you repeat this method over and over you can actually teach them to just nuzzle you with their muzzle without biting. Remember, reward them for their efforts.

When I thought that it was time to slow down from all the hard work that I was putting into ranching and logging, I decided that I would take up breeding horses for a hobby. Unfortunately, the slowdown didn't happen and now I was raising horses as well. I have always had a special love for Appaloosas and cutting horses. I may be biased but I believe that one of the highest mental achievements that a horse can do is to go into a herd and bring out one particular animal and then all on its own, without any assistance from the rider, keep that animal from returning to the herd.

My venture in the horse business started way down in South Carolina, USA, where I purchased an Appaloosa stallion called Ima Lena Too, which was a grandson of the famous world champion cutting horse Doc A Lena.

Ima Lena Too in the barnyard at the ranch.

I'm standing by Brad Peterson, sitting in the saddle on Ima Lena Too after he won the Canadian National Appaloosa cutting in Brandon in 1995. Not only did he win the championship, he also had to beat some good American and Canadian horses to do it. I was so proud of him and Brad.

In 1995, Ima Lena Too won the Canadian National Appaloosa cutting championship at Brandon, Manitoba. I retired him to stud then and raised many good horses from him. Some of his offspring have gone on and won some pretty prestigious shows; i.e., capturing reserved grand champion Appaloosa cutting three-year-old at Fort Worth, Texas. Another young stallion that I sold was reserved grand champion working cow horse at Oklahoma City. I also purchased a few good brood mares; one from California that had debuted in Fort Worth, Texas and lost its cow. She proved to be a very good cutting horse and placed third at Calgary one year.

Pam Harrison photo
Lloyd Antypowich plans to breed his Appaloosas for cutting horses. His breeding operation is located near Horsefly.

Best hoof forward

By PAM HARRISON
The Advocate

Lloyd Antypowich has owned and raised Appaloosa horses for over 30 years, but it is just recently that he has decided to venture off into a new branch.

He is going to breed his Appaloosas to become cutting horses. The sire is a horse called Ima - Lena - II.

In 1991 Ima - Lena - II was ridden by Bill Freeman of Roston, Texas, and won the World Appalloosa Junior Futurity.

This event was held in Fort Worth, Texas. Ima - Lena II then proceeded to win other numerous cutting competitions throughout Texas and Oklahoma. At this time he was only three years old.

Antypowich also has an Appaloosa Filly that won fourth in the halter competition at the nationals in Regina, Saskatchewan. Antypowich is planning on entering Ima - Lena II in three shows in B.C. and also the national, being held in Brandon, Manitoba this year.

He also has a yearling filly quarterhorse that he is anxiously waiting to get into the cutting circle of competition. Currently Antypowich has been getting pointers from his friend Dan Gunderson of Airport Quarter Horses. Now Gunderson likes to ride his quarter horses just for pleasure even though he is 81 years old. He also sold Anty-powich a two-year-old filly quarter horse out of Peppy-Cue-Bar and Sara Tuckers. This filly is currently learning the basics from Brenda Dickie at Gunderson's place for cutting and Antypowich eventually hopes to get her in the cutting circle as well.

When Antypowich decided to take on this new venture of raising Appaloosas for cutting, he had to find himself a sire. He travelled to Oklahoma to see his friend Jaimie Miller Smith. She put him in touch with another friend in South Carolina. This is where he got Ima - Lena - II. Antypowich is looking forward to having six colts in the spring of '96 all sired by Ima - Lena - II. These horses will definitely have "cow" in them.

Both Lloyd and Gloria are excited about this new venture they're heading into. They are currently raising performance working horses with lots of "cow" in them, but they are mainly going to concentrate on breeding Appaloosa horses that can cut, team pen, rope-dog and steer.

Anyone interested in this new venture is more than welcome to come out and share this hospitality that they have to offer. They are located eight kilometres from Horsefly.

Antypowich commented that even though he now has Ima - Lena - II, his favourite is still a 21-year-old Appy that he uses for hunting when he goes out west into the mountains. So you know that Appaloosa horses are very reliable.

A writeup in the Williams Lake paper about the stallion Ima Lena Too

A stallion I bred and raised, Spot Me Too, whom I sold to a fellow in Iowa

Another stallion I bred and raised, Doc's spitting image, went to Vancouver Island

I purchased several quality mares to build the foundation of my herd. Among them were Fergie Straw, out of Strawman; Doc's Reba, out of Doc A Lena, the famous cutting horse, and a quarter horse called Sweet Young Lena; Sassafras Cue Bar, a quarter horse out of Cue Bar. My breeding program gave some outstanding foals.

A couple of outstanding foals sired by Ima Lena Too

These are two more outstanding foals from my breeding program

I am showing a filly in a show at Vernon

Many people that bought horses started out with very good intentions, but in most cases the higher performance horses were too much for them to handle and as a result didn't always get the chance to prove how good they could be in tough competition. At one time I had as many as fifty-six horses on the ranch and nearly all of them were sired by Ima Lena Too. Gloria always was and still is deathly allergic to horses, and eventually I decided the horse hobby had to change as she wasn't able to go to shows or sales with me. One time we went to a sale in Minnesota, USA, where I had several horses to be sold, one of which ended up being the second highest selling horse of the sale. Gloria had to stay in the motel all the time because of her allergies. She never complained about it, but while I knew from the beginning that it had to be that way, it lessened the pleasure for me.

Dogs are probably my next most favorite animal as they are also very intelligible and very loyal to you. When I see someone working with other animals it's not hard to understand how well they speak their language. Some have become masters at this and it is such a gratifying feeling when you can see someone putting a horse or a dog through its paces with such smooth and gentle efforts. I believe that I have just scratched the surface of learning how to communicate with animals and could go to school for a long time and enjoy every minute of it, because there is so much to learn.

CHAPTER 51

Rescuing a Fawn

One spring day I was driving my diesel pickup in the fields out back by the lakes. Gary Knoke and his friend Marie Corbett were visiting and we went out to check Birch Lake, then we drove around looking at the hayfields. The hay was about a foot tall and we were driving along the trail that led down to the bridge I had built over Niquidet Creek where it flowed out of Tommy's Lake. I had the windows open and right beside my door I heard this little squawk; in fact, we all heard it. I stopped and backed up to see what had made the noise, and there was a little fawn lying flat on the ground about a foot from where the wheels had passed. I imagine the sound of the truck and the movement of the wheels had frightened it. The poor little thing was so wet and cold, all it could do was make a little squawk. It had been raining and was quite cold for that time of year, but I did not want to interfere with it for fear that the mother would not claim it when she came back to find it.

That afternoon it started to rain again, and I kept thinking about that little fawn. At about four o'clock in the afternoon we all got in the truck and went back to see if it was still there. Sure enough, it was. When I saw how weak it was, I thought I had waited too long. I picked it up and put it on the seat of the truck, turned the heater up to high, and took it home. I put it in the little box on some towels and used a hair dryer to warm it up and dry it off.

Then I went to the barn for some formula that I used for my foals. I mixed it up with warm water and fed her with an eyedropper. Her mouth was tiny and very cold inside, but I tried a few drops, and lo and behold, she thought it tasted pretty good. She would try to suck it right out of the eyedropper. I gave her a little bit more and it was amazing how it revitalized her. I didn't give her very much to start with, because I was afraid it might cause her to scour. I had no way of knowing if she had even sucked her mother and got the colostrum that she needed. I continued to massage her and use the hairdryer to warm her up. Then I gave her some more formula and she was able to hold her head up.

Right after supper we heard a commotion. She was trying to stand up in her little box, so I went and helped her. I massaged the tiny legs and eventually she was able to get up. Then I had to find a bigger box to put her in.

Gary Knoke and I with the fawn in our kitchen

I knew we wouldn't be able to play mother to the fawn. That was a full-time job, and Gloria and I were both too busy to keep up that schedule. So we phoned around and found a family up Black Creek who were happy to take her. Cathy Sukert and her daughters came and got her and I gave them the little bit of foal formula that I had left.

They kept her until they were too busy to manage the schedule. Then they gave her to Tom Bunn, a bachelor who lived down the road from them. He looked after her until he went to work, then Cherie and Darcy took over. They all thought she was the cutest little thing and were very happy to be able to care for her. It wasn't long before she really took to them and would go bouncing along wherever they went. Soon it was starting to nibble on little bits of grass and leaves, and I can remember when they first started to feed her pellets it would come into the house and lie down on the rug in front of the door and eat the pellets out of a plate.

She really liked that little rug, as it had good traction compared to the hardwood floor, which was very difficult to walk on. But as it got older it would come into their house and walk into every room, looking for the kids. It pretty much had the run of the farm, and sometimes everyone wondered if it was going to come back. However, I'm sure the taste of those pellets was the deciding factor in that.

One time when it was about six months old, the kids had let her into the house to feed her some pellets and forgot to make sure she was out when they went to school. Darcy and Cherie had gone somewhere for the day, and when the kids got home the big living room window was broken. They called me, all excited, thinking that someone had tried to break into their house. I went right over to check things out and I realized that the glass had been broken from the inside and not from the outside. That told me something had tried to get out of the house, so I asked them where their little deer was and they said they didn't know because she was nowhere around. They called and called and looked for her, but she did not show up. I told them that I thought no one had tried to break into their house, but possibly the deer tried to find them and had jumped out through the window.

Later that evening the deer came back and there were two little kids that were worried about what their mom and dad were going to say about them leaving the deer in the house and having it break the window, but so happy that the deer came back that even if they had gotten into trouble it wouldn't have mattered.

That fall there were other deer that would come into the pasture fields right near the house and Whisper would go out there with them, but she always returned to the yard. It was beginning to be quite a novelty as other people that came to visit would see the fawn come through the fence and be totally comfortable with everyone around, showing no fear.

At Christmastime they let her in the house when they were unwrapping their Christmas presents. She seemed to sense the festive mood and their excitement and she jumped around in the wrapping paper, joining in the joyous spirit of the day.

When she was about two years old, they realized that she was going to have a family. One day she didn't come around and she was gone for several days. Then one day she came into the yard with two little fawns trailing behind her. She was still comfortable with Cherie and Darcy, but she did not appreciate anybody trying to pet her babies. She continued to bring them back to the yard but she spent more time out in the bush and pasture than she had before.

She would come down to the ranch and pay us a visit. Quite often we would find her standing in the garden, eating the strawberry plants. As each year passed there would be another set of fawns, and there were times when we would wake up early in the morning and see six or seven deer standing on our lawn. I think she figured it was a safe place for her to bring her babies as well as her friends, because she had the run of the place.

She had Bow, my big German shepherd dog, buffaloed. If he got too close to her she would chase him and strike at him with her front feet, so he wouldn't go near her. He wouldn't chase any of the deer out of the garden or away from the yard either.

What had once been cute became a problem because they were eating the shrubbery around the yard and they would go to the garden and nibble on everything. Some plants could handle that, but others were damaged badly. They were murder on the strawberry plants, eating them right down to the ground, fruit, leaves, and all. One day my daughter, Cindy, went after her with the broom to try to chase her out of the garden. The rest of the deer left quickly, but Whisper defied Cindy and refused to let her chase her away.

She was well known in the neighborhood and everyone looked out for her safety. Bob and Marlene Gardner found her in the shade of their shop during the heat of the day more than once. She would come down and go into my barn or hay shed or shop. She liked the shop because it had a dirt floor and that would help when the flies were bad. Even in the past few years, if she was unsettled by something around Darcy's place, possibly coyotes, wolves, or even cougars, she would still come up on the deck of his house, where she felt safer.

I think she might have died by now as it doesn't seem that anyone has seen her during the past couple of years, but she lived many years after I rescued her, and raised many generations of fawns.

CHAPTER 52

My Granddaughter Gives Me Buddy, My Faithful Companion

In about 2000, my dog Bow got run over by a logger driving on the public road that went past the house. Because the road ran through the middle of the ranch, Bow often ran out to "protect" his territory. Those who went by regularly knew that, but he was a big dog and I guess it annoyed some people. Anyway, one day he got hit and died.

That winter Jennifer gave me a border collie for Christmas. I'd always had German shepherds and had never had a border collie before. I called him Buddy, and he truly was my buddy. He went everywhere with me. He was a fast learner and turned out to be excellent with cattle.

When he was just a pup he would go with me when I fed the round hay bales with the tractor. He would run right by the tractor wheel. It used to worry me because some of those old cows did not take kindly to him being there, and I was afraid that one time when he was making a mad dash to get out of their way, he would get too close to the wheel and I would run over him. But I couldn't get him to stop no matter how often I scolded him, and he was so agile and quick that he never got hurt. It was a natural instinct for him to move cattle and horses, and he really missed all that when I sold the farm.

In the bush, he watched everything I did. If I was moving logs to the landing, he was running right along beside the skidder. When I was cleaning off the landing he would be right in there, pulling branches away.

When I ploughed snow around the ranch or on the bush roads with the cat, he would be right there next to the track. At first I watched to make sure I wouldn't get him under the track, because when the snow was deep the road wasn't any wider than the cat blade, which left him only inches. Finally I just had to leave him to his own senses because he wanted to be right there at the edge of the track. He would go all day with me.

When I was out felling trees, he watched me for so long that as soon as I was finished making the undercut he knew which way the tree was going to go. One day when I was wearing snowshoes to stay on top of the soft snow, he got under my foot continually because the snowshoes were a new thing for him. I was in the process of falling a tree and I stepped back to turn and take a few steps away from the stump. I snagged a branch and tripped myself. He was on me in a flash, licking my face and whining, trying to get me up. I don't know what he would have done if I had been seriously hurt, but he sure did everything he knew to try to get me on my feet.

Buddy hated bears and would chase one every chance he got. It started when he was just a pup and I took him with me, checking for beetle-infected trees in the woodlot. Gary Knoke and Bob Smith had come from Quesnel, British Columbia to go shooting gophers. We went out into the 100-acre field that I used for pasture.

Buddy and I left them hunting gophers and went on foot into the woodlot, where we encountered a black bear. The bear came toward us and I hollered at it. Buddy thought I wanted him to chase it. He ran after it and chased it up a tree. The bear didn't want to stay up the tree and kept coming down. I ran to the base of the tree and grabbed a stick and started beating at the bear, trying to keep it up there. I guess I was hollering quite loud and calling him all kinds of names. Bob and Gary heard me, as we were still close to the fence line of the 100-acre pasture. They came running, thinking the bear might have attacked us.

When they got there, I told Gary to shoot the bear. He said his gun was for hunting gophers, not shooting bear. I finally convinced him to shoot the bear. When the bear fell out of the tree, Buddy was there and I encouraged him to chew hell out of it. This was his first real encounter with a bear that he could actually get hold of. From then on he thought he had to kill every bear that came within smelling distance of him. The bad thing was he had no fear of a bear and the live ones were much more dangerous than one that had been shot with a .22.

He was quick and agile, and one time I even saw him take on an old mama bear with two cubs. He chased them off the landing, down a skid trail. Probably the babies went up a tree and then mama bear turned on him and chased him back to the landing. In the clearing of the landing, he would dart in and nip at her heels. She would wheel around and swipe at him with her paw. Had she ever hit him, she would probably have killed him, but she never connected. This wild and furious battle went on until he darted in and grabbed that old sow on the side of her face. She whipped her head and threw him off and he flew through the air a good twelve feet and he landed bang on the landing. I had been sitting in the truck with a friend, Mel Hynes, watching this whole episode.

My truck had electric windows, and Mel was enthralled with the excitement until the bear got within fifteen or twenty feet of the pickup. Then he started looking for the window crank to close the window. He couldn't find one and kept saying, "Good god, Lloyd, that bear is going to come right into the cab." I had to laugh as I pushed the button and the window went up on his side. Finally I felt I had to take action to distract the bear, because she was trying to kill my dog.

Another time I was driving in from the back field and Gloria was with me. We saw a black bear on the landing and Buddy spotted it at the same time. He was out of the truck box before I got the truck stopped, and was after that bear. The bear ran down a cow trail and Buddy sneaked right in after him. I guess he must have nipped him a good one, as the bear headed for the first tree he came to. Buddy was right on his ass, and when that bear made a jump for that tree, Buddy had a hold of him. The bear dragged him up the tree a good six or eight feet before Buddy let go, and no matter how hard I tried to get him to come back to the truck, he would not leave that tree. I finally had to walk right to him and tell him that it was OK to leave the bear up the tree and that he should come with me back to the ranch. I guess he thought that I should shoot every bear he put up a tree.

Another time Leo and I were sitting on the landing in my truck eating our lunch. It was a nice warm sunny day and we had both doors open, the seats laid back, and the radio playing quite softly. I looked down the road and there was a black bear not more than 200 feet from the truck. I just reached into the backseat and grabbed my rifle. I shot the bear a little too low in the chest. When the bullet expanded, it simply disemboweled him. I told Buddy to get him. In a flash he was on him and they were wrestling around on the ground, with the bear being very much alive. The bear had a death grip on Buddy's neck and would not let go. The bear was about four times the weight of Buddy and my little dog was having some trouble handling him. I hurried over to them, and Buddy looked up at me with pleading eyes, as if to say, "Help me." I kicked the bear in the ass a good one and that caused him break the stranglehold that he had on Buddy.

Buddy was up and now had a good hold on the bear. I could see this fight wasn't going to last to much longer, as all the innards of that bear were on the ground. I kept encouraging Buddy to finish him off and finally he did manage to roll him off the haul road into a little creek that had gone dry. Buddy did manage to strangle him there. However, he didn't come out of that fight without any rips and tears, but he learned that bears could be a very tough opponent and that it was no piece of cake to kill one.

For years, if you said "Where is the bear?" he'd run and bark up the closest tree or attack a post. Stuart Maitland, our son-in-law, is a guide and outfitter, and in hunting season he often has strong bear scent on his clothes. Buddy always associated Stuart with bear and had a barking fit when Stu and Cherie stopped in.

I'm sitting on the water trough with Buddy and Fritz the cat

Buddy was my constant companion when he was younger. He loved me and he could never get enough affection, and he went everywhere with me.

The first summer that we spent time at Plato Island was really hard on him. He always had food and water, but there was no one around most of the time. One time I came home to find he'd been kicked in the shoulder. There were no cows around but I had horses, and I think he must have been down at the barnyard. After that his arthritis started getting the best of him, but before that there was no stopping him from a bear or a coyote.

After Leo died I logged by myself for several years. At first I never thought anything of it; in fact, I loved being out there by myself. Gloria constantly worried about me though, and as I was getting older I had to admit that it would probably be wiser if I had someone with me. So I hired a fellow to help me.

Logging is a job where you can get hurt if you don't keep your mind constantly on the job. One day I was felling a large fir tree right next to a skid trail. I'd made my undercut and noticed a small dry leaner that was hung up against the fir tree. I was about to buck it off when I saw that my new helper had hooked onto a fir that was too much for him to pull. He was seriously abusing the skidder and it was just a matter of time before he would've broken something, so I went and bucked a peeler off the tree and then he had no problem pulling it.

I went back to finish felling the fir tree that I'd been working on, but I forgot to go and buck the leaner first. I made the back cut, set my wedge, and as the tree started to fall, I stepped back from the butt. Then there was one hell of a bang on my head and I was knocked to the ground. My hardhat came off and I fell on top of my power saw. I guess you can't hurt a Polack by hitting him on the head with a stick, but that sure was a good wakeup call.

Another time when I was felling a beetle-infested schoolmarm spruce, part of the tree brushed a large fir and broke a good-sized limb off. A piece about sixteen inches long and two inches thick hit me on the hardhat, then glanced off and stuck in my arm. It drove a hole big enough that I could have put two fingers into it. I saved that piece and I'm going to gold spray it and call it "Lloyd's Bonker."

CHAPTER 53

Traveling with Stu Maitland from Eureka Peak Lodge and Outfitters

In around 2000, Stuart Maitland and my daughter, Cherie, got together. Stuart owns Eureka Peak Guide and Outfitting. He loves to hunt and trap and fish as much as I do. Through the years we have done a lot of things together. I've gone out on snowmobile with him to check his trap line in the dead of winter, with snow up to our eyeballs. It was great fun but now that is an activity for a younger man than me. I love to ice fish and have gone ice fishing with Cherie and Stuart several times at different places. I've also crossed Quesnel Lake with Stuart in his boat to check his camp up the North Arm. One time early in the spring, Cherie went with us and we saw goat near shore on the East Arm. Another time Stuart and I went up the East Arm and came upon a good-sized black bear that he shot on a spring bear tag. Later when we visited them at Eureka Peak Lodge, we ate bear roast from that hunt and it was really good, although generally I have never been a fan of bear meat.

A couple of years ago, after their last hunt, I was with Stuart when he went across Quesnel Lake to bring in his horses. I was amazed at the number of logging roads there were and how far we traveled to find the horses. Once we got them headed home, they came right back to camp. We tied them to trees overnight and the next day the barge came in to pick them up.

The barge was also carrying trucks and equipment for West Fraser.

I was doubtful about how it was going to work, but Stuart knows what he's doing and those horses are old pros. They just loaded on among the vehicles with no problem and rode with ease across the lake.

Stuart's horses loaded on the barge on Quesnel Lake, heading for home

Stuart is a pilot and he loves to fly. I haven't gotten to go up as often as I would like, because it often doesn't seem to work out, but I have been fortunate enough to go a few times. He is a good pilot and I really enjoyed the day with him.

Stuart standing by the plane that he flies

In 2001, Cindy and Gary and their two girls sold their home in Abbotsford, British Columbia and moved to Horsefly. Their intent was to help out with the ranching and logging, but after about a year and a half it became clear that there just wasn't enough money for two families to make a good living, so Gary went back to trucking.

Gary worked in the bush with me and did very well. In this picture are me and Gary on the tailgate of his truck, Bill Isaac (Gary's dad) standing by the truck.

Gary gave it a good shot and accomplished a lot. He learned to work with my old equipment, worked cattle, helped make fence, made hay, and generally everything else on the ranch.

Gary working with calves in the corral at branding time

I believe he enjoyed it. They lived in town in an apartment that they rented from Farqhuarsons until they bought a mobile home and put it in the trailer court.

After Gary went trucking, I hired another fellow. As a person he was a nice guy, but because he drank so much he became a poor employee. At first when he was sober he could work and I tried to encourage him to quit drinking, but over time it became far worse. I think he thought he had me over the barrel because I needed help, and one time after we had disagreement he threatened to quit. I quickly told him that was a good plan and that as of that moment he no longer worked for me. I think he expected me to beg him to stay and he was clearly shocked when I told him it was over.

He'd underestimated how much I had come to despise his drinking and how angry I was at how he handled the equipment, etc. It had simmered inside me for a long time, and when he opened that door, I didn't think twice. He told everyone that he had quit, and in a way he had, but I hadn't given him a chance to change his mind.

It actually turned out to be the best thing for me in the long run, because I realised that I shouldn't be working that hard anymore, and for a while I hired people to do all the logging operations on the woodlot and I stepped right out of the working end.

CHAPTER 54

Herman Howard and Hank

Next to my woodlot there were two very large trees. I wanted to protect them, so I wrote a verse about them, framed it, and put it in the bush by the trees. I added a mailbox and put a guest book in it so people who stopped to read the verse could sign the book. It read as follows:

Herman, Howard, and Hank

Howard and Herman

Hi! Thanks for stopping by to share your time with us. I'm Howard, that's Herman over there behind me on the right, and on the left is Hank, resting peacefully where he has been for many years.

Hank

We have lived a lot in our time. We have prevailed through many changing conditions. We have survived many perils: fires, drought, thunderstorms with tremendous winds and hail, heavy snows that sought to break our limbs, cold that chilled us to the core, root diseases that caused some of our siblings to pass on, the ever-persistent little beetle that could cause us to become weak and die, the loggers' saw and axe. Through all of these dangers, over hundreds of years we are still here. Thanks to the loving hand of the creator and owner of woodlot no. 504, who has promised to never do us any harm, we will continue our contribution to nature.

We have been shelter to many animals through the years. Moose and deer have sought refuge by our roots during snow and rainstorms.

Bear cubs have exercised their muscles, climbing up into the safety of our branches, while their mothers curled up at the base of our trunks to nap. Fox, lynx, coyote, and even cougar have slept on our doorsteps. The pine martin has run up our trunks and through our branches many times. The wolf has serenaded us with his howl and we have listened to it echo through the hills and surrounding forest.

We have fed the squirrels with our cones and given them shelter in our branches. We have shared our time with many of our feathered friends. The whiskey jack has stored its summer pickings for later use in the cold of winter in our branches. The wise old owl has perched on our strong limbs with a sharp eye, looking for its next meal. The majestic bald eagle has occupied the penthouse suite to survey his domain. The crows and the ravens have had many meetings discussing their various concerns in life here. The wren and chickadee have groomed our trunks, looking for insects and beetles, and to them we are very grateful. The woodpecker has knocked on our door many times.

And to you, my friends, please be careful with your matches and fires, as you can see how much our existence depends on you.

Thank you for stopping by to visit! Please sign the guest book and tell others about us. We enjoy making new friends.

Happy hunting or hiking and have a great day!

Herman, Howard, and Hank

CHAPTER 55

It's Time to Enjoy Life and the Fun Things a Bit

In about 2003 I bought a boat from a local, Arnie Erickson, and took it out to Mitchell Bay Landing. Don and Connie Hughes still own and operate the resort. Taking it there worked well for me. I could go over there for the day or rent a cabin and stay for the weekend, and Don kept the boat there year around in a covered, secured holding. I had several problems with the boat, largely because the motor was too small to handle it, but Don was very handy and knowledgeable about motors, so he did a lot of work on it for me. I eventually put a different motor on it and I got a couple of years of decent fishing on the lake with it. Don was an avid fisherman and he went out with me a lot.

In the spring of 2005 I had an opportunity to buy a 19½-foot Marlin with a recently reconditioned 350 Chevy inboard motor that had been rebored with a big cam. It came with a trailer and was a good boat for Quesnel Lake because it had lots of power. I quickly snapped it up.

Shortly after I got the boat I decided I wanted to put a full topper over it. Don said he could build it, so I told him to go ahead and order the material for it.

*A lake trout that I caught in Quesnel Lake while out fishing
with Don Hughes from Mitchell Bay Landing*

My boat after Don and I got the topper put on it. I'm sure it is the only boat on the lake with a skylight in the top. Actually it is not so bad, but it can get pretty warm on hot sunny days when the sun comes burning in through it!

Family is an important part of my life. I wanted my kids and grandkids to be able to come and visit. Although the site at Mitchell Bay Landing is beautiful, the resort rules did not cater to having children staying with us or friends stopping in to visit, so it did not serve my needs. Even though it was and still is the least expensive resort on Quesnel Lake, I looked into getting a lot at Plato Island.

All of my kids and their spouses and children booked a corner of the camping area at Plato Island for a family reunion in 2006. Dan and Bonnie McFarland owned Plato then. The grounds were lovely and Dan did everything he could to accommodate all of us. Everyone had such a wonderful time that we booked the same spot for 2007. In 2006, while I was at the resort, I looked at a shelter and a deck that was for sale on a trailer pad, but I wasn't sure that I wanted to make that kind of a commitment yet.

After the family reunion in 2007, I decided to buy it, and late in August I put the camper in the lot but only got to spend one night in it because I was just too busy. I left the boat at Mitchell Bay for the rest of the year because I had already paid for storage there and the lease went from May to May of any given year, so the next spring I took it out.

In October 2007, I found a 1997 29½-foot wilderness trailer for sale in the paper. I went and looked at it, decided it was a good deal, so I bought it. I took it out to Plato and put it on the pad under the shelter. That winter we had a lot of snow. I drove out and checked on the trailer and shelter because I was thinking possibly I should shovel off the shelter. It looked OK when I was there and I had coffee with Dan, because he stayed at the resort all winter for security. He told me I had nothing to worry about, that shelter had been there for five years and never shown any sign of collapsing, so I went home. It snowed more and then it rained. One night Dan phoned to tell me the shelter had collapsed. He said the trailer was totally destroyed, but fortunately it had not damaged property belonging to anyone else.

Fortunately, the insurance that I had on it was the top-of-the-line, all inclusive, and it guaranteed that the trailer would be replaced with a brand-new one of the same quality. The insurance company tried to give me one of inferior quality, but I wouldn't take it and held out for one with a winter package, a four-foot by fourteen-foot push out, two exit doors, a queen-sized bed and a hide-a-bed, which was what I'd insured. In the end I got a very nice 2007 Cougar trailer with a large push out and two exit doors.

The one I picked had a large window at the rear and I set the trailer on the lot so that window looked out on to the lake. I was able to salvage the deck, which I moved to the other side of the lot. Dan McFarland used his loader to help move it in two sections and set it up. Then I backed the trailer into place and got everything set up.

It was almost hard to believe that I could have been so fortunate; it was one time insurance actually paid out the way it said it would. They even paid me $5,000 to rebuild the shelter anywhere I wanted to, so I built it at the ranch and I take the trailer home every winter.

When I turned sixty-eight in 2005, I knew it was time to slow down. In the fall of 2006, I sold the woodlot to Ian Lanky from 150 Mile. I listed the ranch with a real estate agent and Gloria put up a website on the Internet to advertise it as well.

I became more interested in gardening when I slowed down in the bush. I never could stand to see weeds in the garden and I loved to water and see things grow. During the past five years I'd planted apple trees and plum trees, cherry trees, and raspberries and strawberries. Now they were bearing fruit, and that was very exciting to me.

I'm standing in my corn in the garden

A sample of the corn from the garden

I am watering in the garden and my grandchildren,
Lydia and Colin, are out there with me

I had two kinds of apples trees, these were the largest ones

The abundance in the greenhouse; tomatoes ripening

Peppers prolific in the greenhouse

Buddy and me by the cherry tree loaded with cherries;
boy, they sure did make good pies

CHAPTER 56

It's Time to Think about Retirement

In February 2006, I received a phone call about the 220 acres at Alaha (Birch Lake) and Tommy's Lake. The caller said he wanted to come on a specific weekend. We had a lot of snow that winter, and when the appointed day came we had a nasty storm. I really wondered if he would show up, but he did, along with his young son and small daughter. I drove them out to the property and showed it to them, thinking that it was a total waste of time. When we got back to the yard, he asked if he could come in and give me a deposit. I could hardly believe what I heard.

The buyer was from Bellingham, Washington, USA. Later he told us that his son Ryan had seen the property on the website that Gloria had put on the Internet, and they had decided immediately that if it was anything like it looked they were going to buy it. He has built a beautiful home that will be totally self-sufficient as far as heating and power go and the views are spectacular.

The main ranch had changed a lot since I first bought it. I'd added on to the doublewide and put vinyl siding on it, built a new shop, a hay shed, cattle shelter, and a barn. The entire corral system had been replaced, and while there were other things I could have done, I really had simply run out of energy.

The house as it was when I sold it

The barn with the metal-panel round pen beside it

*These are my cattle coming up the alleyway from the shelter
in the background to the feeders along the hay shed*

A view of the house and the shop and the white fence

*This is an aerial picture of the ranch in winter; I took this picture
while flying with Stuart Maitland one January day*

FROM MOCCASINS TO COWBOY BOOTS 377

In the fall of 2006, I sold the main ranch to the MacDonalds from Williams Lake. One of the provisions of the sale was that we would stay on the place until the end of April 2008. This worked well for both of us.

I kept 100 acres with the intention of subdividing it and giving half of it to Cindy and Gary as her inheritance because they had come up from Abbotsford to help on the farm, but I ran into a snag with this because the Caribou Regional District wouldn't let me subdivide. In the end I decided to give the 100 acres to Cindy and Gary. I put in the water, sewer, and hydro, and they built a beautiful home. Gloria and I live on the ground floor, which is bright and open. Cindy and Gary and their two daughters live on the top floor. It is a good arrangement for all of us.

On May first 2008, a son of the new owner moved into the house where we had lived for most of thirty-five years. Unfortunately, the home where our family had made so many wonderful memories burned to the ground in April of 2010. It was replaced by a new modular home, and in the fall of 2010, the parents started to build a beautiful new house down by the river. They are industrious people and have made many changes to the place. They tore down the old homestead house, added on to the shop, built new corrals and new fences, and generally cleaned up. It is nice to see new owners develop and improve the place, and they certainly have done that.

RETIREMENT AND WONDERFUL MEMORIES

2006-

CHAPTER 57

Life in Retirement

During the five years before I quit logging and sold the ranch, I bought several toys that would go into retirement with me. I got a snowmobile, boat, ATV, and a camper. Of course, I used the ATV and the snowmobile around the ranch and for logging as well.

My grandson Colin on the backseat of the Arctic Cat 500 2-Up

My Ski-Doo that is a 2-up also so Gloria can go touring with me. Here I am out ice fishing on Birch Lake.

My granddaughters Annie and Katie, and my faithful dog, Buddy, in front of my ice fishing hut on Birch Lake

My Bigfoot camper on my Ford Dually truck

My new thirty-foot trailer on the pad at Plato Island

Now that I have sold the ranch, I have taken up fishing as my hobby and I am going to learn how to catch the big one.

In 2007, Gloria and I went to Ocean Falls to a fishing lodge operated by Jim and Joanne Walls.

Jim took me fishing on the ocean, and I will always treasure that time we spent together out there. There were times I wasn't too sure if he wasn't trying to drown me! But we sure had a good catch though. We'd had little contact for more than thirty years, but it was just like old times again. Joanne is a real sweetheart and made us feel very much at home. Walls Fish Camp provided great fishing for big spring salmon, halibut, lingcod, red snappers, and prawns, and we got our limit!

This is the welcome sign at Ocean Falls

*I'm holding a thirty-four-pound spring salmon that
I caught; Jim Walls standing beside me*

I'm holding the second spring salmon that I caught on this trip

I'm holding a halibut; I caught four on this trip

CHAPTER 58

Our Summer Hideout, Beautiful Quesnel Lake!

Gloria and I have spent the last four summers on Quesnel Lake. In 2008 and 2009, we had our trailer at Plato Island.

We really liked Plato Island. It was a beautiful place and we really enjoyed the people who stayed there. George and Ruth Campbell were there and I have known George since I ran Black Creek Ranch. Sid and Darlene Bell, Bill and Darleen Belziuk, Bill Bernath and Carol Macgregor, Jennifer and Mark Loewen, Bob and Nan Loewen, Vi and Carlos Bellizia, Dennis and Doris Evans, and Brian and Ingrid Wanamaker are all people we became friendly with. It was like a big family and everyone pitched in and helped anyone who needed help. In the evenings we often sat around someone's fire pit and had a drink or two and told lies, mostly fish stories!

We traveled up the North Arm with Sid and Darleen Bell, who were our next-door neighbors. We went in our own boats and fished from Plato Island to the end of the North Arm and stayed overnight at the Penfold docks once and at Long Creek another time. They were fun to travel and camp with.

This is my fishing buddy Carlos Bellizia at Plato Island. Carlos and I just clicked when it came to fishing and I was really looking forward to hunting and fishing with him. In August of that year he was diagnosed with cancer and he passed away early in 2008. It really hit me hard to lose his friendship so suddenly.

Sid and Darlene Bell's boat and mine tied up for the night at the
Long Creek docks on the North Arm of Quesnel Lake

In 2010, I moved my trailer onto a lot at Elyshia Resort. Elyshia is at the junction of the North and East arms and that is where I prefer to fish. The management wouldn't let me put up a permanent structure of any sort, so I put a new twenty-five-foot awning on my trailer and bought a patio room that attached right to the awning. Then I put down outdoor carpet, and it worked great; it even kept the mosquitoes and black flies out. I also had a picnic table and a fire pit and room to put out several chairs.

The resort supplied power, water, sewer, and high-speed Internet, which Gloria liked. I could have the propane tanks for the trailer filled at the resort. The docks were solid and I could buy gas for the boat at the docks. They provided garbage bins and recycling bins and I just had to take the garbage to the bins and they took it away. The food at the restaurant was great and it was a really nice place to go to eat once in a while, and it was a bonus that they offered free coffee at any time.

The service and the attitude of the staff were wonderful. Harmony Becar, the manager, kept a running tab of all our expenses—the monthly rate for the camping spot, moorage, boat gas, propane, and meals—and put it on our credit card at the end of the month.

The view from the restaurant at Elyshia

Here I am in front of the patio room and trailer on my lot at Elyshia

Bill Bernath and Carol McGregor moved their trailer to Elyshia from Plato too. We had a lot of good laughs and got to know them better. Although they lived right beside us at Plato, we didn't spend a lot of time with them. Bill and Carol are always good for a party and no one could ever forget Bill's "Moose Milk." It was as smooth as silk, as sneaky as a fox, and as deadly as a snake when you'd had that one glass too many.

In August 2010, my siblings and their spouses, Roman and Arleen, Ben and Shirley, and Clifford and Joyce, all came to our house for a family reunion. It was the first time that had ever happened at my place in all the years I'd been in British Columbia, and it was nice

In 2010, my sister and brothers and me at the family reunion: L–R, Roman, Shirley, me, and Cliff. Ervin had passed away in 2002 at the age of seventy-two.

I took the four of us siblings and my brother-in-law out in the boat on Quesnel Lake for two days. One day, everyone went up to the lake. Arleen, Joyce, and Gloria stayed at the trailer, and when the rest of us came off the lake, we all had dinner at the restaurant.

Benny with the fish he caught on Quesnel Lake

My oldest brother Roman enjoying himself at the helm

My sister Shirley and I enjoying ourselves in my boat on Quesnel Lake

My brother Clifford at the wheel of my boat

Cliff brought his crokinole board and everyone enjoyed it. We took family pictures and then we finished the visit by going up to Eureka Peak Lodge on Gotchen Lake. Cherie and Stu were leaving to take a trail ride out in the mountains, so our group went there for the evening and then everyone left for home the next morning. Gloria and I stayed for three more days just to rest and relax and "housesit."

One week near the end of August 2010, I took my boat up the North Arm to the Penfold docks. Brian and Ingrid Wannamaker and their teenage daughter came up in their boat too and we stayed overnight. It was so peaceful and beautiful there even though there was a wildfire being mopped up on the mountainside above us. We couldn't see the fire from the docks, but that evening there was smoke in the air and we could see helicopters flying in to pick up the fire crews who were staying at Elyshia Resort.

Brian Wannamaker and me with fish we had caught on our way up the North Arm. Here we are standing on the West Fraser docks at the Penfold.

Here I am cooking breakfast on the dock the next morning

A spectacular morning view from the north end of the lake

The Penfold docks on Quesnel Lake; L–R, Brian Wannamaker,
my wife Gloria Antypowich, Ingrid Wannamaker (standing),
and me; we were eating breakfast on the Penfold dock

The morning was beautiful and calm at the docks. We left at around 9:30 in the morning and started fishing our way back. The Wannamakers went down one side of the lake and I went down the other, working my way back to Elyshia Resort. Suddenly storm clouds started to come in and a brisk little squall popped up. I pulled into the shelter of the limestone cliffs, thinking it would blow over. The down riggers were down and I had the little trolling motor going. Then all of sudden it was a full-blown storm. I realized I had to get the tackle up, the downriggers in, get off the trolling motor, and get the inboard started. Things were a little interesting for a few minutes, but once I got the big motor going I figured everything would be OK.

I had often heard about the storms that could blow up on Quesnel Lake, but in all the years I had spent on the lake I had never experienced one. It took me three hours to get home on a trip that usually took about forty-five minutes. There were ten-foot waves most of the way in. It was a good experience to have when I look back on it. I learned what my boat could handle and that I could handle my boat.

When I got back to Elyshia, there had been some damage at the docks and a few people had come in to seek refuge from the storm. The waves had broken one section of the breakwater loose and it kept drifting toward the docks. The only thing that was holding it was a boat that was anchored to a buoy. The Van Cleaves, a family that lived across the junction, came in with their jet boat and anchored ropes on both ends of the boat. They tossed one rope to me on the dock so I could pull it alongside the dock and they held the rope at the front end tight so the boat couldn't bounce around too much on the waves. Once we got it to the dock, I helped Harmony and some young friends of the Van Cleaves tie on the buoys and tie the boat to the dock. Then Van Cleaves went out and threw a rope on the breakwater logs and pulled them out, but they were not able to anchor that section until the next day.

CHAPTER 59

Looking Back

Now that I'm getting a little longer in the tooth, I have learned to take it somewhat easier and not get overly excited at how much I can do in one day. I look back at the years gone by and can honestly say I wish I had spent more time with my wife and family. Although Gloria and I have traveled a little, I wish we had done more. During most of the years of our life we did very little holidaying because I was very involved in reaching my goal to be a rancher, the dream that never died and eventually became a reality.

I took her to Fiji twice; once, my daughter Cindy went along. The first trip, I actually bought a lot in Fiji, which I owned for a number of years.

Cindy and I on the beach

Me with some Fijian children

Two of the Blue Lagoon cruise ships in the background

I went fishing with the crew from the cruise ship, not approved by the higher-ups

Dancing on the cruise ship with a Fijian performer

In 1994, I went to Madeira with Gloria, as well as my brother Cliff and his wife. Madeira is an island just off the coast of Spain and Portugal.

This is a picture of the incredible terraced fields in the mountains of Madeira

*Gloria and I sitting in one of the sidewalk sleds that
slide down the steep streets of Funchal, Madeira*

In 2003, we went on an Alaskan cruise with my eldest daughter Cindy and her husband Gary Isaac, his parents Gladys and Bill Isaac, as well as a very good friend of mine, Peter Zahzcy and his wife Shirley from Edmonton, Alberta. We traveled on the *Norwegian Wind*.

The vessel we traveled on when we went on the Alaskan cruise, the *Norwegian Wind*

Me pulling the American eagle's tail feathers in Alaska

In November 2010, I went to Los Algodones, Mexico. I needed some dental work done and so did Gloria. When I got a quote for a root canal at home, it made me sit back and wonder, because I had more than one to do. Raine Powell, a long-time friend, told me her brother had gone to Algodones for dental work and saved close to two-thirds of the price he was quoted by two different dentists here at home. Once I started looking into it, I found lots of people who had gone down there for years and have been very satisfied.

We drove to Vancouver and caught the plane to Yuma via Phoenix, arriving there at about 9:00 p.m. We took a taxi to the Mexican border at Los Algodones, then found a taxi to take me to the little hotel, Hacienda Los Algodones, where we stayed. We went to a different dentist than we'd planned to when we left home. When we got to the *hacienda*, the people who owned it had two dental businesses, and if you booked at one of their offices they gave you a free night at the *hacienda* and shuttle service to and from the dentist every day. So we decided to go to Tracey's Dental. I was totally impressed with everything, the dentist, the *hacienda*, the staff!

I've got the bull by the horn in Mexico!

*I'm sitting in the shade in Mexico, with a few old
bandits on the wall and a few bales of straw.*

All my grandchildren are growing up quickly.

In October of 2012, my oldest granddaughter, Jennifer Jackson, married Tyler Maitland. They are ranchers, and the wedding had a country ranch theme and was quite spectacular. Jennifer had her brother Jason stand as her bridesman along with my granddaughter Lydia and a couple of other girlfriends. Jennifer and Jason are the children of our daughter, Cherie.

I anticipate that we'll see great-grandchildren within a few years; it is so wonderful to watch the cycle of life starting all over again.

*My son's children, fourteen-year-
old Colin Antypowich and fifteen-
year-old Lydia Antypowich*

*These are Cindy's (my oldest daughter)
children, fourteen-year-old Annie
Isaac and eleven-year-old Katie Isaac.*

My oldest granddaughter Jennifer and Tyler Maitland at their wedding

This is my oldest grandson, Jason Jackson, and his fiancée, Sarah Nightingale. They are getting married in June of 2013.

It's taken me seventy-five years to live this life, but when I look back to where I started and where I am now, living in a new modern home with in floor heating and all the modern conveniences, I am so grateful that I live in Canada. Who knows what the future holds, however. Life is made up of memories, and these are my memories. Because I too will be just a memory one day, I have taken the time to leave a trail from where I came to where I've gone and to where I am now.

A good book is like a good glass of wine; it should be smooth, make you feel good, and go down easily. I hope you enjoyed traveling with me on this journey as much as I have had living my dream. And although there is still a little time left, I take it one day at a time. And if the sun keeps shining and the river doesn't rise too high, I plan to live it happily to the end.

ABOUT THE AUTHOR

Lloyd Antypowich

Lloyd Antypowich has always given his all in everything he has chosen to do. Although he was born to be a rancher, he wore many different hats on the way to achieving that goal: he worked in a sawmill, did oilfield construction, was a farmer, a miner, owned his own logging trucks, and had his own logging operation. When he ranched he raised registered Limousin cattle and Appaloosa cutting horses. He is a natural when working with animals. He is a horse lover and has always had a favorite dog by his side. He was president of the Horsefly Cattlemen's Association for seven years, president of the BC Limousin Association, and sat on the board of directors for the Canadian Limousin Association. He started the first 4-H Club in Horsefly and was its leader for seven years. He also worked on several fair boards.

From his youth, he was an avid hunter and loved being in the wilderness mountain country. Today he is retired and lives at Horsefly, British Columbia, Canada. He loves to garden and fishing is his pastime. The last hat he plans to wear is that of storyteller and author.

Edwards Brothers Malloy
Thorofare, NJ USA
April 17, 2013